SPIRITUAL TREASURE OF SAINT RĀMADĀSA

SPIRITUAL TREASURE
OF
SAINT RĀMADĀSA

V. H. Date, M.A., Ph. D.

MOTILAL BANARSIDASS
Delhi :: Varanasi :: Patna

MOTILAL BANARSIDASS
Indological Publishers & Booksellers
Head Office : BUNGALOW ROAD, JAWAHAR NAGAR, DELHI-7
Branches : 1. CHOWK, VARANASI-1 (U.P.)
2. ASHOK RAJPATH, PATNA-4 (BIHAR)

ISBN 0 8426 0805 2

First Edition : *Delhi*, 1975

Printed in India
BY SHANTILAL JAIN AT SHRI JAINENDRA PRESS, BUNGALOW ROAD, JAWAHAR NAGAR, DELHI-7 AND PUBLISHED BY SUNDARLAL JAIN, MOTILAL BANARSIDASS, BUNGALOW ROAD, JAWAHAR NAGAR, DELHI-7

To
My Spiritual Teacher

PREFACE

To write about the nature of God from the philosophical point of view without reference to any concrete mode of worshipping Him is not very difficult. To write about the different modes of worshipping God and to say about the relation between the devotee and God without reference to the speculative problems in philosophy is also easy. But to take into consideration both the intellectual quest of the philosopher and the actual devotional interest and practice of an aspirant and the experiences and the mature wisdom of a saint, and then to construct a philosophy of religion which will satisfy both the philosopher and the devotee is not at all easy. This becomes all the more difficult when one has to deal with the polytheistic belief of the Hindus, and then to reconcile it with monotheism and monism, and to synthesize it further with mystical realization. This however is the task which we have to do so far as the present work is concerned. The saint Rāmadāsa had reached the acme of spiritual realization by worshipping the deities—Hanumān and Rāma; but he has given us also a philosophy which, according to us, is of the highest value.

I must straightway acknowledge with all humility and gratitude that the credit of whatever I have been able to do goes to Rāmadāsa and to my spiritual Teachers, Bhāusahib Mahārāja, Amburao Mahārāja (the saints of Umadī and Inchgiri) and to Professor R.D. Ranade, the philosopher-saint of Nimbal. Had not their grace come upon me in the manner in which the waters of Gaṅgā would flow over an idle man sleeping on the bank, the world would never have seen the face of any of the books which I have been able to write. It is no exaggeration to say that I have been throughout my literary career as well as in my material and spiritual endeavour and achievement a mere instrument which they have moulded and used as they wished. It will be more correct to say that a particular plan is being fulfilled through me on account of the power of their grace than to say that I am fulfilling it through my efforts.

It was a mere stroke of fortune, I now feel when I look back on my life, that I happened to begin the reading of the Dāsabodha of Rāmadāsa in the year 1918. I was then eighteen years of age and was staying at Jamkhandi with my sister and her husband. One day I happened to go to meet my teacher Mr. Yashwantrao Lele in his house known as Lele-wada. I remember even now how when I stepped into the front-gate, I saw before me at a distance of about fifteen feet, Mr. Yashwantrao Lele standing and talking with a stranger. When they both looked at me, I was simply dazzled and felt immensely happy in seeing the glowing face and the most attractive and the beautiful eyes of the stranger. I stopped where I was, and did not go forward; whereupon the stranger asked my teacher, "who is this boy ?", and he looked at me with affection and interest. I bowed down before him and there ended my first meeting with a great saint. That stranger was none else but Professor R.D. Ranade, who since then has become to me the guiding-star of my life. Reading of Dāsabodha I continued upto 1924 without any exception on a single day; but when I stopped doing so, I came in direct and intimate contact with the Professor. For, immediately after my graduation in 1924, I went straight to Nimbal and stayed with him for a few months. There it was that I came to know that the Dāsabodha of Śrī Rāmadāsa was the principal book which was being read for the purpose of imparting spiritual knowledge, three times a day almost since the beginning of the century in all the places which were sacred to Professor Ranade, to his Guru and to his Guru's Guru. Indeed, how wonderful it is that the Dāsabodha which I began to read in 1918 as a mere chance, was made known to me in 1924, as if by a second chance, as containing in it a very great treasure of spiritual knowledge ! The place of Dāsabodha was taken by my spiritual teacher, and I came to know that there was vital connection between the two. In my association and contact with my Guru, I must have had the unconscious feeling that I was in contact with the teachings of Dāsabodha. Perhaps, as a result of this, for the next eighteen years my reading of Dāsabodha was not regular. It again became so when I wrote my doctorate thesis[1] in 1941-42. For, I must be candid in saying that my thesis which was quite a fresh study of the mystical life as also a careful analysis of it, was based mainly on the teachings of Rāmadāsa. Again for eight years more, there was no regular reading; but since 1950, I have been reading it regularly and discussing various problems in it with some of my spiritually-minded friends almost on every Sunday. There was no idea of writing a book on Rāmadāsa, but during the four months when I was in America between April and July 1972, I had no other work on hand and also no other inclination except to write regarding the philosophy and spiritual teachings of the saint. By the grace of God, the writing of the teachings in Dāsabodha was over during the four months, and after returning to Jodhpur I finished the writing regarding Rāmadāsa's other works also.

In what I have written, I have been absolutely faithful to Rāmadāsa, but I have also added my own comments and explanations wherever I thought this to be necessary. Let me hope that this work of mine would please my spiritual teacher and that aspirants, if any, be benefitted by its study.

This preface of mine will be properly concluded, I think, by the prayer which Śrī Rāmadāsa addresses to the Lord, Rāma; for it will bring out the purpose for which Rāmadāsa strove hard throughout his life, and after achieving which he wrote all his works so that the same might be achieved by others.

"Let the spirit of the divine Incarnation of Rāma be triumphant everywhere; let all unbelief and ignorance be wiped away from the face of the earth; and let the minds of all beings be filled with divine consciousness.

"As I have lost my feet of egoism, I have chosen to be your servant (dāsa) O Rāma, because I have heard that ever since you ruled in Ayodhyā, a city in the continent of Bhārata (India) which is situated on the bank of the river Sarayu, you have shown your grace to all who are miserable and helpless

1. The thesis was first published in 1944 under the title "Yoga of the Saints," and has again been recently published in a revised and enlarged form in March 1974.

and to those who have surrendered unto you. Therefore have I come to you singing your glorious Name and qualities with love and joy, so that you should shower your grace on me and destroy my sense of duality between you and me.

"You are the sole donor of Spiritual knowledge which will put an end to all sorts of beggings, O Rāma. Teach me the several ways of being devoted to you with faith, love and gratitude; lend me your stick of spiritual illumination for my support, and the garment of Vairāgya (disgust for God-less things) to cover my body, and to protect me from the shivering cold of the temptations of Māyā; give me such bread of desirelessness as will satisfy my hunger for lust and other objects of sensuous pleasure; and give me the butter-milk of spiritual instruction, so that when I shall drink it, my silent meditation alone would show that I am satisfied.

"But, kindly, O Lord, do not send this all to me through your maid-servants in the form of your miraculous powers; I shall never accept it. Nor shall I accept any charity which will create the feeling of duality or of imperfection in me; nor again that which is offered to me piece-meal. I know you are the fulfiller of all desires. Therefore grant me such grace, and grant that yourself directly to me, as will make me as great and perfect and free from desires as you are.

"O, what a miracle ! when my Lord, Rāma gave me, this lame Rāmadāsa of his, whatever he wished to give out of His grace, I forgot that I was a beggar and that He was the donor. For, He made me as perfect and whole as He is. Verily, there is neither any beggar nor any donor within the bosom of that eternally One blissful Spiritual Consciousness."

I have virtually finished my preface by acknowledging that what I have done is nothing but what the great Saint Rāmadāsa has bestowed upon me by showing his grace. But before putting down my pen, I must do my humble and precious duty of giving expression to my sense of thankfulness to all those who have helped me in bringing this long-cherished work of mine to a happy conclusion. Dr. Mohanlal Sharma, M.A., Ph. D., Reader and Head in the Department of Philosophy, University of Jodhpur, Mr. M.P. Vyas, M.A., LL.B., Lecturer in the same department and Mr. Jagannath Vyas, M.A., have almost corrected the entire proofs and gave me very valuable suggestions. The latter especially was very useful in preparing the Index Mr. Kanhiyalal Joshi B.Com.,LL.B., who has ever been helpful to me in doing all sorts of work connected with the execution of plans of writing and publishing my books, has as usual obliged me greatly by preparing the typed copy for the Press. To my sons, Dr. Vishvanath, M.R.C.P., and Dr. Raghunath, Ph.D., I cannot be less thankful inasmuch as it is on account of all the facilities which they provided me while I was with them in America, that I could finish the whole of the manuscript of this work. To M/s Motilal Banarsidass, Publishers of Delhi, I offer my heartfelt thanks for coming forward and undertaking the venture of publishing this work. The Printers also have a rightful claim on my thankfulness for having done their job so nicely and without any flaw.

V.H. DATE

CONTENTS

SPIRITUAL TREASURE OF ST. RĀMADĀSA

CHAPTER I

LIFE, SĀDHANĀ AND RULES OF CONDUCT

A. *Life of Rāmadāsa.*

Rāmadāsa was born at midday on Tuesday, the 9th day of the bright half of the month of Chaitra, in the year Śake 1530 (15th of March 1608 A.D.). A strange coincidence that Śrī Rāmachandra, the renowned Avatāra of Viṣṇu is also believed to have been born thousands of years ago on the same day of the month, and at the same noon time, which since then has come to be known as the Rāma-navamī day. The place of birth of Rāmadāsa was Jāmba, a small village situated on the bank of the river Godāvarī, in the district of Aurangabad, in the present State of Mahārāshṭra. He is the second child of Rāṇubai and of Sūryājipant Ṭhosar, a Ṛgvedi, Deshastha Brahmin bearing the ancestral gotra (family name) as Jamadagni-vatsa, and devoted to the worship of Rāma and of the Sun-god. The family was a well-to-do one, since Sūryājipant was the Kulkarni (Revenue Officer) of twelve villages. But he had no issue for a very long time; and it was only after continuous devotion and repeated prayers both to the Sun-god and to Śrī Rāma that Rāṇubai gave birth to her eldest son, Gaṅgādhara, on the 13th of Mārgashīrsha in Śake 1527. As ill luck would have it, Sūryājipant died when Nārāyaṇa, (for, that was the name of their second son, before he became known as Rāmadāsa) was only seven years old.

Two things were remarkable about Rāmadāsa even at this tender age. Though not naughty, he was a very frolicsome boy. He would climb to the very top of a tree and from there jump like a monkey on the top of an adjacent tree, or throwing himself down in the river below, would swim with great pleasure. On one such occasion, he got his forehead severely hit and the protuberance caused thereby became as if a life-long ornament to him. It was on account of this agile, enthusiastic and fearless nature of the boy that people might have begun to call him out of joke as the incarnation of Hanumān. Indeed, this came out to be true later on when Nārāyaṇa became, as Hanumān before him, the greatest of the devotees and servants (dāsa) of Śrī Rāma. Equally remarkable were his love for thinking in solitude and his quest for God. Indeed how wonderful it is that what he later on in his life taught as the outcome of his mature wisdom, namely, that a man's life should revolve round the two poles, namely, of activity and contemplation, he should have exemplified it in his early boyhood. That he should often keep awake till late in the night and think about the well-being of the world, that even when he was eight, he should request his elder brother, Gangadharpant, to instruct him in the spiritual lore and that, when his request was not granted, he should go straight outside the village and sleep in the temple of Hanumān with the prayer that he should be shown the way to realize God, and that being pleased with this Rāma should appear in his dream and give him the 'mantra' for meditation,—all this strikes as a great wonder. The four years intervening between Śake 1538 to 1542, Rāmadāsa must have utilised in getting some education at the school, as well as some knowledge of Sanskrit and religion from some Pandit in the old orthodox manner, as was common in those days. All the same, he must not have neglected his meditation on the Name of God, as he was instructed to do in his dream. Otherwise, his running away from the marriage hall in Śake 1542 for the sake of realizing God would not have taken place at all so easily.

A new chapter lasting for twelve years opened in his life in Śake 1542. This was the period of his great penance, of meditation and realization of God. From morn till noon, he used to stand waist-deep in the waters of Godāvarī, at Tākaḷi, and meditate upon the Gāyatrī-mantra, and again in the afternoon meditate on the Name 'Rāma'. This he did regularly for twelve years, without a single exception. Naturally, it must be during this period that he can be said to have realized the immaculate and the permanent vision of the Lord, Rāmachandra, along with Sītā, Lakṣmaṇa and Hanumān. Considered from his own personal point of view, there was nothing to be gained beyond this. God-realization, the realization of the Self or the Ātman, and the experience of the identity of the Self and Brahman, were all achieved by him. None could have said a word against him, if he had stopped his spiritual activities only with this personal achievement, and not gone beyond to improve the ethico-spiritual conduct of the people around him and of the humanity at large. For, as the Bhagavadgītā says, "one who sports with the Ātman with love and is satisfied by living in the Ātman, may or may not engage himself in other activities" (3.17).

But Rāmadāsa like Yājñavalkya and King Janaka before him, or like the incarnations of the Supreme Being, namely Rāma and Kṛṣṇa, or like the Antarātman himself whom he worshipped, was one of the most active saints the world has ever seen. He wished to create as many saints as possible like himself, so that within his lifetime or after his passing away, they should continue to do the same ethico-spiritual mission of bringing people on the path of God-realization which he himself was doing in the manner in which Rāma and Kṛṣṇa and the sages of the olden times had done. "I shall not call myself a servant (dāsa) of Rāma, if like him I do not save the souls of others", says he with great confidence. That was both his ambition and his vow.

Therefore, for twelve years again, from 1554 to 1566, he was ever on his feet, and travelled far and wide throughout the length and breadth of India. It is said that he went into Nepal (probably to visit the temple of Paśupati) and touched even Kabul and Kandhar. Even during his stay at Tākaḷi for twelve years Rāmadāsa must have had several occasions to hear about the woeful condition of the Hindus under the oppressive rule of the Muslims. Naturally, he must have thought to see things for himself and be convinced about the same, so that he could think of finding out some means to counteract the evil and make life secure and peaceful. What however was in store for him was utter gloom and despair. Wherever he went he found heart-rending situation. Hindu temples were being demolished, and along with this the Hindu culture, skill and arts were almost destroyed. Women were not safe in the least; and conversion to Islam was being done through temptation or force on a very large scale. To a certain extent, the Hindus too were responsible for their downfall. They became cowards and sought the shelter of the Muslims, or embraced Islam of their own accord.

They became so selfish and treacherous that they deserted their own kings and sardars, and joining the enemy fought against them in order to usurp power and wealth. The Kṣatriyas lost their valour and took pleasure in serving at the Muslim courts. The Brahmins became the most pretentious and the meanest of the lot. Excepting a few here and there who were really both learned and pious, the majority of them did not know their own religion. Parrot-like they repeated the Vedas without understanding the meaning and made the sacred mantras as commodities for sale. Thus the two chief upper classes of the Hindu society cared only for their belly and the satisfaction of having wealth and power. Even most of the sannyāsins among them were a pack of scoundrels, wandering over the earth under the guise of pious sādhus, but engaged in cheating the people. Under such circumstances, it became very easy for the Muslims to be more and more oppressive and to secure whatever they liked through persuasion, loot and plunder. As the result of this all, life became intolerable for those who were morally good and God-fearing. Everywhere there was the dark shadow of dread, gloom, despair and insecurity; and to his great horror and disappointment, Rāmadāsa was constantly hearing the groaning of the millions of the Hindu slaves.

Was there any way for Rāmadāsa to get out of this dangerously sensitive plight ? Was there any hope for him, single-handed as he was ? Yes, his hope and his remedy lay in what he had already achieved in his twelve years' concentrated spiritual sādhanā. He had the full faith that God's grace was on him, and that therefore he was not alone. Silent meditation in the presence of God and constant rumination in seclusion over the single thought of how to liberate the country from the foreign yoke, had given him certain guiding principles about which we shall say more later on. For the present, we only note that he was convinced about two things. One was, there would be no security, peace and happiness under the Muslim rule, that is, until it is replaced by Swarājya. The second was that the Hindu society as a whole was in need of repair, of such a strong shake-up that it would be roused from its lethargy, ignorance and its habituated insensitiveness to slavery and dishonour in every respect. To attain this twofold task of achieving political freedom and of moulding and strengthening the moral courage of the Hindu society, he must have thought of having a twofold remedy. In the first place, the ruling power must be in the hands of those who have the highest esteem for the moral and the spiritual life, and who would strive for the common weal of all. Secondly, the people in general must be so trained morally and spiritually, that there would be no disharmony of intent and action between the rulers and the ruled. Of course, both these remedies are interdependent and must co-exist both as means and ends on the solid foundation of a selfless life of devotion, dedication, and service to God and to mankind as a whole. Rāmadāsa never intended to have the Hindu religion as against the religion of Islam; nor did he think it proper that Islam should wipe away Hinduism by cruelty and atrocities. He wished to have a free religious life for all, whether Hindus or Muslims. But there was nothing wrong in protecting the Hindu religion against the onslaughts of the Muslim fanaticism. Thus, in view of the prevailing horrible condition of the country, Rāmadāsa must have concluded that the application of the first remedy was a greater necessity. For, if once the political power is there, and if it is in just and worthy hands and is not abused, persuasion, training and instruction in the moral and spiritual fields would be very easy and smooth. And yet, Rāmadāsa was keen enough to understand that a band of selfless persons like himself was the minimum necessity for starting his twofold mission.

Now the next problem for Rāmadāsa was to find out a place where he should try his experiment. No part of the country was absolutely safe to do this. Especially, the whole of the northern India beyond the rivers Godāvarī and Narmadā, as also the whole of the southern India beyond the river Kṛshṇā was occupied by the Muslim rulers. In the north, there was the power of the most unscrupulous rulers. Shahjahan and Aurangzeb were the contemporaries of Rāmadāsa. And in the south, there was the Bahamani Kingdom which lasted for 180 years (1347 to 1526 A.D.), but which was not a whit behind in the cruelties and atrocities wrought by the Muslims in the North. Afterwards it split up into five different kingdoms, but it spelled as if five times more misery and oppression on the Hindus. Together, they destroyed not only the most flourishing Hindu empire, so to say, of Vijaynagar, but also several small kingdoms of the Hindus in the south. Mahārāshṭra also was not safe. But there were two favourable considerations which must have made Rāmadāsa to choose Mahārāshṭra, as the venue of his new activities from Śake 1566 to the end of his life, in Śake 1603. Rāmadāsa himself was a Mahārāshṭrīya. He knew the people and their hearts and their aspirations more than he knew of any other people. Another consideration was that Shāhji, the father of Shivāji, and a notable Sardar at the court of Bījāpur, had taken under his powers the Jagīr of Masūr, that is, of a strip of the country extending from Satārā to Mirāj and Kolhāpur. Shāhji and Rāmadāsa must have known each other very well, since during the period when the latter was doing his penance at Tākaḷi, the country surrounding Nasik and Trimbakeśvara was under the jurisdiction of Shāhji. So, the most natural and correct inference would be that it must have been after consultations with Shāhji, that Rāmadāsa decided to shift from the bank of Godāvarī to that of Kṛshṇā. Shivāji too was slowly and gradually becoming more and more active; and Rāmadāsa must have thought, as also received the sanction of his Deity, that Shivāji would be the most proper person who would put an end to the foreign rule, and then relying on the growing strength of morality and spiritual knowledge of the people in general, bring about security, peace and happiness.

Chāphaḷa near Karāḍa was thus selected by Rāmadāsa as the headquarters of his multifarious activities; and he made the beginning by the most daring acts of that time, namely, the setting up of eleven images of Hanumān at Shāhpur, Masur, Chāphaḷa and other places, and the celebrating of the anniversary of the birth-day of Lord, Rāma, at Masur in Śake 1567 and at Chāphaḷa in 1569. When throughout the whole of the country, woeful tales of the destruction of hundreds of the Hindu temples were being daily heard, the setting up of new idols and the building of temples was both a challenge to the power of the Muslims and the test of his own strength. People were infused with courage, and they got the first lesson of becoming united for the common cause of the worship of their gods. Without being paid any wages for their labour, they even built the temple of Rāma at Chāphaḷa. And to ensure it as if against being pulled down, Rāmadāsa managed to have the gifts of land for the erection of the temple and for the worship of God from the Hindu Sardars at the court of the Bījāpur Durbar itself. This was indeed the most triumphant augury of the huge task ahead, namely of establishing a Hindu Raj in order to have a check upon the atrocities of the Muslims. Soon afterwards, in Śake 1571, in the garden at Shingaṅāwāḍi near Chāphaḷa, Rāmadāsa accepted Shivāji in his spiritual fold. It was this act of initiation which made Rāmadāsa not only the Spiritual Teacher of Shivāji but also the best guide and counsellor in matters concerning politics.

The view that the act of initiation took place in Śake 1594, and that Shivāji and Rāmadāsa came together for the first time in that year, and that therefore, Rāmadāsa was only the Spiritual teacher of Shivāji, but that he was in no way concerned with the political career of Shivāji, is altogether wrong. In this connection we shall simply note what Mr. S.S. Deva, a great scholar of the works and literature about Rāmadāsa, and Professor R.D. Ranade have to say. It will be absurd, says Deva, to believe that Rāmadāsa and Shivāji, did not meet till Śake 1594, when Sambhāji, the son of Shivāji, in his Sanada of Śake 1602, whereby he donated some land to Vāsudeva Gosāvī, a prominent disciple of Rāmadāsa, makes mention of another Sanada whereby Shivāji had given to the same Vāsudeva Gosāvī a piece of land in Śake 1593. It looks very strange that Shivāji should not know Rāmadāsa in the least till Śake 1594, and yet donate land to the disciple of Rāmadāsa in 1593. Professor Ranade brings forth another formidable evidence to show that Shivāji had come in contact with Rāmadāsa since the foundation of the temple at Chāphaḷa, that is to say, since Śake 1569 though the meeting took place in Śake 1571. Professor Ranade refers to the most important Sanada[1] which Shivāji passed on to Rāmadāsa with utmost respect and gratitude in Śake 1600, wherein Shivāji sums up his relation to Rāmadāsa, during the past thirty years. Besides, it was in Śake 1577, that Shivāji offered the whole of his kingdom to Rāmadāsa, though Rāmadāsa declined to accept it, just as he had declined before this Shivāji's offer to build the temple

1. This Sanada is given at the end of this Chapter.

at Chāphaḷa and to meet all the expenses in connection with the daily worship and other festivals of the Lord, Rāma.

Thus, if we are once convinced that Rāmadāsa and Shivāji were intimately bound together by spiritual ties, it will be easy for us to understand that they were not working in two different watertight spheres, though apparently politics is different from spiritual life. We may add a third sphere to this, namely, the sphere of social ethics in general; for without this as the basis there would be neither untainted spiritual life, nor the adequate dispensation of justice at the hands of the rulers, Shivāji produced his veteran warriors and soldiers to vanquish the enemy and acquire new territory, but not to molest and abduct any women. Rāmadāsa produced hundreds of Mahantas and thousands of disciples whose main duty was to make people morally good and spiritually devoted to God. They were not beggars in the sense of being parasites on the society; they begged not so much to fill their belly as to glorify the Name of God and to feed the people who would assemble at the time of festivals or ceremonies connected with the worship of God.

So, being encouraged by the extraordinary success which he achieved in carrying out his initial spiritual activities at Chāphaḷa, Masur and several other places within a radius of about 50 to 75 miles from Chāphaḷa, Rāmadāsa began to take more and more daring steps of establishing various other similar centres to carry on his twofold mission of instructing the people to live an untainted ethico-spiritual life, and thereby flock together with strength and unity under one political banner of one mighty, just and benevolent Hindu ruler. These centres, which he called as Maṭhas, were spread by him all over the country. There was hardly any important town or place of pilgrimage where a Rāmadāsī Maṭha was not to be found. From Rāmeśvara to Badrikedār, and from Dwārakā to Jagannātha Puri, these Maṭhas, on the authority of Giridhara, numbered not less than one thousand. Each of them was given in charge of a Mahanta who was instructed and tested by Rāmadāsa as being strong, efficient, wise, good, just, compassionate, and above all extremely devoted to God. Every such Mahanta was expected to do the same work as Rāmadāsa did. He was allowed to have his own band of faithful, selfless disciples, everyone of whom was potentially a Mahanta, just as every Mahanta was, at the time when he was appointed, potentially a Rāmadāsa. The disciples were expected to beg alms for their own maintenance and for the growth and upkeep of the Maṭha itself, so that it should develop into a strong ethico-politico-spiritual outpost of the Kingdom of Rāmadāsa and Shivāji. Naturally, the disciples were also expected to act like soldiers as if, and to protect the outposts and all those who would come for shelter, from robbers and attacks from any other alien power. Shivāji's escape from the prison at Agra and his safe arrival at Satara can never be properly explained unless it is presumed, that he was being helped at every step by these Mahantas and disciples. The Mahantas, therefore, were expected to act in unison with each other, by constant communication and exchange of views; and they had to send their reports regularly to Rāmadāsa and meet him at least once in two or three years. In short, like the Monads of Leibnitz, each disciple and each Mahanta was expected to represent the Central Monad (Rāmadāsa) in respect of all his characteristics and activities. The whole network was thus a unique and harmonious combination of aristocracy in its ascent, and democracy of equal rights and opportunities in its descent. None could disobey Rāmadāsa; or else, the punishment was sure to come heavily upon him. Vāsudeva Gosāvī, one of the most trusted Mahantas, for instance, was once beaten by Rāmadāsa in the presence of several persons for having misused the spiritual mantra. In his Dāsabodha Rāmadāsa has described at several places how a Mahanta should behave, and how he himself used to behave in order to collect people around him for the common cause of establishing a benevolent Swarājya. Let us, therefore, mention some of the important directions which he had given to both the Mahantas and the disciples; for, that will necessarily give us a picture of how Rāmadāsa himself behaved. In fact, they were the characteristics first of Rāmadāsa; and so, they can be considered as the guiding principles of any Mahanta or an ideal saint who wishes to be active even after God-realization for the moral and the spiritual good of others. In other words, they constitute the entire ethical code of an active saint.

The first and the foremost duty of a Mahanta or an ideal

saint is that he must realize God. He should then try to make this easy for others by initiating them in the spiritual life. To be able to do this, he must attract the people towards him by his soft, sweet, but truthful speech. They must first know that there exists a man who is God-fearing, morally upright, compassionate, forgiving, trustworthy and helpful, and that if they approach him he would be ever prepared to instruct them and make them gradually know the things which he knows. Of course, he must be very intelligent to know who is who, that is, to know if a person is a pretender, an enemy, a spy or a wicked man, and then treat him as he deserves, without letting him know that he has been found out. The Mahanta should not trust in anyone unless he is tested in several ways. Then alone according to the capacity and competence of everyone he should be asked to do something or be kept at a distance. But one should never allow himself to be known by others. Therefore, not everything should be made known to others, and certainly not to all. One must always keep something which he can call his own, and which he alone can deal with. If however others should test him, he should never be found wanting and fall in their esteem. The same people then, who might have formed wrong opinions about him, would correct themselves and flock around him, and wait to do as he would bid. No greatness can be had, or nothing great can be achieved unless one undergoes utmost trouble first, and unless one resorts to seclusion and to meditation on God, and thinks about the problems he wishes to solve. Then alone a Mahanta can produce another Mahanta like him.

There are also other characteristics of an ideal saint. Like Rāmadāsa, he should also first do and have thee xperience for himself, and then preach others to do the same. Never will he be tired of putting forth efforts; for, this to Rāmadāsa, is absolutely a divine quality. How will a saint then afford to give up his daily meditation ? To do so is to cease to be a Mahanta. Of course, in the case of an active saint like Rāmadāsa, meditation would be followed by activity, and activity followed by meditation. Will there then be any time left for him for idle gossip, disputations, lethargy and for long hours of sleep and merriment ? Desires of his own, he has none; his only desire is to be content with the life in the Ātman. He is, therefore, ever engaged in doing some kind of good to others. He knows that life is too short, lasting as if for a couple of days; and so, living like a guest in this world, he does the maximum use of it by means of meditation for the moral and spiritual upliftment of himself and others. This he feels he can do better by remaining unknown in mountains and valleys, and only occasionally coming down amongst the people to preach and set them right. He might look and live like a beggar on alms, but neither is he dependent on anyone except God, nor would he ask for anything even from his disciples, except that they should meditate on God after his passing away. It is worth remembering in this connection how Rāmadāsa refused to accept any financial aid or even kingly power from Shivāji. In 1570-71, Rāmadāsa himself dug the earth, cut the trees and the thorny shrubs and helped his innumerable, faithful disciples in building the temple of Rāma in Chāphaḷa, when Shivāji was prepared to bear all the cost of it. Again in 1577, Rāmadāsa refused to accept the whole of the Kingdom which Shivāji had offered him, saying to him that he should rule over it as a trustee of God and protect all his subjects with justice and mercy.

A few more qualities came to stay in Rāmadāsa on account of his constant and direct contact with the Ātman. Like the Ātman, Rāmadāsa too was the doer of all things, but remained aloof and hidden at the back of all as the prime mover and support of all. He lived in all sorts of environmental conditions and difficulties, but was neither daunted nor disturbed or contaminated by anyone of them. We shall do well not to say in advance all that will necessarily be told as we proceed. It will be sufficient if we direct the attention of the readers to Sections 52, 61,64,70,74,87, and 88 of Ch. II on Dāsabodha and verses 47 to 56 from those addressed to the Mind, in order to know how the Mahantas and disciples should behave like him.

Rāmadāsa's Upāsanā of Rāma as the Antarātman of all was the only source of his strength, courage, hope and success. Depending on this, he used to do whatever he thought to be proper, and to advise and forewarn Shivāji on several occasions. To quote some instances, it was through his foremost disciple, Kalyāṇa, that Shivāji was cautioned about the impending attack and treacherous visit of Afzulkhan of the Bījāpur Durbar (Śake

1581). His going over to Tanjore in Śake 1577 was not so much with the view to visit the holy temple of Rāmeśvara, as to meet Shāhji and have talks with him regarding the future plans about the activities of Shivāji as also to bless king Vyankoji and appoint Bhīmaswāmī as the Mahanta at Tanjore Maṭha. Rāmadāsa did attend the ceremony of the auspicious entrance into the fort of Pratāpgaḍha in Śake 1579. And in Śake 1594, he went along with Divākara Gosāvī to Pāragaon near Panhālā, at about a distance of twenty miles from Kolhāpur, in order to have a secret meeting with Shivāji, regarding probably the capture of the fort Panhālā. For, in the end of this very year, Konḍāji Pharjada, a warrior of Shivāji, took only sixty men of the mountains, and conquered the fort in one night only.

The point to note in this context is that Rāmadāsa did not even mind his remaining absent at Chāphaḷa for the celebration of the festival of the Rāma-navamī day, the anniversary day of the birth of the Lord, Rāma. He celebrated it at Pāragaon. This shows how his spiritual mission was inextricably bound so much so with the political mission of Shivāji that he knew very well as to which he should give his immediate attention and which not. The equanimity of mind which he had attained by his having realized the Ātman was so great that it could not be shaken whether he was to be at Chāphaḷa or at Pāragaon. And, as the chief aim of his life was to make all men happy, the people of Pāragaon were not alien to him. They too were fortunate to attend the Kīrtana which Rāmadāsa had performed at the residence of Rāmachandra Amātya. In Śake 1596, Shivāji was crowned King; and though opinions differ whether Rāmadāsa went to stay at Sajjanagaḍha in Śake 1598 or was already staying there, as the most reliable Vākenaśīprakaraṇa tells us, since Śake 1572, one thing is certain that Shivāji went over to Sajjanagaḍha soon after his coronation ceremony was over and spent a huge amount in feeding the poor during his stay there for about a month and a half. It is said that several Mahantas, saints and prominent disciples had also assembled there for the first spiritual conference, so to say, (and perhaps the last in the lifetime of Rāmadāsa and Shivāji), and that Kīrtanas were being performed daily by someone of them, including both Shivāji and Rāmadāsa. Now, whether this happened in Śake 1596 or 1598 is not of much importance;

for, as said above, Rāmadāsa must have had made Sajjanagaḍha as his permanent residence since Śake 1572, though he might have made it a point to visit Chāphaḷa every year for the festival of the Rāma-navamī day. Sajjanagaḍa must have provided a far better vantage ground to Rāmadāsa than Chāphaḷa to have an easy survey upto Poona and beyond on one side in the north, and upto Karāḍ, Mirāj and Kolhāpur, on the other, in the south. It seems, he intended to make another headquarter up in the mountainous region to the west of Karāḍ, in the valley of Heḷavāka with the view to have his keen and protective eye on the country lying beyond the western side of the Sahyādri mountain, and stretching far and wide from Chiplun to Ratnagiri along with the seacoast. Rāmadāsa went to stay at Heḷavāka in the very winter of 1596, that is just a few months after Shivāji was crowned king. But unfortunately, he suffered very much from fever and bronchitis at Heḷavāka, and he had to return to the hot climate of Chāphaḷa. Rāmadāsa acknowledges with gratitude how he was attended upon with great care and affection by Raghunāthabhaṭa at Heḷavāka, and how the deity of Hanumān to whom he was offering prayers cured him from illness.

Before proceeding to the description of the Sādhanā which Rāmadāsa himself practised and which he preached to others, let us make two observations regarding Rāmadāsa's mission in life as a whole, and his relation with Shivāji. As we have already seen, his one mission in life was to make people in general morally and spiritually enlightened. In this, he made no distinction of caste and creed, not even between Hindus and Muslims. People who wish to accuse him of being pro-Hindu and pro-Brahmin should consider how Rāmadāsa has severely condemned the Brahmins, as no other non-Brahmin could do, by saying that the Brahmins had lost all contacts with God and had become morally and spiritually bankrupt. A Brahmin is one, says he, who knows the Brahman. Pitying the Brahmins for having lost all wisdom, learning and self-respect, and seeing them as mere belly-fillers by means of flattery and service of the mean-minded, he says that they should take a lesson and improve their conduct. Rāmadāsa appears to be pro-Hindu, and one must admit that he was to some extent in favour of a Hindu Raj; but this must be assessed on the background of the inhuman atrocities committed by the Muslim fanatics and the utter destruction of the Hindu temples, and their culture, religion, art, as well as the molestation of the Hindu women, for centuries together in his own lifetime and before. But he never encouraged fanaticism among the Hindus. On the contrary, his spiritual message was equally addressed to Muslims as would be clear from several of his Hindi songs where he has pointed out without any equivocation that there is no difference between Rāma and Allah. Here, it will be appropriate to say about Shivāji with equal justice that he too had no ill will against the religion of the Muslims. In fact, to show equal respect to their religion he built a mosque at Raigaḍha opposite to his own palace. As G.S. Sardesai tells us he "revered the saint Bābā Yakuti of Keḷsi as much as he did Rāmadāsa". He was a protector of all faiths. He had Muslims in his service "on high posts of trust and honour".

Regarding the other point we know that there are people who, on account of bias, presupposition or for some other reason, do not like that a Brahmin should be the Guru of a non-Brahmin. But historical conclusions do not depend upon wishful thinking. The life of Rāmadāsa apart from the political activities of Shivāji in which he had engaged himself would have been much poorer than what it was, and the life of Shivāji, bereft of his spiritual involvement on account of his close association with Rāmadāsa, would have been equally poor. It would be futile to say that Rāmadāsa was more dependent upon Shivāji, or that Shivāji was more dependent on Rāmadāsa. Both were independent monarchs in their own spheres; and yet both of them depended upon each other voluntarily for the common object of regaining the honour of the country, for the prosperity and the moral life of the people living in it, as also for the glory of God. Rāmadāsa represented the divine wisdom and the strategy (Yukti), while Shivāji represented the nobility of character and bravery (Śakti). They both were necessary to establish a Hindu Swarājya in opposition to the tremendous and oppressive power of the Muslims. It must be noted that Rāmadāsa's going over to Mahārāshtra in Śake 1566 for the propagation of spiritual mission synchronized with Shivāji's capture of the fortresses of Koṇdanā and Purandara.

Rāmadāsa did not go even to Jāmba to meet his mother

whom he had met in Śake 1562, except suddenly at the time of her death in Śake 1577. This was the year when Shivāji offered his whole kingdom to Rāmadāsa, but which Rāmadāsa refused to accept. Six years later, in Śake 1583, when Rāmadāsa went to Pratāpagaḍha, he set up there the image of Tuḷajā Bhavānī, the Goddess whom Shivāji used to worship. Rāmadāsa implored her to protect Shivāji, to make him a great King in his very sight, and to destroy the enemy, as she had destroyed the demons on several occasions before. He tells us further in the verses describing the 'region of bliss' (Ānandavanabhuvana) how the Goddess who had bestowed a boon upon Rāma was equally kind to his servants, namely, Rāmadāsa and Shivāji, how in a vision he saw her with a bludgeon in her hand, and walking along with Shivāji and destroying the mlecchas. Does this not show that Rāmadāsa had taken up the cause of Shivāji as his own, and that he wished to secure the blessing of the Goddess for this purpose? The one firm belief of Rāmadāsa was that power resides in putting forth efforts over efforts, but that they would be crowned with success only when they get the support of the grace of God. Shivāji too learnt this great truth from Rāmadāsa. And there would be no shame in accepting that he became a follower of Rāmadāsa not only for acquiring spiritual wisdom but also for securing the divine sanction, strength and protection both from Rāmadāsa as his spiritual Master and from his patron Goddess, Tuḷajā Bhavānī.

In fact, for both of them, the inordinate growth of sins, injustice, cruelty and oppression had become too intolerable to bear any longer. Of the two, however, Rāmadāsa had the clear idea that notwithstanding the divine power which was definitely on his side, he was still in need of an earthly, physical instrument in the form of a morally good, brave, intelligent and powerful person. On the other hand, Shivāji, as a pious and a God-fearing person must have assumed that the invisible hand of God would surely come forward to help him in his noble cause of freeing the people from slavery, ignorance and poverty. As destiny would have it, both came close to each other in Śake 1566; both used to hear with great pleasure what the other was doing; and both became exceedingly eager to meet each other. Shivāji sent his men to know the whereabouts of Rāmadāsa; and Rāmadāsa too after meeting them sent a letter to Shivāji in which he says, "Blessed are you in that you possess excellent qualities of a pious and benevolent King; you are a mountain of courage and have become the support of innumerable, helpless people on account of your bravery and daring. Many a wicked enemy, you have destroyed and have filled the hearts of many with terror. It is on account of you that to some extent at least Mahārāshtra has been saved from being totally destroyed, and that the Hindu religion is still living. And yet much is to be done. It is with great hope that I have come to stay in your territory, but I wonder why you have not as yet taken cognizance of this." Upon this, as Bakhara tells us, Shivāji went immediately to meet Rāmadāsa. And, since then, as their acquaintance grew into a friendship of mutual trust, it became possible for Rāmadāsa to initiate him into Spiritual life in Śake 1571.

Two more incidents in the life of Rāmadāsa are most important, in our opinion; for, they shed more light on the nature of the relation that existed between Rāmadāsa and Shivāji. In the month of Chaitra, Śake 1602, Shivāji died. Of this, Rāmadāsa had given, it is said, a hint to Shivāji some two months before the event. This kind of foreknowledge ought to have prepared Rāmadāsa himself to bear the tremendous loss, and yet to carry on his mission of turning men to spiritual life after the death of Shivāji. But this he could not do. It appears that he felt a vacuum in his life. He came to know that the death of Shivāji was an end of his mission also. Thereupon he almost stopped his activities; he became too sad to talk with others; he used to retire in seclusion and meditate. Another incident. when however Sambhāji went to meet Rāmadāsa, he was told that he should place before him the ideal life of his father, Shivāji, and that he should do as his father did to protect his subjects from being molested by the enemies. After one year, that is, in Chaitra Śake 1603, Rāmadāsa went to Chāphaḷa for the Rāma-navamī festival and came back to Sajjanagaḍha, soon after it was over. Probably, he was waiting for the arrival of the images of Rāma, Sītā and Lakṣmaṇa from Tanjore. These were installed on the 5th day of the dark fortnight of Māgha, Śake 1603. Rāmadāsa then totally refused to take food and water; and only four days afterwards, that is, on the 9th day he gave up the ghost after ejaculating loudly the Name Rāma, three times.

In short, all these above-mentioned facts in the lives of Rāmadāsa and Shivāji ought to convince us that they had no two separate missions. To sever the two lives and to consider each of them in isolation will be unhistorical, unjudicious, unpolitical and unspiritual.

B. Sādhanā of Rāmadāsa

Before proceeding to describe the routine of Rāmadāsa's own spiritual discipline in the earlier years of his life and the gradual changes which occurred in his mode of worshipping his Deity as he advanced in age, it is very necessary to keep in mind constantly a few of the fundamental features of his dynamic life as a whole. Rāmadāsa tells us very often that he never preached anything unless he had first an experience about it. Knowledge which does not stand the test of one's own direct experience is like a vomit of a dog, he says. Even so, is the preaching of how one should behave. His advice to others about anything, especially in matters of social and moral conduct and spiritual discipline is only a reflection of his own experience and example. As the ethico-spiritual life is necessarily a growth, a process of development, it will not be wrong to say that like all other great saints, Rāmadāsa too was a saint in the making. Naturally, what he philosophises and says on the basis of his own observation and experience is not a dull repetition of what others had said before him, but a valuable addition to it. To a superficial reader who will not understand the importance of these additions, the works of Rāmadāsa will appear as replete with contradictions and counter-statements. But if, as hinted above, one would remember that the life of devotion also is amenable to growth, organization and unity, the contradictions will be found not only as reconcilable but also necessary to eke out the deficiencies of the earlier statements.

We must not also lose sight of two more facts, namely, the method of Rāmadāsa's writings and his motive in not disturbing the faith of others without giving a substitute for it. His method was intended to shed more and more light on the various problems of spiritual life, by retaining what is valuable in the old notions of the past and by linking it with what is more valuable and comprehensive in the present, so that instead of contradiction, there would be coherence. The method was the instrument of fulfilling his motive namely, to give to his followers and to the humanity at large a substitute which would be more real, more enduring and more congenial and satisfying than what they possessed before. His earnest yearning to raise the thinking and the devotional section of the humanity to a higher level of truth, goodness and reality is reflected both in his teachings and in his own example. So, it will be on this background that we shall narrate how Rāmadāsa could himself ascend by the grace of God from the worship of images, idols and that of the incarnations of God to the worship of the Ātman and the Lord, and from that to the realization of the Brahman.

There is a belief that Rāmadāsa had realized God even at the tender age of eight. But this seems to us quite improbable. It must have been based on a current anecdote that Hanumān, the celebrated devotee of Rāma once entered the house of Sūryājipant, the father of Rāmadāsa, and seeing Sūryājipant alone, lifted and carried him in the jungle outside the village and showed him the beautiful forms of Rāma and Lakṣmaṇa. The story goes on to say that Rāma blessed Sūryājipant and gave him the assurance that he would have a son who would spread the gospel of the devotion of God far and wide. This might be relied upon because Rāmadāsa himself makes mention of it. But he continues to tell us that he too like his father had a dream of this kind in that very temple of Hanumān outside the town and had received directly from the Lord, Rāma, the 'mantra', as also the instruction that he should worship the image of Hanumān. Had there been the realization of God in his early boyhood in Śake 1538, there was no point in his being deeply disappointed when his elder brother, Gaṅgādharpant, known as Śreṣṭha, refused to impart him the 'mantra'. Besides, the great penance which Rāmadāsa underwent for twelve years at Tākaḷi on the bank of the river Godāvarī near Nasik from 1542 to 1554, loses much of its significance, if he is to be credited with having the Rāma-darśana without any efforts at the age of eight only.

On the contrary, his extreme anxiety to have the vision of God, and on that account his anguish in not having the 'mantra' from his elder brother, must have been the two great incentives which had kept him restless for four years afterwards, till he got a suitable opportunity to run away from the 'mandap' where he was about to be married. Perhaps, he wished to please his mother who insisted upon his being married, and so he came into the mandap; but the words 'Sāvadhāna, Sāvadhāna' (Beware, Beware), which the priests and the relatives chanted while singing some devotional songs, made him conscious of his mission in life, and forthwith he ran away. It appears that he had a very clear idea of that mission. He had not wasted the four years that intervened between the disappointment at his brother's hand and the time of his running away from the marriage hall. For, when, on one occasion, he kept awake and was sitting alone for long hours at night, his mother asked him as to why he was sitting that way and what he was thinking about. "I am anxiously thinking about the well-being of the whole world, mother," replied Nārāyaṇa. (For, that was the name of the boy before he became known as Rāmadāsa.) And, as the whole of his life is a pointer to what kind of well-being he must have been thinking about, we can very easily say that his only mission in life was to realize God for himself, and then by placing his own example before the thinking humanity, turn them towards the single ideal of God-realization, by being morally and spiritually disciplined.

The earliest form of worship which Rāmadāsa therefore adopted at Tākaḷi was a combination of devotion directed to both the Saguṇa and the Nirguṇa aspects of God. Following the instruction given by the Lord in the dream, Rāmadāsa set up the first image of Hanumān at Tākaḷi and began to worship it. At the same time, being a Brahmin, he also used to repeat the Gāyatrī-Mantra which is a very valuable and efficacious means of propitiating the Sun-God. Besides, this was the form of worship which his forefathers also had adopted before him. So, these two, the worship of the Sun-God and of Hanumān, constituted the Saguṇa-bhakti of Rāmadāsa. In addition to this, he was also repeating the mantra which the Lord Rāma had imparted to him in the dream. The mantra must have been no other than the divine Name of 'Rāma'; for it was this as also the Gāyatrī which he was repeating at Tākaḷi daily from early morning to noon, for a period of twelve years (1542 to 1554) by standing waist-deep in the waters of Godāvarī. The Name however should not be construed as being the name of Rāma, the son of Daśaratha, but as being the symbol of the eternal, immortal God. The name therefore constituted the Nirguṇa Bhakti of Rāmadāsa.

But, after coming over to Masur in Mahārāshṭra, and after he had established himself at Chāphaḷa near Karāḍ, he set up eleven images of Hanumān in different places within a radius of about 50 to 75 miles, and thereby awakening the people from sloth and torpor, made them turn their attention to the worship of Rāma. This was polytheism no doubt, but he knew that it was only the first step towards being spiritual. He wished that the people should put their faith in Rāma; and so, he started the festivals of the birth of Rāma and that of Hanumān and created around him a band of ardent and courageous disciples who used to go forth and spread the devotion in exactly the same manner in which Rāmadāsa did. This was of great help in bringing about people in one camp as if.

Rāmadāsa himself acknowledges with great pride that it was his devotion towards Hanumān which made him realize the real nature of Rāma, and this he wished in the case of others also. So, not only did he recommend the worship of idols including the images of the incarnations of God, but he had also spent one whole 'Samāsa' (section) in his famous work, 'Dāsabodha' in mentioning about 40 to 50 deities and in recommending the people to worship anyone or more of them. Rāmadāsa does not stop with this, but recommends the people to worship any particular deity even mentally, if it becomes difficult to worship it physically. Even the material for worship, he advises them to create mentally and then offer it to that deity. Thus we see that he wishes the people to turn gradually from polytheism to monotheism and from physical worship to mental one.

As against this, paradoxically as if, with the view to raise the people to a higher level of devotion, Rāmadāsa denounces as forcibly as possible both the physical and the mental worship of the idols and images. How can images which are made of clay, stone or metal, and which are broken into pieces by the iconoclasts or stolen by thieves or thrown away into water, create the universe or save the souls of men? Similarly, after having recommended the people to visit the places of pilgrimage in order that they may increase the sattvaguṇa in them and purify themselves, Rāmadāsa asks them again very boldly if they can find anything else except stone and water in the places of pilgrimage or in the holy water of rivers. To move from one such place to another will only bring fatigue to the body and weariness to the mind. What Rāmadāsa intends to achieve by this criticism is that one might perhaps turn his attention to the worship of the Avatāras or the incarnations of God. But as they are no longer living, one has only to re-create them by his power of imagination after the pattern of the description of them in the Purāṇas. This too, says Rāmadāsa, though good and very useful, will not enable any one to discover the real God; for, here also, one has to fall back on one's own imagination as suggested by the descriptions of the authors of the Purāṇas. Perhaps, to those sagas of the olden times, the descriptions might have been of actual visions and not due to any imagination, which occurs in the worship of the idols, corresponding to the ideas of the goldsmith, or of the stone-cutter. No doubt, the reading or the listening of the glorious deeds of the incarnated gods is highly useful and meritorious, since it purifies the mind; but in no case can it be said that there can emerge on that account the concrete and the direct realization of God. One might excel in his power to visualize mentally what he would like to see or what is described to him by way of imagery. Rāmadāsa however says that there is a world-wide difference between what is visualized by imagination and what is actually seen with open eyes. What seems to be present before the mental vision vanishes when the eyes are opened. Dubious is the credit-value of a thing; the cash value is certain. That is why a person who is engaged in trying to visualize the image of a particular deity as it is described in the Purāṇas for his mental worship, might be bitterly disappointed, if in course of his mental creation of the image a particular limb of the deity becomes disproportionately larger or smaller. A garland of flowers, for instance, which he might intend to throw round the neck of his deity may prove to be too short on account of the sudden increase in the height of the neck or the head of the deity, or of the crown over its head. The devotee may thereby become all the more restless and unhappy by his mental worship.

Matters will not improve, says Rāmadāsa, even if one

goes beyond the worship of the images of the Incarnations of God and begins to worship the highest deities, namely, Brahmā, Viṣṇu and Maheśa, who are supposed to be the Creator, the Protector and the Destroyer of the universe, respectively. For who is that God, asks Rāmadāsa, who is the creator of Brahmā, the protector of Viṣṇu and the destroyer of Maheśa ? That God is the real God who must be worshipped. He is immanent in all, as being the inner Self, the Antarātmā of all. It is this God whom I worship, says Rāmadāsa. We shall not be able to verify this statement, if we simply believe that Rāmadāsa himself set up and worshipped the images of Hanumān at several places, or that the stone image of Rāma which, as was directed to him in a dream, was found by him in the river Kṛṣṇā at Aṅgāpur, and was then set up and worshipped by him for several years at Chāphaḷa. We shall be able to see the veracity of the statement by following very carefully, how Rāmadāsa in describing Hanumān in a 'stotra' (a verse of praise) is giving the description of his own experience of a vision. No longer it was the idol of stone before him, but the omnipresent, omnipotent vision of Hanumān who, he says, was his own inner Self. Rāmadāsa sees the vision first as small as a particle or a speck of dust, but as becoming afterwards larger and larger until it occupied the whole space; and the tail of Hanumān in the vision, he tells us further, as becoming longer and longer and as encircling the universe as if several times. The vision then looked like emitting fire from its eyes and as having swallowed the very disc of the Sun. Its speed was tremendous, even greater than the speed of the mind; and its jumps were so high, quick and incessant that even the tallest mountains were no obstacles to it. Fear itself, including that of Death, trembled before it. And yet, says Rāmadāsa, the vision was very pleasing to look at. It appeared to him as the most purifying and the life-giving principle of the universe. And he tells us finally that the vision of Hanumān changed into that of the Lord, Rāma. who was not only the Self of Rāmadāsa and Hanumān, but who is also the self of the whole of the Universe.

We thus see how Rāmadāsa had gone beyond both the physical and the mental worship of the deity of Hanumān, and seen him as being identical with Rāma, and as the universal Ātman of all. The creeper of the physical worship of the deity of Hanumān he did not allow to wither; but, on the contrary, he tells us that he made it ascend through a mental counterpart of the same, right upto the bower of the universal vision of the Lord, Rāma, whom he afterwards recognized as the only one creator, the protector and the destroyer of the universe. But, what must have been his upāsanā or the form of worship at this stage? Was it limited to the application of the sandle-paste on the foreheads of Rāma, Lakṣmaṇa, Sītā and Hanumān? Was it the waving of lights, the ringing of bells, and the offering of flowers, fruits and sweets to them, as before? Rāmadāsa had no hesitation to do all this, so long as he had the images of stone before him, even though he had no necessity to do so. Both at Chāphaḷa and at Sajjanagaḍha, and at other places wherever he went, he did worship to the end of his life the images of Rāma and others, so that people might be encouraged to do the same and rise higher and higher to have the experience of the direct vision of God. His instruction to his disciples and to the people at large was that they should not talk about God being Nirguṇa and Nirākāra (qualityless and formless) so long as they have in their presence the image of some deity, but that they should worship it in the same old, usual manner and sing its glorious deeds with devotion, and pray and prostrate before it. For, it is by taking one's stand on the devotion of the Personal aspect of God, that the devotee can rise to the Impersonal aspect of Him, and then come to know that the Personal and the Impersonal are fused together in the immaculate and the imperishable vision of the Lord. It will be only at this final mystical stage of experience that there would be the identification of the devotee with God; and then the form of worship would be nothing else but the meditation on the Name of God and contemplation on His visions. Rāmadāsa could maintain the balance between the saguṇa and the nirguṇa forms of worship, because to him Nirguṇa did not mean the absence of the qualities and forms of the visions of God, but the inclusion and the transcendence of them all, and so, the incompetence of any of the qualities or forms to bring any limitation on the nature of God. To him, Nirguṇa means Bahuguṇa (Bahu=many; guṇa=quality), that is a collection of infinite qualities none of which is capable to define adequately or to limit the nature of the Absolute. God is this, that or any other quality or form, no doubt; but he transcends all of them put together. Rāmadāsa was fortunate to begin his upāsanā at Tākaḷi both as saguṇa and nirguṇa, as we have already seen. The Lord Rāma himself was his Guru; for He had given him the mantra, namely, the Name 'Rāma', which, when meditated upon by Rāmadāsa for a number of years at Tākaḷi, ultimately resulted in the 'Rūpa' or the vision of Rāma, that is, the universal Ātman or Brahman. The meditation on the Gāyatrī as also his worship of the deity of Hanumān, as directed by Rāma, were simply ancillary to this. Thus, it is for Rāmadāsa, and therefore in the philosophy of Rāmadāsa, that Bhakti, that is, the sādhanā or the upāsanā culminates in the illuminational kind of Jñāna and becomes the progenitor of Vairāgya or disgust for all God-less things.

Should therefore one conclude from what we have said so far that the proper way to realize God would be to begin with the worship of the idols which might be made by artisans or created by imagination? Well, this may be permitted for some time; for, that might create the desire to know the nature of the real God. But there are several pitfalls and dangers in doing so for a very long time. The rituals and the modes of worship, which ought to be considered as only aids for creating the attitude of devotion and surrender would become the ends in themselves. The idols might cease to command reverence, love, awe and fear, if the worship of them ceases to yield the desired fruits. A grocer-like attitude would follow in its wake, and man may change the idols one after another with the wrong notion that an idol of another deity would bring to him more quickly the desired fruits. Idols might be broken or stolen, and the worshipper might become totally disheartened. And, supposing this does not take place, one might continue to worship the idols and idols only till the end of his life, but achieve nothing from the spiritual point of view. Rāmadāsa tells us that all that is accepted as true with blind credulity might not lead us to the discovery of God, unless the worship of a particular deity is recommended by the spiritual teacher, as had happened in the case of Rāmadāsa himself. But this kind of initiation, which took place in the dreams of saints like Rāmadāsa and Tukārāma through the vision of God or of a saint, is a rare phenomenon. What is necessarily required in a general way is that one must be initiated into spiritual life by another person who has realized God and who has the power of making others realize God by the means of meditation on the divine Name.

Here ought to begin the real Sādhanā of an aspirant, whatever else he might be doing as additional incentives for strengthening his spiritual life. Meditation on the Name of God sums up within it other eight kinds of devotion. It involves (1 and 2) Śravaṇa and Manana, if the Name that is uttered is at the same time heard mentally. It becomes (3) Kīrtana when it is uttered or sung loudly along with the singing of the glorious deeds of God. It implies (4) service, (5) worship, (6) and salutations to God and to the Guru. Constant meditation is the only means of (7) befriending God. And finally, it is the royal gateway which opens into (8) complete surrender to God. Rāmadāsa calls this last kind of devotion as the Ātma-nivedana, and says that this alone will confer on the aspirant the everlasting liberation known as Sāyujya-mukti, which when attained, the devotee becomes one with God. This, to Rāmadāsa, is both the means and the end. This is the only kind of Upāsanā which culminates in Jñāna, which is nothing else but the vision of Lord Rāma, or the realization of the Brahman. What remains then is the Brahman alone, (which we might indifferently call as God or Rāma) and not Rāmadāsa or any other aspirant, much less the world at large.

One cannot however reach to God-head at one stroke. He must first travel little by little like an ant, and then hope to fly like a bird to that point of his spiritual journey to which he has first made his progress like an ant. Even assuming that there is the constant devout, regular and concentrated meditation on the Name of God, the aspirant has still to cross necessarily two stages of Ātma-nivedana, before, he can hope to reach the final destination. This is because Rāmadāsa makes a three-fold distinction of Ātmanivedana. It is 'jaḍa' (gross though devotional), 'Cañcala' (dualistic though Intuitional) and Niścala (Beatific). We may call them as three stages of the realization of God, so that we can determine the particular stage of a devotee from the kind of the surrender of the self he makes. In the first, there is the awareness of the distinction between the Self and God. But the combined forces of devotion and of philosophical thinking make one realise that all things in the world, including his body, senses, mind, intellect, egoism and his possessions belong to God. As such, he offers them all continuously to God. 'Not I, but thou'; 'not mine, but thine', this is the attitude with which he continues to make his life-long sacrifice of all that he has. All the same, what he offers to God is not sentient (jaḍa). However, it cannot be said that a devotee on this stage of spiritual life is no better than a mere temple-goer on account of his dualistic belief regarding the relation between himself and God. For he might have had also seen various visions of God and experienced various auditory, tactual and other kinds of mystical phenomena. He might have also tested the trustworthiness of these divine experiences and come to know that all of them are real. He might have seen and verified for himself that the divine vision is neither burnt by fire, nor drowned or moistened by water, nor swept away by wind, nor cut by weapons. And with all this, he might always feel that he is different from God. Especially, this sense of dualism would come upon him forcibly when he is not meditating or when he is deeply engrossed in the joys and sorrows of his daliy life in the world. The maximum he can do under these circumstances is that he would say and behave with full conviction and sincerity that he is nothing but that God is all-in-all.

When, however, as instructed by the spiritual teacher, he comes to realize the truth of the great statement, 'Tat tvam asi' (that thou art), on account of his having realized that the vision he sees outside his body is just the same vision which he sees inside the body, he comes to realize that there is one Ātman only, who is both the seer and the seen. In other words, he comes to realize that it is not the individual soul who sees the Ātman, but it is the Ātman who sees the Ātman. The so-called individual soul is not there at all. The 'tvam' (thou) is lost in the 'Tat' (= that—Brahman); equally so, is the 'I' (ego) lost in the Brahman. Therefore the other great statement, 'I am the Brahman' also comes to mean that there is nowhere the 'I', but that Brahman is everywhere. The artificial walls which had created the false notion of the Jīva known as the 'I', namely, those of body, senses, mind, intellect and egoism are broken by the power of meditation on the divine Name and of contemplation on the divine Forms; and then what remains is nothing but the Ātman. With this, the consciousness of the phenomenal world and of the Prakṛti as separate from the Ātman also goes away. What is now on this second stage of surrender, offered or sacrificed is the very consciousness of the individual soul as a separate entity.

Here we must pause a while, and before we proceed further, get ourselves fully acquainted with what Rāmadāsa means by the Ātman or the Antarātman whom alone he worships, as he himself very often tells us. To understand this correctly is to understand the entire spiritual philosophy of Rāmadāsa. Unreservedly and un-compromisingly like Śrī Śaṅkarācārya before him, he accepts the Advaitic view of the Vedānta that there is only one Ātman, and that this very Ātman is to be realized afterwards as the only one Nirguṇa Brahman. But unlike all others before him, he gives us a novel picture of the Antarātman in altogether a new setting. His own experience is a guide to him in this matter also. On the one hand, he equates the Ātman with the Brahman, and on the other, with Ākāśa, though the latter is one of the five elements. If the Upaniṣadic seer finds no difficulty in saying 'Khaṁ (Ākāśa) is Brahman', Rāmadāsa also finds it easy to say that the same Khaṁ or Ākāśa though a product of Brahman, is necessarily the Antarātman. Following the Advaita Vedānta, Rāmadāsa tells us that in the Brahman there first arose the desire of 'becoming many', as if it was a breeze of wind in the still infinite space (ākāśa). Therefore, says Rāmadāsa, the Antarātman is not simply the Ākāśa or the nirguṇa Brahman, but possesses two characteristics one of which is the motion or activity of the wind, and the other, the consciousness of Brahman. This, he says, is corroborated by what takes place in the human body, namely, that it is sustained by prāṇa (vital breath or wind), and is also full of conscious desires. Various are the names of this Antarātman, though he is only one. He is the Mūlamāyā, the Jīvātmā, Śivātmā, Paramātmā, Viśvātmā, Guptātmā, Jñānātmā, Śiva-Śakti, Kṣetrajña, Kūṭastha, Śuddhasattva, Mahattattva, Mahadbhūta, consciousness, God, Nārāyaṇa, Puruṣottama, and so on. He is also known after the manner of his manifestations such as, Nādarūpa, Jyotirūpa, Sākṣarūpa, Sattārūpa, Caitanya-rūpa and Sasvarūpa. He is the only active principle, swifter than the wind, at the back of all changing phenomena, the original Prakrti, the Guṇamāyā, the all-doer, the Creator, the Preserver and the Destroyer of the universe. It is he who enables all the creatures to see through their eyes, taste through their tongues, smell through their nostrils, hear through their ears, and so on. He is immanent in all as consciousness and force, and yet transcends them all. He is the giver of fruits and the enjoyer of them. He is both the devotee and God. To this Antarātman Rāmadāsa is paying his homage at all times.

We shall explain some of the above-mentioned names in order to show that the Ātman is one only, in spite of its appearing as many. Popular usage may speak of four Ātmans, just as space (ākāśa) though one, is spoken of as being four. Break a jar, and the space inside (ghaṭākāśa) becomes indivisibly one with the space within the house, because it was already one even before the jar was made. Break the walls of the house (Maṭha) and the space within it (Maṭhākāśa) becomes one with the space in the universe. Break the frontiers of this (Mahadākāśa) further by the power of imagination, and then it will merge and become one with the transcendental space known as Cidākāśa (the Pure Caitanya). Even so, the first two Ātmans, known as the Jīvātman (the individual soul) and the Śivātman (the Cosmic soul) can be transcended by means of meditation. The artificial walls that have been created on account of ignorance around the real Ātman, are broken. Cease to suppose that you are the body, senses,mind, intellect and egoism by constant meditation on the Name of God, and then what you will always and everywhere see before you will be the most immaculate and effulgent Being known as the Paramātman (the most transcendent Ātman) who is at the same time the Antarātman of both the individual and the cosmic souls. He who was hidden (Gupta) will manifest before you in various forms (rūpa); now as light (Jyoti), now as the unstruck sound (Nāda), now as the witness of all (sākṣī), now as presence and force (sattā and Caitanya), and now in your own bodily form (svarūpa). There will be no end to his creative power, to his swift motions, and to the perpetual and infinite changes wrought about by him in the organic and the inorganic worlds and in man. Rare indeed is a person, says Rāmadāsa who can keep company with this Paramātman and understand his plans, purposes and activities in details. Like the Upaniṣadic seer who says that the realized soul, though sitting in one place, moves in a far-off land, Rāmadāsa says that one who lives alone in the valleys and caves of mountains—obviously referring to himself—and is engrossed in doing silent meditation on the Name of God and contemplating always on the Divine Forms will alone be able to move with the Ātman and witness the glory, fame and power of that Ātman spread everywhere.

This indeed is a grand picture of the great Upāsanā of Rāmadāsa. But he does not stop with this. For, after all, says he, the Antarātman is the principle of change and activity. Why should a man worship God at all and be devoted to Him asks Rāmadāsa, if he cannot make himself free from Karma which is both jaḍa, and cañcala (inert and full of change)? One who worships the changeable God will himself become changeable, while one who worships the unchangeable Brahman will himself become unchangeable, says he. Besides, there will remain the constant fear of falling down from the giddy heights of the experience of moving with the highest and as well as the changeable Ātman. All-pervasive as the Ātman is, it has the roots of its being in the transcendent, changeless Brahman, and its branches and off-shoots, as the Bhagavadgītā also says (15.1), down in the phenomenal world, and in the good or bad motives and actions of the human beings. One peculiar characteristic of this Ātman is that it appears to assume the form of anything with which it comes in contact, even though it remains uncontaminated by anything. Man, therefore should be on his guard even though he has attained the knowledge of the Ātman. For, notwithstanding the power of the Ātman in him, he will rapidly fall into vice and sin, and turn his back towards the Ātman itself, if he, for instance, allows himself to be allured by the beauty of a woman, or tempted by the prospect of having ill-gotten money. Soon will such a man lose control over his mind and senses, cease to meditate on God, and avoid the company of the good and the holy. This will amount to leaving the company of the Antarātman; and yet, such a man will be impudent enough to justify his wayward conduct by saying

'All this is Brahman', 'All this is the sport (vilāsa) of Brahman', though in fact it is his own vilāsa and not of the Brahman. Falsely will he say that he has gone beyond the three guṇas and beyond sin and merit, and continue to go by the wrong and the sinful path.

To realize the Ātman is to have as if a wish-yielding tree in the court-yard of one's own house. Therefore one has to exercise all the more caution not to entertain any evil or sinful thought after one has taken his shelter under its protective and wish-yielding shade. The Ātman is the giver of all that one would want, of all that one would pray for, and of all that one may even wish in his mind to have. Rāmadāsa exhorts the devotee not to be anxious or sorrowful about anything while he is standing under this tree of the Ātman; for, in spite of the very natural kindness and the consequent protection of the devotee which the Ātman will yield, it is also very likely that sorrows and anxieties might multiply, if the devotee gets himself unnecessarily plunged into them. Just as water will equally help the trees to bear sweet fruits, as also the poisonous herbs to maintain the poison in them, even so the Ātman which is immanent in all as the inner sap of life, will equally be the cause of flourishing what is latent in everything. It is therefore on the second level of Ātmanivedana that one is likely to be more egoistic than what he would be on the first level of Ātmanivedana. There, man is at least conscious that he is either only a partner with God or an instrument in the hands of God in whatever he does. Here, notwithstanding the devotee's knowledge that the Ātman is the only All-doer, the latent egoism in him may unconsciously (though backed by the power of the Antarātman) grow to such an extent that he would soon forget that the Ātman is the doer, and begin to proclaim that he himself is the doer of all. How appropriate it is that Rāmadāsa who is aware of this possible self-deception, says at the end of his great work Dāsabodha, that "it would be dishonest on my part to say that I am the author of the work when, as a matter of fact, God or the Antarātman alone is the doer of everything." He therefore tells us emphatically that his Dāsabodha is only a collection of 'words which came out of the mouth of the Lord, Śrī Rāma.'

It is on this account that Rāmadāsa advises us to go beyond

the changeable, phenomenal world, and beyond the changeable nature of the Antarātman and be lodged in the restful peace and unspeakable ānanda (joy) of the unchangeable Antarātman or Brahman. Occasionally, however, as he himself used to do, he asks us to alternate our active life by silent meditation on God. For, thus alone, one can come in contact with God and give the benefit of it to those who are eager to have the knowledge of God. Whether he lives alone in the mountains or lives amongst the people, a saint like Rāmadāsa would alone be able to have his eye, mind and soul fixed in the contemplation of God, and live like God, uncontaminated by anything whatsoever. In him will live devotion, illumination and disgust for Godless things at one and the same time, and in him will live activity and inactivity (contemplation) without any contradiction.

Such was the great saint Rāmadāsa and such was the ever-rising height of his sādhanā. Like Alps over Alps, his forms of devotion rose upon one another, but without demolishing any one of them. His polytheistic worship gave room for Pantheism; out of Pantheism, grew in succession his monotheism, Pantheism and ecstatic Beatificism.

C. *Advice regarding conduct*

1. The body and the house we will live in, and the wealth we might possess are meant for us for a couple of days, as if.
2. One who confides his secrets to a woman is a fool.
3. Do not frequent the place where you are honoured.
4. Too much discussion will not bear any fruit.
5. Do not have any obligations from any one; but if you have them sometime, repay them in some form or other.
6. Let not the tongue abuse or utter harsh words.
7. Make your heart as large as the sea, so that you will be able to swallow the insults hurled at you as also the faults of others.
8. Do good even to those who censure you.
9. Be happy with the happiness of others and miserable when they are in misery.
10. Measure your greatness in terms of humility, and your efficiency in terms of non-egoism.

11. Respect that musician who sings for the glory of God, and that minister who is morally good.
12. Do know the opinions of all but you need not accept any one of them.
13. Have cordial relations with all but do not sacrifice your independence.
14. What is the good of your learning if you cannot refute falsehood ?
15. Unbridled action can be a sign of a learned fool. Even so mere reading of books, if not digested, may make anyone a pedant.
16. Miserliness has no end. One might rob even the ants of the particles of grain from their mouths.
17. The characteristic of all worldly happiness is that it ends in misery.
18. Egoism can be ended if one compares himself with those who are superior to him.
19. Jealousy however is difficult to be rooted out; for it is interested in censuring others. Himself being crooked, one who is jealous calls the kind-hearted as a weak person.
20. Do not harbour idleness at any time.
21. First do and experience, and then preach to others.
22. Try to please all; at least do not displease anyone.
23. Always be doing some good to others.
24. One who finds pleasure in solitude will be the first to solve the riddle of the world.
25. Whatever one wishes to achieve must be achieved while he is young.
26. Mind should be free and open.
27. If you come to know what is right, then you must do accordingly.
28. Be always in the company of those who are superior to you.
29. The leader must himself be above corruption and sin; and then he should try to save others.
30. Distinguish between the deserving and the undeserving persons, and then worship only those who deserve the respect.
31. Strive, strive and strive till the end is achieved. Only

supplement it by right kind of thinking.

32. Come in contact with all but observe them minutely, so that you should know who is who.
33. If you wish to give something to others, give the best of what you possess.
34. While you speak, use the most appropriate words suitable for the occasion.
35. Do not forget that you have to die one day.
36. Keep your mind calm and composed, whatever might be the circumstances.
37. Do not shirk your duties and responsibilities, even if others do so.
38. Do not say about a fool that he is so. Teach him also gradually, if possible, as if he is a child.
39. Suffer first even a defeat, if it is necesssary to defeat others finally.
40. For oneself or for the followers, there must be so much work that there should be left no time even to think about doing any mischief or bad action.
41. Sometimes, it is even desirable to hand over the keys of the treasury to a thief, provided the thief has the potentiality of gradually being turned into an honest person.
42. One should set a thief to catch a thief, and remain himself unnoticed.
43. One should not advertise all his plans except to the trusted few.
44. Procrastination is the surest way of defeating one's own purpose.
45. What you have to do, do it yourself. If you depend upon others, they may not perhaps do it.
46. Keep the main thing under your control and let all the subsidiary things be done by other persons in accordance with their capacity.
47. If the tent is to be a strong one, then the supporting ropes of it must also be very strong.
48. Be alert at all times and remove the defects if there be any.

49. Keep yourself away from the greed of money and lust for women.
50. Have your eye upon your mission without minding what others may say.
51. Do not allow all people to come very close to you.
52. People will respect you only when they find you above any desire.
53. Increase your activities and social contacts if you must, but remain uncontaminated.
54. Do not give any piece of advice to anyone unless he requests you to do so.
55. Do not ask for anything from anyone.
56. Divine knowledge is not a commodity for sale.
57. Have not any equivocation in your speech.
58. Do not give false promises.
59. Neither be puffed up with pride nor harass your opponent in any discussion.
60. Avoid extremes in everything.
61. Do not allow the cause to suffer, nor the disintegration of those who support that cause.
62. Make your intellect sharp enough to infer what is to happen in future.
63. Do not be impatient to trust anyone even though the first impression he makes about himself is good.
64. Decorate your mind by wisdom rather than your body by dress.
65. There should be no limit to the desire for acquiring knowledge.
66. Have such self-confidence as will not be shattered by the words of censure from others.
67. Have excellence in whatever you do and not simply a lukewarm satisfaction.
68. Avoid all artificiality.
69. Do not allow any loop-holes in your efforts.
70. A householder who lives a morally good life is no worse than a devout Sannyāsī.
71. Repentance has got the greatest value in moral life.
72. Do not advertise your spiritual experiences with egoism; for you may not have them again.

73. Even if you are a Brahmin by birth, you should know that one would be entitled to be called a Brahmin if he has realized the Brahman.
74. Distinctions are real in the day-to-day worldly life. How can then saints and scoundrels be of like nature ?
75. First learn to swim well, and then try to save others from being drowned.
76. Spiritual life can be introduced as a new current in the stream of worldly life; but what should take place in course of time and gradually is that the spiritual nature should permeate and eclipse the worldly life altogether.
77. Cover up the faults and sins of others; forgive them and transform their lives by your own example of virtuous life.
78. You should no doubt first dine to your heart's content. But what is left over after you have dined should be distributed among others, and not wasted.
79. Search your own heart, and find out whether you wish to get your desires fulfilled or whether you wish to meet God.
80. Be honest in saying whether you want to use the power of God for being famous and prosperous, or you want the grace of God.
81. What is the good of simply fattening the body ? Sooner or later it will hardly be a morsel of food for Death.
82. Instead, drink the ambrosia of the Name of God, and as the result of it the body will shine with a lustre which is unique.
83. To be merely active without being devoted to God is to become subject ever to the law of Karma and to all that it implies. It will lead to egoism and fatalism.
84. But if activity is turned into devotional activity of worship and meditation or is combined with it, it will lead one to the realization of God, and then to the dislike of all other things but God.
85. Therefore the best way in which one should lead one's life is to be alternately active and contemplative. This will put an end to egoism and fatalism ; then only man will live as God wishes him to live.

86. This means that instead of being at the mercy of blind fatalism man will accept the divine determinism, in which case, he can be only an instrument in the hands of God.
87. And finally, man will realize that the instrument also is not something separate from God, just as the hand and the will of man are not separate from man himself.
88. At this stage alone, there will be no difference between activity and devotion, and between devotion and the realization of God.
89. Who then is the author of any form of activity which takes place in this world? It is God and God alone.
90. In the realization of this there lies the whole Truth, the whole Reality, and the whole of Freedom, Liberation, joy and peace.

(Extract from Prof. R.D. Ranade's "Mysticism in Maharashtra" pp. 368-369, First Edition, 1933)

The SANADA in which Śivājī sums up his relation to Rāmadāsa, dated Śake 1600 (1678 A.D.) Āśvina Śuddha Daśamī, reads as follows:—

"Obeisance to my most high Teacher, the father of all, the abode of all bliss. Śivājī, who is merely as dust on his Master's feet, places his head on the feet of his Master, and requests : I was greatly obliged to have been favoured by your supreme instruction, and to have been ordered that my religious duty lies in conquest, in the establishment of religion, in the service of God and Brahmins, in the relieving of the misery of my subjects, and in their protection and help, and that I should seek to obtain spiritual satisfaction in the midst of this duty. You were also pleased to say that whatever I wished from the bottom of my heart would be fulfilled for me.

"Consequently, whatever business I applied myself to, whatever intentions I cherished in my mind, for example, the destruction of Turks, the creating of fastnesses by spending enormous wealth in order to assure the continuance of my kingdom, have been fulfilled for me by the grace of your Holy Self.

"Then, whatever kingdom I earned I threw at your feet, and bethought of applying myself all the while to your service.

Then you ordered me that what you had already asked me to do by way of my religious duty was alone the service of your feet.

"Then, when I implored that I should enjoy the close proximity of your company and should see you often, that somewhere a temple of God might be established and the spiritual tradition made to grow, you were pleased to live near-about in the caves of mountains, to establish the image of God at Chāphaḷa, and to spread your spiritual instruction far and wide.

"Then, when I implored that now that the deity at Chāphaḷa had been established and that the Brahmins and the guests had been entertained, that buildings had been erected, and that ceremonies were being performed, I should be ordered to assign lands for the upkeep of these, you were pleased to say, 'What is the use of this all? But if you are really determined that you should serve God, then you might assign whatever lands you please according to your convenience, and should extend them only as your kingdom would grow.' Hence, wherever the images of God were established, therever I assigned my lands.

"Then, when I again implored that I intended to make over wholly 121 villages to the temple at Chāphaḷa, and eleven Vitas of land in each of the other 121 villages, and when I said also that I intended to give eleven Vitas of land for the continuance of worship in each of the places where God's image had been established, then you said that all these things might be done in course of time. Consequently, I have at present assigned the following lands for the service of God....I take upon myself punctually and without fail to present at the time of the annual religious festival of the Deity all the corn that may be grown on these lands, or else an equivalent amount of money in cash. Dated Rājyābhiṣeka Śake 5, Āśvina Śuddha 10."

Chapter II

IN THE HEART OF DĀSABODHA

Contents :

1. The aim of Dāsabodha ; 2. Salutations to God and to the Spiritual Teacher ; 3. The saint and the saintly poet ; 4. The spiritual Assembly ; 5. The highest Good; 6. The human body as an instrument of Spiritual gain ; 7. What can a fool achieve? 8. Do this then to save yourself ; 9. The Demoniac Heritage ; 10. Begin somewhere on the path of Devotion ; 11. When Rajoguṇa (the drive of selfish activity) dominates ; 12. When Tamoguṇa (the drive of stupid inactivity) dominates ; 13. When Sattvaguṇa (the drive for purity and spiritual illumination) dominates ; 14. The Divine Heritage ; 15. The virtues of the Dispassionate ; 16. The learned fool ; 17. Without God-realization, life is but the weariness of flesh; 18. The threefold affliction ; 19. Death levels down all except those who have realised God ; 20. Make haste to meet God ; 21. Hearing and singing of the Name and the glories of God; 22. Service and salutations to God and to Guru; 23. Befriending God and the Guru ; 24. Self-surrender as the apex of devotion ; 25. Four kinds of liberation ; 26. Necessity of the Spiritual Teacher ; 27. The false and the real Gurus ; 28. Who is a true disciple ? 29. Nature of spiritual initiation ; 30. Spiritual knowledge as distinct from the phenomenal ; 31. The slaves of pleasures ; 32. Repentance followed by aspiration to become free ; 33. The baptised soul ; 34. Only by degrees man becomes one with God ; 35. The search after God ; 36. To know God is to become God. 37. The worldly distinctions vanish with the realization of the identity with God ; 38. Not longevity, but spirituality as the test of greatness ; 39. Contrast between the Brahman and Māyā ; 40. Are gods many or one ? 41. The sensuously perceived is short-lived, the non-sensuously perceived is Real ; 42. To describe the Brahman is to describe the experience of Brahman; 43. Contradictory characteristics of the Brahman ; 44. Contemplation and activity should alternate; 45.

Mystical experience as being beyond wishful thinking; 46. Listen to the Name of God as it is mentally uttered ; 47. The Saint's estimate of his body; 48. God is different from his creation ; 49. Puzzles of speculation and their solution ; 50. Hindrance and aids to Spiritual life ; 51. One Ātman and one liberation ; 52. Characteristics of a great Saint ; 53. The wise too fumble in their search for God.

1. *The Aim of Dāsabodha* (1. *i.* 1-38)

The saint, Rāmadāsa tells us at the outset that the aim of his writing the Dāsabodha is to show how by the path of devotion alone one can realize God easily and necessarily. Along with this, there will also be the discussions about problems such as Brahma-jñāna, Ātma-jñāna, Māyā, Immortality, Vairāgya, the relation of God and his devotees, the nature and kinds of devotion, the effects of God-realization, and several other subsidiary topics.

2. *Salutations to God and the Guru* (1. *ii.* 1-30; *iii.* 1-26; *iv.* 1-31)

The traditional way of saluting God as the very source of knowledge and intelligence in the beginning of a noble pursuit, is not without meaning. It is to invoke the blessings of God so that our efforts for realizing the Ātman and the Brahman may be crowned with success. Nothing can be achieved in the spiritual field, unless there is the divine grace even at the start. As Rāmadāsa was fortunate to have the direct visions of God in the forms of Gaṇeśa and Śāradā, he describes them as he sees them actually before him, and advises others who have no such visions to put faith in him and invoke the blessings of God. Rāmadāsa describes Gaṇeśa, as is usually done, as having a large body, four hands, and the head of an elephant. But he sees the vision as being beautiful in all its limbs, and as nodding its head with joy.

His description of the Goddess of Learning is superb. She is at the back of all the four kinds of speech; it is she who reveals what is contained in the Word. She is the samādhi of the yogins; destroys both vidyā and avidyā; the consort of the Great Puruṣa; the power and the desirelessness of God; perceptible though, inscrutable even to gods; the source of intelligence, inspiration, beauty, splendour, light and of the very life; the very grace of the Sadguru which destroys the evils and saves man from being drowned in the floods of saṁsāra, by the power of the Divine Name. Known as Māyā or Śāradā, she is omnipresent, even as the pure and the undisturbable, Svarūpa (one's own Form) during the samādhi of the Siddhas and the yogins. Without her presence and grace, no spiritual life is possible, neither devotion, nor Bhajana nor any kind of liberation.

So far as my spiritual teacher is concerned, says Rāmadāsa, I wished to praise him by resorting to speech, the power of Māyā; but he transcends that power. Māyā herself turns back with the feeling of being defeated in doing so. Therefore, I too have become helpless. And yet, I shall praise Him anyhow with the help of Māyā alone. The spiritual teacher is the Sun of Reality who, once he rises, never sets, and never allows the darkness of ignorance to come in again. He is like the river Ganges from which, like a stream which has entered into it, the disciple can never be separated, once he is accepted by the Guru. The 'Pārasa' stone is reported to have the capacity to change iron into gold, but it can neither change iron nor gold into itself; the Guru, on the contrary, makes his disciple grow into a spiritual teacher like himself. He can be said to be as unperturbable, imperishable and Nirguṇa (transcending all sorts of qualities) as the Brahman whom he has realized; and yet, he feels compassion for the afflicted. In short, the secret that he is beyond any description constitutes his description, and it is known to the saints only.

3. *The Saint and the saintly poet* (1.*v.* 1-26 ; *vi.* 1-23; *vii.* 1-34)

The company of the saint alone would enable one to realize the Reality which goes beyond the phenomenal world, and which therefore can never be revealed by the light of the Sun or of the fire. How can the physical eyes of even the best among the learned be able to visualize it, when it lies beyond the powers and range of the mind, the speech and the reason ? By the help of the saint alone one can have access to the Reality, because the saint has already realized it ; and though like the Reality he too is beyond description, he is the receptacle and the giver of the highest bliss and the peace of Brahman. Neither the kings nor the sovereigns of this earth, who are as if beggars before the saints, can ever be able to bestow upon others this treasure of great merit and of final liberation.

Those who listen to spiritual discourses will be continuously reminded of the Brahman, and will become as pure as the fire is. They will be bliss incarnate ; and there will be nothing which will pass beyond their ken.

Had there been no poets like Vālmīki and Vyāsa among the saints to proclaim the nature of the knowledge of God and of the ways and the means to realize Him, the whole world would have remained ignorant about God. Had they remained silent with their own self-realization and not spoken or written a word of the vast spiritual poetry they have composed, we could have never known the secret path by which great yogīs and devotees of the past have attained the Godhood. Therefore, says Rāmadāsa, that these great poets of the spiritual realm hold the keys to the divine knowledge, and can show us, if we just surrender unto them, an ocean of spiritual pearls and mines of spiritual treasures that belong to the Primeval Being. Let us therefore approach them with humility and prostrate before them; for, they will then fix us permanently in the knowledge of God, create in us a disgust for Godless things, and sustain our devotion and loyalty to God. Their poetry will enlarge the capacity of our intellect and intuition, and fill our ears and mind with joy which is unique and sweet.

4. *The Spiritual Assembly* (1. *viii.* 1-29)

God has left his home, the so-called Vaikuṇṭha, says Rāmadāsa, and has come to reside in his new and real Vaikuṇṭha, namely, the Assembly of the saints. For, it is there that He can listen to his Name being sung with joy. 'Victory to the Name of God' they sing in chorus ; and contemplating always on the visions of God, they engage themselves in describing his various qualities and deeds by means of sermons, lectures and discussions. Among the members of this assembly are saints and ascetics of various hues and professions. All of them are meritorious, self-controlled, courageous, pure, compassionate and full of grace, though some of them are used to go on pilgrimage, some in doing sacrificial and other works of charity, some in writing books and composing poetry, and some in living as householders or as sannyāsins. There is no restriction of age, sex, creed or caste in joining this assembly, if only one wishes to know and to love God. It is here, in this assembly of saints, who are verily the images of God, that one is sure of realizing Him.

5. *The Highest Good* (1. *ix*. 1-27)

The realization of Brahman or God is the highest Good of man. This is not something which can be had on credit; this is to be achieved on paying the hard cash of one-pointed devotion to God, which will then not only save him but give him the power to save others also. This Brahmayoga, the highest among all the yogas, appears most difficult to be achieved ; but, as a matter of fact, it is very easy to be had, provided one gets his entrance into the company of the good and the holy. Brahman is everywhere, but it is not visualized in the least except by one who is prepared to follow in the foot-steps of a Brahmayogin by the secret path which runs through the empty space within and without the heart. For, in the eyes of such an one alone, the Guru applies the ointment whereby God manifests himself once for all and never again becomes invisible, if the devotee keeps on meditating on Him. None can then deprive the devotee of his unique possession; neither the kingly power, nor the robbers, nor again the fire can destroy what he has gained, namely, the condition of liberation which is beyond birth and death. Naturally, as the Brahman is the only Reality which remains the same, unmoved and unperturbed, the young Brahmayogin also looks upon the phenomenal world of the five elements, and upon his mundane life which is only a part of it, as a transitory or unreal something with which he has no concern. And the more he becomes one with Brahman, the more is he convinced of this, and there remains ultimately no trace of doubt in his mind.

Thus when one becomes lodged in Brahman and attuned with the life in it, he gets all the rest and calm he wishes to have. One who has got this has got the Kingdom of God ; all others are no better than beggars. Or, to put it differently, one may be said to have fulfilled the end of his life by realizing God; the others are sinners only.

6. *The human body as an instrument of Spiritual gain* (1. *x*. 1-62)

The body is the base of all that can be willed and done successfully in the human life. Lover of freedom as he is, man does not wish to be a slave and to live like an animal at the mercy of others. To be free from any defects such as dumbness or deafness, and to possess a sound and healthy body is itself a great boon of nature, and one must be thankful to God for this, above everything else. For, a defective body is not only an object of pity to others, but also a great handicap in achieving anything great in life. So, instead of despising the body, one should utilize it for achieving the Spiritual Good by following the path of devotion in its various aspects. It is on account of the immense help of the body that man could achieve innumerable miraculous powers over nature, mind and speech. To become of the nature of fire or water and so to become free from the fear of being burnt by fire or drowned in water ; to become invisible all of a sudden, and to appear at a distant place ; to obtain whatever one wishes; all such and other miraculous powers, man has achieved by possessing a sound body.

On the other hand, the body is not all in all. Like the house in which the man lives, the body too does not belong to him only. Scorpions, rats, flies, dogs and guests consider the house as their own. Even so, lice, germs and diseases like to live in the human body, as if it is their own abode. And, the wonder is that this fool of a man also considers the house and the body as belonging to him alone. On the contrary, he should think that as a traveller he has come to stay in the house and in the body for a short time only, and that he has to seize this opportunity to have the only real gain of his life, namely, to have the realization of God. Considering thus, he should neither fondle the body too much, nor despise it too much. He should look to its great utility and try to preserve and protect it from disease and vice, so that God-realization might become almost a certainty before he becomes too old and therefore unable to put in the necessary efforts.

7. *What can a fool achieve*? (2. *i.* 1-74)

Look to the undesirable leanings of his mind and his actions in order to be convinced that he is too ignorant to have the knowledge of the Ātman. Being extremely egoistic, he thinks that he is equal to the wise and the great, but does not open his mouth in the assembly of the learned. He is averse to learning, and takes delight in being idle; and yet is bold enough to give his counsel to others. A glutton, a coward, one given to too much of sleep, a flatterer of the rich, and an ungrateful person as he is, he is never kind, and never serious about anything. He will not hesitate to betray his mother, father, friend or even his teacher, but will be very friendly with any woman, and will have no scruple in amassing money by any foul means. Naturally, he will have no forgiveness; but he will take delight in punishing others even for their small faults and in causing them pain and misery. How will such an ungrateful, ignorant and wicked person think about the existence of God, much less about the possibility of realizing Him ?

8. *Do this then to save yourself* (2. *ii.* 1-42)

Behave with others in a straightforward way, without any self-conceit, hatred, deceitful intent, or an evil eye on the wealth and women of others. Bid good-bye to idleness and to indulgence in pleasures and sleep, and work hard in order to discharge your duty faithfully, and in sticking to what is morally and spiritually true and good. In doing so, try to please God and your spiritual teacher by your devotion without feeling the sense of shame in the least, and without wasting your time and energy in arguing with those who are merely talkative and unbelievers. You can do so if you are very careful in not accepting unnecessary obligations of anybody by putting your burden upon others. But whenever there arises an occasion to return the obligations, or you are required to help anyone, do not be miserly in the least. Do not give a word if you cannot keep it, nor say to others to do a thing unless you have first done it yourself. Why should you be cross with others if you have no love for them ? Lose not your courage and patience, and be not angry with them beyond a limit. For, in case, they come round and approach you with humility, you should teach them again as if nothing has happened. Naturally, to maintain this calmness of the mind, you must remain far away from all the evil habits, such as overeating, smoking, addiction to drugs and the company of the wayward and the wicked persons. Neither should you dine at the table of a miserly person; for, that might spoil your discriminative power.

If these be the guiding rules of your conduct, there will be no need for you to be anxious about anything. This will help you to be secure and happy both in your worldly and spiritual life.

9. *The Demoniac Heritage* (2. *iii*. 1-40)

This abounds in a man who is both stupid and arrogant. Desire, anger, arrogance, jealousy, greediness, pretentiousness and egoism make him always discontented. He is a wonderful mixture of opposite but equally undesirable deficiencies and habits. He might be both ugly and evil-minded, weak and wicked, poor and miserly, idle and gluttonous, foolish and wrathful, ignorant and faithless, sinful and yet censuring others, a coward and yet a bully, least intelligent and yet a disputant, and so on. Will such a person hesitate to be treacherous to anyone? Will he not go even the long way of being a murderer of anybody, whether he is a relative or not? He is as away from one who is born with the divine heritage as the north pole is from the south pole.

10. *Begin somewhere on the path of Devotion* (2. *iv*. 1-27)

The whole life will be a waste if it is not directed towards God-realization. Hence, one must begin to tread somewhere on the path of devotion so that he might some time reach the goal. Let him read the scriptures or any other spiritual literature and guide his intellect thereby. Or, if he be interested in the sacrificial ritualism, and in the practice of penances, let him do so; or let him move in the company of the saints from one place of pilgrimage to another, and thereby purify his body and mind, and become fit for receiving the knowledge of God. Let him do acts of charity, kindness and benevolence, shed his selfishness and do the service of the needy and the miserable, so that he might easily do the service of mankind also. Let him further join the devotees of God who assemble together for the purpose of celebrating and glorifying the Name of God, so that he might come to know how to love God and realize Him.

11. *When Rajoguṇa (the drive of selfish activity) dominates* (2. *v.* 1-42)

Then, the chief interest in life is centred round oneself, one's own family, and the desires and the pleasures of eating, drinking and sex. Utter selfishness makes him blind to the claims of freedom and pleasures of others; and so he wishes and struggles hard to usurp their belongings for his own pleasure. Sex, fun, recreation, delicious food and intoxicating drinks being all that he wants, he does not mind to be deceitful, jealous and crafty. Naturally, such a person turns his back against all moral rules and religious discipline of any kind.

12. *When Tamoguṇa (the drive of stupid inactivity) dominates* (2. *vi.* 1-41)

The person then becomes blind on account of his unsatisfied desires, and he becomes angry with all, and loses the sense of propriety and reason. He may do anything out of jealousy, hatred and anger—kill himself, his wife, his children, his won brother, mother or father. He takes delight in the miseries of others, in the killings of the battles, in burning houses and property, and in doing any destructive work. Slothfulness incarnate, he eats a lot and sleeps and sleeps. Memory leaves him, and delusion overtakes him forever. If he becomes active at all, it is for the purpose of practising black magic, or for tormenting his own body in various ways, such as fasts, speechlessness, etc. in order to please the lower deities and get his desires fulfilled. This only means that the Tamoguṇa only degrades a man to the level of the beast. He would not only be indifferent to God, but also break the images of God out of hatred and anger. All this however would make him most miserable.

13. *When the Sattvaguṇa* (*the drive for purity and spiritual illumination*) *dominates* (2. *vii.* 1-88)

The person then not only gets victory over the two other drives of selfish activity and blind stupidity, but also finds in the moral goodness and the purity of heart the basis and support for a higher life in God. The evanescent nature of the worldly life becomes obvious to his discerning eye, and he hungers more and more for the permanent and joyful life of spiritual illumination. His heart leaps up with joy when he sees a saint, and he comes to know through his grace that the way to realize God is to meditate on His name with love and regard. Regularly, then, with full faith, he begins to meditate on the divine Name, and utilizes all the energy of his body, senses and mind for the single aim of real zing God. Thinking that his highest allegiance is to God only, and there being no other worldly motive for his devotion, he considers everything else as being far inferior in importance to the knowledge and love of God. So, whenever there is an opportunity to serve God and the saints who have realized God, he will not hesitate, and if need be, to sacrifice everything else for their sake. Nothing will be below his dignity ; he will take a broom and sweep clean the courtyard and the premises of the temple of God, and apply the dust of the ground on which the saints have treaded to his forehead. And when by the grace of God, he would look at Him with a steadfast gaze, his body will sweat; hair will stand on ends, and with love added on to love, he would dance with joy and clap his hands, and almost forget the consciousness of his having a body at all. Thus, having achieved this all by means of Sattvaguṇa, he will engage himself constantly in mentally uttering and hearing the divine Name, and will come to have the fullest satisfaction of having realized the Ātman. Why would he then heed what the people might say about him ? If they call him God-intoxicated, he would all the more be devoted to God.

As a result of this all, he will naturally be endowed with several other divine qualities. Being free from egoism and desires, he will have no enmity with anybody. On the contrary, being full of compassion, he too will be able to bring salvation to others. People might speak harsh words to him, but in return, he will be soft and humble to all. He will not expose their faults, but oblige them in several ways. Forbearance, forgiveness and compassion will be ever present in him. Determination to lose all for the sake of God, firm courage in spite of calamities, control over the senses and mind, and undeviating love for God will be his foremost characteristics. In short, being sorrowful with the sorrows of others and joyful with the joys of others, he will show that he exists for the good of others only.

14. *The Divine heritage* (2. *viii.* 1-32)

Here, we find a rare combination of two opposite but equally commendable virtues. One who possesses the divine heritage is at once strong and courageous ; wealthy and generous; a devotee even after the realization of God; very learned and yet humble and without egoism; serene and calm even after having practised a great penance; brave and thoughtful; young and conforming his conduct to rules of behaviour; a musician and yet in the company of the saints; enjoying all prosperity and yet a devotee of God; or a minister to the King and yet morally upright.

Always joyful and contented, he is free from greed; and being pure at heart, he brings consolation to all by his sweet and truthful words. As he has no desires of his own, he is in fact independent of all things, and yet tries his best to remove the miseries of others, and to save them by bringing them on the pathway to God. This he does because he feels that they too like himself are a portion of God.

An innate quality like beauty or complexion of the body cannot be acquired by efforts; but all the above-mentioned virtues must deliberately be practised by all, and especially by one who wishes to go beyond the temptations of this worldly life.

15. *The Virtues of the Dispassionate* (2. *ix.* 1-43)

A dispassionate person is neither expected to be an idler nor a parasite, nor a recluse who has no social duty to perform.

On the contrary, he is expected to uplift the humanity by his direct contact with it. He can therefore live in society and live as a member of a family, though his duty and interest might go far beyond a particular family or society. He should consider himself as a friend to the whole world; for then only can he be truly independent of the petty, worldly interests, and try to establish the Kingdom of God by instructing the people to go by the path of devout meditation and moral uprightness. He should move as a pilgrim from one holy place to another, so that he can meet and form friendship with saints, and strengthening the bonds of spiritual ties with them, spread the gospel of God even among the wicked and the sceptics.

But in doing this all, he must be true to himself and never fail to practise the virtues which he wishes to inculcate in others. He must possess always the sāttvika qualities of forbearance, forgiveness, compassion, courage, discrimination, dispassion, self-control and purity. To add to this, he must be acquainted with all the several opinions and practices that might be current as the so-called spiritual ways of reaching the Godhead, but which might prove ultimately to be one-sided and defective. Therefore, he must be very wakeful and alert to see that people do not go by these blind alleys, but by the royal path of surrender, meditation and love for God. And yet, with all the increase in the range of his activities, the dispassionate servant of God should retain his freedom and independence. He must not get himself contaminated by anything which is likely to sever his contact with God.

16. *The learned fool* (2. *x*. 1-41)

A simple fool can be taught; but a learned fool is incurable. His excessive egoism and selfishness make him too arrogant to listen and to learn from anybody. He might have been born in a noble and righteous family, might have read the scriptures and other several books, and might therefore excel in preaching verbal knowledge about God; but in practice, he would neither believe in anything nor do any 'sādhanā' such as meditation or prayer; nor would he hesitate to root out the faith of others in God. He will blame others for the blemishes and faults which he himself possesses. He will speak one thing and do just the opposite; he would flatter men but not say a word of praise about God, in spite of his great learning. If he attends any lecture he would belittle the speaker by attributing ignorance to him. Having regard for the physical body only, he would like to have the company of women under the garb of having spiritual discussion with them. This only shows that he makes the spiritual knowledge as a means of attaining his selfish ends. But so far as his own non-spiritual lineage is concerned, he would not be ashamed to hide the fact, if thereby he would be able to advertise that his prosperity is due to him only. In short, a learned fool is more dangerous to the society than what a simple fool is.

17. *Without God-realization, Life is but the weariness of flesh* (3. *i*.1-53; *ii*.1-65; *iii*.1-48; *iv*.1-54; *v*.1-56)

A child is born, let us suppose, in a perfectly good condition. It grows into a strong and good-looking boy after causing great anxiety to its parents. Unfortunately, it became the victim of several diseases one after another; once, a limb of his body was broken; at another time an injury was caused to his eye; once, he escaped from being drowned; he fell into bad company, picked up evil habits and neglected his studies and health, making his parents very miserable. Fortunately again, he was saved from all this and became a respectable man in the society; but soon after his marriage, he centred his affection on his wife to such an extent that he not only became a tool and a slave in her hands, but a victim of the ever-increasing sexual passion. He became a profligate and spent his money on women, wine and merriment. Soon was he reduced to poverty, and overcome by diseases of the worst kind. He could not provide sufficiently for his wife and his too many children. To add to his calamities there came a terrible famine, and after it an invasion of an enemy, during which period some of the members of his family died, some were taken away as prisoners, and then being destitute of his parents, wife and children, he became the most miserable and the pitiable creature of all. He became too old to earn anything, and too impotent to enjoy the pleasures of life, though his greed for food and sex was all the more on the increase. All his organs of knowledge and action became incapable of doing their functions; his whole body began to ache; it became a store-house of several diseases; constant suffering, sleeplessness, coughing, indigestion, as well as mental anxiety and repentance for having wasted his life became intolerable for him. He wished to die, but could not; for, in his heart of hearts he wished to live the longest life possible for any human being.

Such being in general the story of all, whether rich or poor, it appears that birth itself is a gateway into misery, disease, old age and death, and that there is no escape even if the story is repeated a thousand times. Whoever is thoughtful and not blind to the facts of experience will admit that the sum-total of human life, notwithstanding the sprinkling of happiness and joy here and there, is verily frustration and misery. And yet, there is one way of escape into full freedom, joy and peace; and that is the way of surrender, love and worshipful meditation of God.

18. *The threefold affliction which overtakes a man* (3.*vi*.1-56; *vii*. 1-87; *viii*. 1-29)

The afflictions which are due to one's own body, mind or life are of one kind. All the aches and the diseases of the various parts of the body; affliction due to hunger, thirst and the sexual desire; as also those due to the various other emotions such as fear, love and hatred go to form one kind of afflictions. The other kind consists of those which arise out of our contact with other beings in the world, whether they are creatures like serpents and scorpions; or animals like bulls, bears or tigers; inanimate objects like trees, walls, rivers, fires, poisons, medicines and human beings including one's wife and sons, as also robbers or enemies. The loss of wealth, prosperity, reputation, or of one's kith and kin also comes under the second kind of afflictions. And the third kind of afflictions is that which goes beyond human understanding and control. It is the fatalistic visitation of misery which is hurled at man by an unknown force for his previous sins and ingratitude, probably in a life beyond death, and in the regions of hell.

All these three kinds of afflictions are not without any purpose. They are, in a sense, blessings in disguise. They make a chastening effect on the mind and make us aware that the only aim of life is not to eat, drink and be merry, but to find out the Real which, as the saints have declared, is the permanent source of a lasting joy and peace. It is but natural that birds on a tree should leave it when it is on fire; even so, it is natural that all the kith and kin of a man should leave him when he is afflicted in all possible ways. Then alone a man comes to know that all his dearest and beloved persons love him for their own selfish ends, and that the vacuum which is created in his mind after they have all left him is to be filled in by God who will never desert him even while he is suffering.

19. *Death levels down all except those who have realized God* (3.*ix*.1-59)

As the physical body and all that pertains to it is perishable, it is natural that it should become the food of death. It is immaterial whether the body belongs to a child, a youth or an old man, or to a king, a sannyāsin or a saint. Death overcomes it sooner or later. But the saint who has realized God becomes immortal even while he lives, and so continues to be immortal even after his body falls. He had already attained the condition of the disembodied Spirit even though he had a body, and so he continues to live in that very disembodied or immaculate state after he dies.

20. *Make haste to meet God, as this life and its affairs are too short-lived* (3.*x*.1-74)

Our worldly life is like a great river in floods in which crocodiles in the forms of egoism, lust, attachment, arrogance, jealousy and hatred are moving with their jaws wide open waiting to swallow us. And this silly creature of a man clings fast out of egoism and infatuation to his own tiny home, to his sons and daughters and other kith and kin, and to the various objects of pleasure and belongings, even while he knows that he is being drowned in the great dangerous river. He does not take into consideration that his short span of life is being wasted day by day in pursuing the pleasures of life which are sweet to enjoy in the beginning but which end in sorrow; that his wife, sons and daughters would leave him one day when he would be no longer useful to satisfy their interests, or when he would be overcome by great disease and nearing his death; and that if he dies he would be deprived of the opportunity to realize God.

Therefore before it is too late one should remember that to be born with a human body instead of with anyone else out of the millions of other non-human bodies is the rarest chance which can be utilized for achieving the equally rarest prize of life, namely, the realization of God. With equal concern, he should note that the span of human life, though short, ought to be turned into a treasure of precious jewels in the forms of meditations, praises and prayers which can be offered to God with great love and regard. For, it is this emotional attitude of love and regard which is reflected back, like an image in a mirror, as a vision of God. So, it entirely depends on man to keep this attitude of faith, love and regard untarnished by any other contrary idea, feeling or emotion. For, like the reflection in the mirror, the vision of God too will behave with him in the same manner. God too will be sincere and loyal to him to the degree to which he is loyal to God. If one would therefore surrender unto God, seek his grace and love, and depend upon him with full faith, God would certainly jump in the dreadful river of saṁsāra and carry his devotee safe to the other bank. If God be with him, there will be no sorrow or fear of any kind. He would be having the eternal source of bliss and peace which will be denied to others. In short, what one should do is to leave all and hold fast to God alone. If one has to become a slave to another who gives bread for maintenance, should he not be ever grateful to God for bestowing on him a human body, and should he not therefore constantly remember him with love and faith ?

21. *Hearing and Singing of the Name and glories of God* (4.*i*.1-34; *ii*.1-31; *iii*.1-25)

Śravaṇa or the hearing of such literature as would lead to spiritual knowledge is a very important form of devotion. It is both the beginning and the end of Spiritual life. Nothing which is not heard mentally will ever produce any definite knowledge about anything. It will mostly be some diffused state of consciousness. In our ordinary life, words have got meaning either with reference to some sort of activity intended to be done by the listener, or with reference to some further thought or feelings connected with that meaning. The function of language is vitally connected with thought, feeling and action. This is no doubt true of spiritual literature also. It helps us to modify or confirm our beliefs and thoughts and persuades us to act accordingly. But what can we say regarding the divine Name which is imparted by the spiritual teacher to his disciple? We are neither asked to weave an imaginary web of thoughts nor to bring back in memory a bundle of them which are buried in the past. Neither are we asked to do any overt act by our hands or feet. It has however a peculiar mandate of its own. We are asked to carry on some covert acts connected with the tongue, the ear and the mind. The tongue may utter the Name loudly from the house-tops, or silently after shutting the lips; but what is most important from the viewpoint of a devotee is that while the Name is being uttered loudly or mentally, it should be heard mentally. Thus between the simultaneous uttering and hearing of the Name and the repetition of this, there should intervene nothing, no other thought or action. When the mind of the devotee is engaged in attending to the self-same process of the uttering and hearing of the Name in the same moment of time, it becomes non-different from that Name. The subject becomes identical with its object, that is, with the indivisible meaning implied by the Name which is nothing else but God. As the consequence of this, there is produced in the mind of the devotee an habitual attachment or love for the Name of God, and to that extent a disgust for Godless things. In course of time, egoism and consciousness that the physical body alone is real become more and more diminished; the mind becomes purified of its blemishes and crookedness, and there comes about joy and peace.

As the divine Name cannot be meditated upon in the manner described above continuously for a long time, a sādhaka should do well to employ a complimentary device known as Kīrtana. This form of devotion removes the feeling of monotony that is likely to creep in naturally in the mind of the meditator, and it keeps him joyfully engaged in doing devotional activity only. Kīrtana consists in describing the nature of God and his various qualities such as omnipresence, omnipotence, kindness, mercy, grace, beauty, magnanimity and so on. But it is not simply a discourse or sermon. It is interspersed by the singing of the praises and the Name of the Lord, in chorus, or by playing them on musical instruments and accompanied by the clapping of hands. This creates a thrill of joy not only in the person who performs the Kīrtana, but in all those who participate in it. Certainly, God too would like to be present in the midst of such an assembly. One great advantage of Kīrtana is that it purifies the minds of innumerable persons at one and the same time on account of the waves of devotion and joy that pass and repass in and over them all. Not only each of them becomes bound to God with love, but he also becomes so with all of them.

Rāmadāsa sounds however a threefold warning to one who wishes to perform a Kīrtana. He should avoid three things. In the first place, he should not describe the beauty and the bodily form of even the heavenly women; for, this will immediately make him and the audience lose their courage and self-control. Secondly, he should not perform a Kīrtana for the sake of money; for, that will increase his greed. And, thirdly, he should not describe God as being Nirguṇa, when he has before him an image of God or of an incarnation of God, who is necessarily Saguṇa; for, that will defeat the very purpose for which the Kīrtana is performed. How indeed can one win the love of God, if he is entangled by the beauty of a woman? How can he win the grace of God, if while performing the Kīrtana, he is drawn away by the greed for money? And, how can he experience that God is compassionate and full of grace, if he describes God as bereft of any quality? Rāmadāsa does not forget to give the additional advice that music too is only a means and not an end in itself. For, if one becomes absorbed in the melody of the music, God would remain away from him.

If however one takes care to avoid the above-mentioned pitfalls, Kīrtana is an excellent method of increasing one's devotion for God. It purifies one's tongue and mind; it improves one's moral conduct, clears away his doubts, and enables him to realize God. At all other times, that is, when one is not meditating on God with concentration at fixed hours, or when he is not performing a Kīrtana, he should by all means, says Rāmadāsa, remember the Name of God. For, on account of this only, concentrated meditation and disinterested Kīrtana will become more and more easy and joyful. Such a man will be befriended by God.

22. *Service and Salutation to God and to Guru* (4. *iv*. 1-26; *v*. 1-33; *vi*. 1-25; *vii*. 1-28)

Pāda-sevana, Arcana, Namaskāra, and Dāsya are four other modes of devotion through which a devotee should also worship and serve God, and thereby make easy progress towards the cherished goal of God-realization. Pāda-sevana consists in resorting at the feet of the Guru, and in placing one's head upon them with humility and reverence until such time as one is fortunate to have the vision of God's feet everywhere, and then to worship them also. In the beginning, he will have to rest content first with the Saguṇa worship of the feet of an image of God and those of the Guru. For, it is only through this kind of Saguṇa-Bhakti that he will attain to the Nirguṇa-Bhakti of worshipping God's feet revealed in mystical vision. In a way, both these Saguṇa and Nirguṇa types of Bhakti meet in the service of the Guru, since while the physical body of the Guru is the Saguṇa image of God, his experience of the immaculate divine vision constitutes the Nirguṇa aspect of God. Worship of the Guru is therefore the worship of God in both the personal and impersonal aspects; and so, the devotee should serve him both physically and mentally, and think that he is always resting at the feet of his Master. But when the Guru is away at a distant place or when unfortunately he is no more physically alive, how will it be possible to serve him? In that case, the service of the Guru will consist in faithfully following his spiritual instruction, namely, meditation on the Name of God as imparted by him. For, that alone will enable the devotee to realize God. Besides, if Pāda-sevana were to connote the exact literal meaning of washing, worshipping and shampooing the feet of the Guru, it would be possible only for a very few of his devotees, for a short time only, and so long as the Guru is alive.

Arcana or the worship of God as ordinarily understood consists in doing some such things as giving a bath to an image or images of God, applying sandle-paste to the forehead of the deities, offering flowers, sweets and different kinds of fruits and dishes, burning of incense and waving of lights, ringing of bells and singing prayers and glories of God with great love and sincerity. No doubt, God is pleased with the attitude of love and surrender on the part of the devotee, rather than with the materials offered to him. Arcana however need not consist of physical things or acts. Even a mental worship of a mentally created deity with the mental offerings will be equally efficacious in propitiating the deity. Arcana Bhakti will produce dispassion or non-attachment for worldly things, if they are being constantly offered by him to God in the spirit of sacrifice and dedication. It will simultaneously increase attachment to God and detachment to all other godless things. Thus the devotee will gradually rise from the mere idol-worship, where such things as water and flowers are used, to a continuous, life-long, heart-felt worship of God, where the entire current of life, whether good or bad, is dedicated to God or to the Guru without the least sense of egoism.

Namaskāra is another kind of devotion closely allied to Arcana. It means making salutations to God and God-like persons by bowing down or prostrating before them with utmost humility, and without any sense of shame or hesitation. God will surely grace such a devotee and wash away all his sins, and forgive him for all his lapses. Salutations done physically or mentally to God will generate spiritual virtues in the devotee, such as non-egoism, humility, dedication and surrender, and enable him to wait with faith and hope for the grace of God. By means of constant salutations and surrender, the devotee will certainly be lifted into the Kingdom of God.

All the three above-mentioned forms of devotion are in a sense, the expression of the fourth type of devotion, namely,

Dāsya or the service of God which however is something more than Pāda-sevana. What is now required is that the devotee should consider himself as one of the humblest servants of God, and should readily do any kind of service to God which may ordinarily be thought of as below his dignity, such as cleaning the precincts of the temple of God and rendering physical service to the Saints. For, service done to the people of God is service done to God. Dāsya however does not include the service that is rendered to Godless humanity. The building of schools, hospitals and sanatoria may go to form the highest social and moral service, but it is in no way spiritual in nature, unless it turns the people who receive it towards God.

23. *Befriending God and the Guru* (4. *viii*. 1-30)

When the devotee becomes sufficiently advanced by practising the above-mentioned types of Bhakti, he gains insight, faith and sincerity needed for cultivating the Sakhyatva or the Friendship of God. This is almost the culmination of devotion. The devotee now depends wholly on the love and grace of God and of the Guru. They are now his true and only friends. Now it is that his sense of creaturehood and dependence makes room for his friendship with God. For this, the devotee becomes prepared to pay the highest price. He will never think that the giving up of his precious possessions, dearest relatives and even his own life is too great a price for befriending God. For, he knows that friendship of God is altogether different from human friendship which depends on barter, a sort of give and take. Men may desert each other in moments of crises and perplexities. But the friendship of God, based as it is on an uncompromising determination to lose all for the sake of God, may appear for some time to be a one-sided affair in which the devotee gives all, and God appears to remain indifferent. But as Rāmadāsa says, God only watches our little courage with kindness, and is verily an adamantine protection to us. He alone will be our ever-lasting friend, bound with us by the unbreakable bond of love, because He is the ocean of grace and compassion. If He is once convinced of our all-absorbing love for him, in spite of our sufferings and disappointments, He will repay us manifold with His love and grace. But the devotee must remember, that God being nearer to him than his own breath, he should never think of deceiving Him by pretension of friendship. Even the slightest change of heart becomes known to God ; and then there arises a corresponding change in Him. God smiles if the devotee smiles ; God might become angry if the devotee is angry ; and God would be true and faithful if the devotee is so. Thus the key to achieve the friendship of God lies with the devotee alone. He should not hide anything from God, but communicate to Him with confidence, love and prayer every secret of his heart. He should constantly meditate on Him, pray for the grace, and live and move and have his being in God.

24. *Self-surrender* (*Ātmanivedana*) *as the apex of devotion* (4. ix. 1-30)

Ātmanivedana is the crowning phase of the devotional life. The surrender of the self to God is so complete that in the blissful unitive life of God-realization, there remains no trace of egoism or of the consciousness that the body has got any reality of its own. It is as if the cutting of one's own head on the altar of God. There would be no wonder if the whole of the perceptible world would vanish like a dream before the eyes of one who has realized the Brahman. Rāmadāsa tells us that Rāma-bhajana is the surest royal road which will lead us to God-head.

Rāmadāsa knows that there are people who think that there is also the philosophical way of attaining Ātmanivedana. But he warns us by saying that there are great pitfalls on this way, and that one is very likely to fall in one or the other of them. For instance, if one begins to make the search of the 'I' in him, he is advised by the philosophers to eliminate one after another the five elements of earth, water, fire, wind and sky of which his own body as also the entire perceptible world is made up. This has no doubt helped the seeker of the Self to avoid one stumbling block in his way, namely, the perceptible world itself. As the stuff out of which his body as well as the whole of the perceptible world was created is one and the same, namely, the five elements, and as these elements in their turn had their origin in the Prakṛti or the Mūla-Māyā or Avidyā, it is quite natural for the seeker to believe that the body and the world are both real. Like sees the like. The very sense-organs being the products of Avidyā, readily believe in the reality of another portion of Avidyā, namely, the perceptible world. Now, intellectually at least, philosophy has helped the seeker not to be carried away by the appearances only. The negative method of elimination has been very useful to him in convincing that the world and the physical body are not at all real. Even so, he would be successful in negativing the reality of the mind, intellect and egoism, and be convinced that the psychological world of mental states and ideas and egoism also is not ultimately real. No doubt, he will know what is unreal ; but what is the essence of the real 'I' would remain for him still a mystery. To believe that what remains after the process of elimination is over is God or the Ātman, is no doubt logically true. But after all it is a make-believe, born of intellect, and not the conviction born out of experience. How long can the mind be satisfied by a conclusion which is negative in character ? There being no positive content on which it should take its stand, the human mind will soon be fatigued, and in sheer despair it will either fall back again upon the perceptible world and his body as the veritable facts of reality, or be content with a void which means a total annihilation of everything including even the hypothetical existence of the 'I' he was wishing to discover. The first is the pitfall in which fall the commonsense realists, and in the second fall the sceptics and idlers.

Rāmadāsa tells us that there are two more ways in which the intellect tries to make headway towards Ātmanivedana. One is known as the Viveka-pralaya (intellectual dissolution), whereby the very constituents of the world, namely, the five elements are dissolved, one into the other in the manner in which the effect is dissolved into its cause. The Earth, for instance, is imagined to be dissolved in Water, out of which it is supposed to come into being ; Water as being evaporated by Fire, Sun and lightning ; fire as extinguished by Wind, which, in its turn, is blown away into the void or empty space (Ākāśa). And, if the void is to be avoided, as said above, what remains is the eternal Puruṣa or the Brahman. The other way is to imagine oneself as becoming larger and larger, so that the universe will begin to appear as smaller and smaller. As this double process of imagination will continue, the earth, for instance, will first appear to him as if it is a cricket ball, then as an apple, and then again as a mustard seed. This dimension too the earth will soon lose, and it will be as good as non-existent; for one will then imagine himse'f as being infinitely larger than the earth. And what would happen ultimately is that the mental state (Vṛtti) of imagination also will be torn into pieces in its attempt to approximate to the dimensions of the Infinite Being, which alone would remain as the eternal Reality.

This absence of any Vṛtti does not however mean, as Rāmadāsa says, that one has attained the Supramental condition (Unmanī-avasthā) of the unison of the subject and the object (devotee and God). It only indicates a negative state, whereas the unitive life with the Ātman is a positive state, to attain to which one must ceaselessly meditate on God and win His grace. Then will the devotee be rapt up with divine consciousness ; for, God will be both inside and outside of him. There will then neither remain in him the false notion that his body and the world outside are real, nor the egoism of his tiny individuality, nor again the vacuum of a vacant mind. During the period of ecstatic joy and peace, the devotee would become as large as the Infinite, just as the river which enters into the sea becomes as large as the sea. The river loses its name and form ; so does the devotee who enters into God lose the consciousness that he is separate from God. The non-dualistic, Advaitic doctrine of the Vedānta becomes for the devotee a practical life. Of course, it admits of degrees ; even so, Ātmanivedana admits of approximation to God. All this is possible only when the pure idea (Śuddha Kalpanā), that is, the Name of God would gather volume, intensity and strength by being meditated upon constantly, and when all other impure ideas, that is, all Godless ideas are completely shut out.

25. *Four kinds of Liberation* (4. *x*. 1-31)

After we have dealt with the problem of the identity of the self with God through surrender and meditation, there ought to have been no further problem regarding the destiny of man towards which the nine forms of devotion are intended to lead him. But as there occur very beautiful descriptions of the heaven and its pleasures and of the different kinds of liberation after death in the Purāṇas, which will perhaps tempt and mislead the devotee, it will be worth-while to discuss them in brief and find out that the highest kind of devotion is intended to end in only one kind of liberation, namely, the Sāyujya mukti, that is, the merging of the self in the Brahman.

The heaven as conceived by the Purāṇas, is a very enchanting kingdom consisting of the abodes of the several gods, including the Vaikuṇṭha of Viṣṇu, Satyaloka of Brahmadeva, Kailāsa of Śiva, Amarāvatī of Indra, and so on. There are mountains of gold, mines of emeralds, lakes of nectar, forests of wish-yielding trees, herds of wish-yielding cows, dinners of nectar-like dishes, celestial flowers and perfumes, and the melodious unceasing songs of nymphs and dancing girls. All the time, there is unbreakable joy of youth ; there is neither disease nor old age nor death; the bodies of the inmates there complete with each other in beauty ; they are made of light which is akin to that of the Sun, the moon, the lightning or of fire ; and so far as fame, power and success are concerned, they have no limit.

This is the alluring prospect of a life beyond death which the poets say is reserved in the heaven as a prize for the life of the devotees who are gods on earth. This promise given in advance is of three kinds of liberation. First, the devotee is told that he would be lifted to the abode of that deity which he worships on the earth. This is known as Salokatā Mukti, the liberty to stay in the region of the deity. If the devotion is of a higher order, the sādhaka obtains the Samīpatā Mukti, that is, he is allowed to stay after death near the deity. And, if the devotion be still of a higher order, the saint obtains the very Form of the deity, without however becoming one with the deity. This is known as the Sarūpatā Mukti, but which, according to Rāmadāsa, can be had even while living. All these three kinds of liberation are however short-lived. They last only so long as the merit is there ; but as soon as it is exhausted, the devotee is born again in this mortal world, and is placed again on the wheel of karma. The fourth kind of liberation, known as the Sāyujya Mukti is the only one which abides forever, and which can be had even within the lifetime of the saint. This does not terminate with the death of the saint, because the saint has already become one with the Brahman, and has no sense of duality left in him. Naturally, even after his death the saint becomes as immortal as the Brahman.

Sāyujya, which means an intimate and indissoluble contact or identity of the self with the Brahman, does include in it the other three kinds of liberation, but not the defects or limitations of them. It is Salokatā and Samīpatā in the sense that it makes the saint permanently lodged in Brahman. And, it is Sarūpatā in the sense that it makes him aware of his own real Form (Sva = own, and Rūpa = form), namely the Brahman; but once the river of the self meets and merges into the ocean of the Brahman, how can it be separated again? The river becomes the ocean ; even so, the self becomes the Brahman ; the Personal changes into the unchangeable Impersonal Brahman.

26. *Necessity of the Spiritual Teacher* (5. *i*. 1-46)

The realization of Brahman is neither possible by the reading of the Vedas nor by the performance of any sacrifice. Worship the idols as much as you like; ring the bells, wave the lights, sing the praises and the prayers to them, and make as many offerings of precious things, food and fruits as you please; visit the holy places and spend all your wealth in charity, and yet, you will only have the fulfilment of all your cherished desires, but not at all the knowledge of Brahman. No yogic postures and methods of concentration of the eyes and the mind, no attainment of miraculous power, no ritualism of any kind, and no mere external expression without the inner real devotion to God will ever result in the realization of Brahman. The only means to attain it is to have the company of the good and the holy, and the grace of some great spiritual teacher who has himself realized the Brahman and who can show it to others. That spiritual teacher alone who has gone to the end of all desires can truly be addressed as the 'Ātmadeva', since he has already visualized the identity of the Ātman (his own self) with Brahman. Therefore, he alone can impart this knowledge to another and enable him to have the experience of the identity of his self with the Guru as well as with God.

27. *The false and the real Guru.* (5. ii. 1-73)

There are teachers and teachers in every walk of life; the spiritual teacher however is a category by himself and is distinct from them all. Our parents are in a way our teachers; those also who teach bookish knowledge and how to earn our daily bread; those who teach fine arts like music and dancing; those who teach black magic which will work out miracles and hypnotize audience; those who initiate people into the worship of several lower deities by means of uttering hymns to images and their representative diagrams, known as 'Yantras', are all of them, Gurus no doubt. But, of what use are they from the spiritual point of view ? Some of them feel indebted to their disciples who offer them wealth; therefore they do as the disciples wish them to do; some of them use their excellent oratory power while speaking about great principles of Vedānta, but themselves indulge in sensuous pleasures; while some others leave the spiritual path altogether and increase the importance of their body only by pursuing the path of acquiring miraculous powers. How can such selfish men teach the disciples to have control over the senses and the mind and to practise meditation ? One should cast away such pretenders, even if they can be had by giving a penny.

The real Guru is that who, in spite of his having realized the Brahman, never gives up his sādhanā of meditation, and who has got the power of making others realize the Brahman. Rare is the Guru who has got no other desire but to realize God; who being lost in silent meditation on the divine Name and in contemplating upon his own real immaculate Form or on a vision of God, has turned his back in disgust upon the pleasures of the worldly life; and who passes his time in contentment, joy and peace. Morally great, compassionate and full of grace as he is, he alone will be able to reveal to his disciple that the entire spiritual treasure is contained in the Name of God which he imparts to him. He alone will hand him over safe in the arms of Divine Mother, from whom he was unfortunately separated by being immersed in the worldly affairs. One should therefore find out such a powerful Guru who will root out the ignorance and the misgivings about spiritual life, and teach the disciple that there will be no realization of God unless there is morality and self-control on the one hand, and regular meditation on the Name of God, on the other.

In short, one must exercise caution and take great care in finding out a worthy Guru before he surrenders unto him and receives initiation from him in the life divine.

28. *Who is a true disciple ?* (5. *iii.* 1-104)

The foremost characteristic of a true disciple is that he must have absolute and unwavering faith in the Guru. And in order to strengthen this and be able to see the vision of God constantly before him what is equally essential is that he must be, as often as he can, in the company of the good and the holy ; meditate he must daily and regularly with the attitude of humility, love and regard; and being pure, compassionate and generous, he should in his own humble way try to spread the gospel of God with deligence and courage,

And when, in course of time, God would reveal himself in the form of a vision, a true disciple should feel all the more grateful to his spiritual teacher for having shown him the Godhead. And when in course of time, again, he would realize that in knowing the nature of God, he is himself becoming God-like, he would be endowed with such strength of courage as will never shake him with fear or change his conviction regarding the power of the grace of his Guru, even if he be in the midst of the greatest of calamities. The whole world will, as if, vanish from his sight when, being supported by the grace of his Guru, he comes in the very presence of the mighty vision of God.

29. *Nature of Spiritual initiation.* (5. *iv.* 1-36)

Just as there is a vast difference between the real spiritual teacher and a false one, even so the real initiation into spiritual life is vastly different from one which is merely an imitation of it. One may be initiated into the eightfold discipline of the Pātañjala Yoga and taught to practise different postures and the ways in which concentration may be sought. Or one may be taught how to propitiate a deity, how to achieve various powers which will be-friend him with anyone he likes, how to confound and destroy his enemies, or how to have a control over the elements, or undo the deadly effects of the bites of scorpions and serpents. One may be taught how to perform various sacrifices and to obtain his desired objects of pleasure. One is asked to visit the holy places and to meditate upon any name of God which the Guru is pleased to choose at random, or to repeat endlessly till one gets tired some such great statement of Vedānta as 'I am the Brahman', or 'All this is Brahman'.

Useless however is all this from the spiritual point of view. That would be the real initiation which will yield the fruit of God-realization. That which does not so yield is useless like a broken or roasted seed which will never grow even into a sprout. Hence, that word or that divine Name which comes out of the mouth of a saint who has realized God constitutes the spiritual initiation.

30. *Spiritual knowledge as distinct from the phenomenal one* (5. *v.* 1-39 ; *vi.* 1-75)

First, with the knowledge of the phenomenal world which is as evanescent as the phenomenal world itself; and therefore it is not at all the abiding Reality. To know a thing which is hidden and the unknown events of the past, or the happenings of the present and the future might be called by the generality of people as constituting the knowledge of reality. But this is not correct. For it perishes along with the known as well as the unknown perishable things. Similarly perishable is the knowledge of the various arts like music and dancing, of sciences and philosophies, of languages and poetry, of knowing what is passing on in the minds of others, of the auspicious and inauspicious times, of diseases and their remedies, of how to determine the nature and quality of a horse, or of a woman, a jewel, a fruit, or of innumerable such other things. All these kinds of knowledge look like real knowledge but the knowledge of the ultimate identity of man with God is altogether different. And till this is achieved, man will never be fully satisfied.

There is also an erroneous notion among the learned that one who goes beyond the three states of wakefulness, sleep and dream becomes the knower of all that exists, and that this is what is known as the real knowledge. But this also is not correct. For, where there is no such thing as 'all' over and above the one and the only one Reality, the knowledge of the so-called 'all' is, in fact, the knowledge of the phenomenal, perishable world. Even so, the notion that by the constant repetition of the great Vedāntic truth, 'I am the Brahman', the person who repeats it becomes the Brahman, is equally erroneous. For, the repetition will only bring fatigue to the mind. It will not enable the person who repeats it to experience the identity of the 'I' with the Brahman. It will only mean either a grammatical or at the most a logical identity between the subject and the predicate, and never a factual and experiential identity, in which case the 'I' forgets itself and becomes merged in Brahman.

It is this latter kind of identity which, when it becomes the content of experience, constitutes the real knowledge. And, as the 'I' or the self is lost gradually in that process of identification, the Brahman alone remains as the knower of the identity, as also the object which is known, and as the knowledge in which both the subject and the object do not remain as separate entities. In other words, when Brahman knows itself, it is known as the state of the real knowledge.

This comes to saying that real knowledge means the realization of the Self or the Ātman by the Ātman. It is the seeing of one's own Form by oneself, as if in a mirror. This Form it is which in course of time comes to be known as God or Brahman, because it transcends the perceptible, phenomenal world of the five elements, namely, the earth, water, fire, air and ākāśa. Besides, it is supramental and supra-intellectual; and being pure and *sui generis*, it is the source of all that exists, as well as the destination in which all is dissolved. Realizing this, all the great sages of the past, such as Vyāsa, Vaśiṣṭha, Śuka, Nārada etc. became omniscient, liberated and blissful ; and even the great God, Śaṅkara, is said to be nodding with joy on that account. This knowledge is the essence of the Vedas and the conclusion of all intellectual search. It is the sweet fruit of the grace of the spiritual teacher, in the form of the experience of the identity of the disciple with the Brahman, as seen above in explaining the meaning of 'I am the Brahman'. It is but natural that when the fire of this knowledge would become a huge conflagration, the scattered rubbish of the perceptible world should be burnt into ashes. To put it differently, in the presence of this real knowledge, the world, though it may continue to be perceived, would be as good as naught.

This is, in short, the knowledge of the Ātman ; and it can be achieved by resorting to devotion, the crowning phase of which is self-surrender. One must therefore meditate in seclusion on the divine Name imparted by the Guru, so that God will be permanently fixed in the heart, and there would emerge disgust for all the God-less things in the world, and with that, there would emerge the true wakefulness in the knowledge of God. Reciprocally, however, we may say that the true index of such wakefulness is the utter disgust for God-less things. Therefore, in order to have both, namely, the supra-wakefulness and the dispassion, one should mentally and constantly meditate on the Name of God and should listen to it while it is uttered.

31. *The slaves of pleasures.* (5.vii. 1-49)

What is the alternative for men, if they are neither on the path of God nor desirous to go on that path ? The only choice left for them is to allow their natural, hedonistic urge to make them the slaves of nature. The result would be that they will lack the qualities which are necessary for the emergence of the knowledge of God, but possess such qualities as will make them love only three things in life, namely, women, wealth and bodily pleasures. Day and night they will direct their mind and senses to these three objects only. And the qualities, which are very helpful to promote the acquisition of these objects and which they possess in abundance, are anger, pride, arrogance, pretension, greed, jealousy, hatred, treachery, selfishness, miserliness and so on. How can such people like the company of the good and the holy, cherish the desire for God-realization and possess forgiveness and compassion ? How can they think of visiting holy places or spending money in charity or of relieving the miseries of others? They will censure the saints, disrespect them, and being blind to what ought to be the most valuable thing, waste their life in seeking pleasure after pleasure till they become impotent to enjoy them.

32. *Repentance followed by Aspiration to become free.* (5. viii. 1-44)

There comes a time when the extreme and the gross hedonist also becomes old, or perhaps being overcome by diseases, he feels that he has become incapable of enjoying the pleasure which he had once prized most. The pleasures do not however become less attractive, nor does his lust or greed become diminished. But the consciousness of this, if it comes to a thoughtful person long before he becomes old or is overtaken by disease, would create a vacuum in him, and make him more and more uneasy and repentant for having wasted his life in following the will-o'-the-wisp of pleasures. He would recall with grief how being duped by women and wealth, he only censured the saints, despised the devotees of God, and deserting the path of truth and goodness had become the supporter of what was only false and evil. 'All this I did', he would confess woefully, 'in order to fill my belly and to keep up my reputation in society. If I worshipped any deity, I did it out of show ; I sat for doing meditation, but used to think about the ways and means of increasing my wealth. I preached the people, but charged fees from them ; and yet, put them on a wrong track by abusing my intelligence. I am so selfish that I did nothing for the good of others. I have been a mountain of sins, and yet I never thought of visiting any holy place, nor of coming in contact with the good and the holy. How indeed can I save myself now ? What is my wealth or prosperity in comparison to that of the kings and sovereigns ?

Who indeed can protect me now from the mental and the physical afflictions from which I am suffering?' In these and other words, he would censure himself, and thinking that the saint alone can pardon and save him, he would resolve to surrender unto him.

Thus it is that repentance for one's own past, wayward behaviour as also the consequent aspiration and resolution to reverse the steps and to follow the spiritual path of the saints, constitute the first step, or as we may call, the first conversion, on the pathway to God.

33. *The Baptized soul.* (5. ix. 1-62)

The second stage of the spiritual life begins the moment an aspirant is accepted and initiated by the spiritual teacher. That very moment all the chains of bondage are snapped asunder, and the soul becomes one with the Universal God. But, this, at the start, would only be a dogma for the aspirant; for, it is not a fact of his experience. And so, he is required to have full faith in his Guru, and to practise meditation on the Name of God, as imparted to him by his Guru. That Name has the power to reveal out of itself the visions of the Forms of God. And this will happen provided the Guru is a very powerful one, and has himself realized God fully and always. The meditation also has to be done regularly, daily and for a long time with love and regard. The Name might be uttered loudly; but it would be far better if it is uttered mentally and in silence, and also heard by the mental ear while it is being meditated upon. In course of time, the aspirant will come to know that he too is fortunate to have the same experience as has been described in the spiritual literature of the saints in the past, and by his own teacher also.

In order to achieve this, however, the aspirant has to toil in several ways. He has to come again and again in the company of the saints, after deliberately avoiding all the environmental entanglements, attractions and disturbances; he has to cultivate moral virtues and bid good-bye to idleness, misgivings, doubts and evil habits, and to become free from egoism, greed, lust, anger, jealousy, hatred and fear. Ignoring what is perceivable to the physical eye and what can be grasped by memory, imagination, intellect and mind, he has deliberately to hold fast to the Name. And then by the power of his meditation and the grace of his Guru, he will hold fast also to the vision of God which would manifest itself before him, and which would dazzle his eyes and make him tongue-tied on account of its splendour which is unique and novel. This will make him one with the divine Form which is both transcendental and immanent, supramental and suprawakeful, and which, though itself without any name, quality or form, is the source of all names, qualities and forms.

In effect, the aspirant will be without any egoism or attachment to bodily consciousness, though he too will have a body and behave like others. What he is in reality will not be seen by anyone ; because being one with God, he has gone beyond the five elements and beyond the five organs of knowledge.

34. *Only by degrees man bec:mes one with God.* (5. x. 1-45)

While discussing the second stage on the path of God, we have also mentioned the third and the last stage to which an aspirant, or the Sādhaka, as Rāmadāsa calls him, ascends, namely, the stage of being one with God. But this is so in theory only. In actual experience, the unity is achieved only by degrees. Even the greatest of the saints can be said to reach the God-hood approximately only, as Professor R.D. Ranade holds it. Therefore as a corollary, even this approximate perfection is achieved gradually. One who has just begun his spiritual career should not, therefore, be expected to be capable of giving up all his former habits, his defects or even his vices or sins, at one stroke, and on the very first day. This is especially so in the case of a house-holder who has the double responsibility of carrying on his family life with the same status and reputation as before, and of keeping pace with the saints and his Guru by increasing his spiritual worth. So, it must be remembered both by the aspirant and by his critics that perfection in the moral and the spiritual field has to be slowly and gradually acquired, and that none should blame a person if he cannot give up his faults and his bad habits all of a sudden.

There is however one characteristic which we can use as a measure to determine that progress is being made on the spiritual path. There must not only be the absence of the slightest doubt regarding the existence of God who has created all this movable and immovable world, but also the absence of disbelief that the aspirant will realize God by resorting to meditation. The so-called 'way of doing the works' (karma-mārga) and all the speculative philosophies which might deal with the nature of God are full of doubts and counter-doubts. All these must vanish on account of the meditation on the Name and of the direct experience of the vision of God. On the one hand, one must come to know that the immaculate vision of one's own Self is the Form of God, and that, on the other, that Form itself is the source from which the world has sprung up. The criterion here is one's own experience. In the presence of the full-fledged vision of God, the whole world would vanish as it were, and there would be no limit to bliss.

The more the conviction due to the direct experience of the statement, 'I am the Ātman' (Brahman or God), and the more the joy which will follow this experience, the more would be the spiritual and the moral perfection of the devoted soul. The more he becomes free from the considerations of his body and from the belief that he is the body-complex only, the more would he be free from egoism and doubts of any kind.

35. *The search after God.* (6. i. 1-31)

One must first cognize God before he salutes him ; he should not make a mistake and salute someone else. He should therefore consult some one who has already seen God and then do as he would advise. But is it necessary that every man should meet God? Yes, it is desirable to do so. For, will it not be considered as desirable for one who dwells in a village or town to know the chief or the important persons of that place, so that he should not be taken as a suspect? This will be considered more and more necessary, if one should reside in a city or the capital of a country. For to be acquainted with the king or the sovereign will be the greatest asset for securing several other advantages. Even so, will it be to become acquainted with God who is the King of Kings and the Creator of the universe. God will keep his devotees safe from all the dangers and the evil forces which come under the domain of the deceitful Māyā, known as Prakṛti. Whoever fails to realize God will, therefore, be a 'fallen' man. He will fall in the snares of Māyā, and then, in the absence of the knowledge of the real king, he might salute any one of the evil forces. But will this be of any advantage to him ? What can a beggar get if he meets another beggar, or a patient meets another patient? One who is drunk cannot save another who is equally so. Even so, one will never know what God is and how he is to be realized by moving with the people who only know how to fill their belly, and who only protect and fatten their bodies, and die one day without caring to know anything about the existence and nature of God. One must, therefore, meet a saint who has seen the eternal, imperishable God, and who, though living amidst the people of the world, tells us to do something which they do not know, even though they might be the most learned of all. Therefore, if anyone wishes to find out God, he should first find out a great saint, surrender unto him, and be initiated by him, so that by meditating on the divine Name he would realize God.

36. *To know God is to become God.* (6. ii. 1-45)

What would be the advice of the saint, if one were fortunate to find him out? The saint would ask him to do two things ; one is to realize in his own experience that God is indestructible ; and the other, to realize that he himself is identical with God, and, therefore, has no separate existence of his own. This is the essence of all spiritual advice, and of the act of initiation performed by the saint.

The phenomenal world consists of eight parts, namely, earth, water, fire, air, ākāśa (ether) and the three natural propensities in man which drive him to be either stupid and lazy, or selfish and active, or pure and good. The first five are known as the elements, and the next three as the qualities (guṇas). Together, they constitute the eightfold Prakṛti or Māyā which, according to the saints, is perishable in nature. Things of the phenomenal world come into being and vanish after some time. God or Brahman, on the contrary, is neither an element nor a quality, and is, therefore, said to be 'Nirguṇa' and imperishable. Brahman cannot be cut by weapons, or burnt by fire, nor moistened by water, nor blown by wind ; it is not something which can be brought into being, or can be kept hidden. Though it has no specific colour, and though it is not visible by the physical eyes, it exists in a subtle manner everywhere and at all times. It is this Reality, known as God or Brahman, which must be seen, though the ordinary people see only the perceptible world. And the only way to see and realize it is by means of spiritual meditation.

The second thing which the Guru asks the disciple to realize is that in the very process of realizing God, he should also realize that he himself is becoming God. If the first step in the process of realization can be named as 'Deva-darśana' (the seeing of God), the second step can be named as 'Ātma-nivedana' (to realize the Ātman or the Self as God). Ordinary people, and popular philosophy which does not go far beyond the wrong notions of ordinary people, believe that the body itself is the Ātman. But a little thought will tell us that this is not correct. Even the expressions, 'my body', 'my mind' etc. will show that the body, the mind etc. are different from the 'Me' to which they belong. In the same way, the entire perceptible world, whether external or internal, that is, whether consisting of the eightfold Prakṛti, or of the senses, mind, intellect, egoism, as well as of the emotions, feelings, likes and dislikes, etc., is different from the pure 'I' which will still remain as the core of our consciousness, after all the above-mentioned super-imposed things are eliminated. This then is the Nirguṇa 'I' which is the same as Brahman, and which, therefore, is beyond birth and death, merit and demerit, and all other dualities. And, when the sādhaka sees, during his meditation and after, that his own Form is omnipresent, he gets the additional proof that his self or the Ātman is the Brahman. He knows that he is becoming one with God. Why then will he care about what happens or would happen to his body? For, he is no longer the body ; he has attained the immortal condition of being forever lodged in Brahman.

37. *Distinctions vanish with the Realization of the identity with God.* (6. iii. 1-37)

What is known as the Brahman is greater than the great and subtler than the subtle ; homogeneous, spotless, compact and spread-out everywhere without any break; neither perceivable by the eye, nor capable of being imagined by the mind; immovable and indestructible ; having neither beginning nor end ; remains always in front of oneself, and yet envelopes the earth and the heaven. Just as the space in a jar was already there before the jar was made, and will be there after the jar is broken, without being affected in any way, even so the Brahman, which has been already in existence before anything came into being, will continue to exist after everything goes out of being, without itself being affected in any way. In short, there being nothing else which can be said to have any semblance with the Brahman (God or Ātman), the only way to have knowledge about it is to bring one's mind in relation with the experience of some one who has realized the Brahman. God is immanent in the universe, no doubt, like juice in the sugar-cane ; but he must be experienced as transcending the universe, just as the juice is extracted by eliminating the gross stuff in the sugar-cane.

And this is exactly being done by a saint, that is, by one who has directly realized the Brahman. This he does not only with reference to the external phenomenal world, but also with reference to his own body which also is composed of the five elements. He looks to his body, and applying the same logic which he applies to the phenomenal world, he comes intellectually to the conclusion that what would remain after the elements are removed one after another is the Ātman only. The proof of this he gets during his meditation. He sees first the Ātman as having the Form of his own body ; and though it is likely that he might be confused for some time and think that the manifestation of the Ātman is conditioned by his body, he will soon come to know by the power of his meditation and by the grace of his Guru that the Ātman which he sees before him, though immanent in his body, has a transcendental existence of its own, and that it is identical with

Brahman inasmuch as he sees the same Form spread out in all space and in all the directions. Forthwith, the sense of his being identical with the physical body goes away ; along with it goes away all his egoism, and his sense that he is a complex of senses, mind, and intellect. The sense of the 'I' in him is no longer due to the superimposed burden of a physical body, along with the egoism of the senses, the mind and the intellect; it is due to the presence in him of the pure Ātman, who in spite of his being immanent is transcendent in the sense that He is not contaminated by anything which is physical, moral or intellectual.

In short, when the entire false sense which has become unfortunately attached to the 'I' is eliminated by the grace of the Guru and by the power of meditation, there remains no distinction between the disciple and the Guru, and between the saint and God. The answer to the question, 'Who am I' or the question 'Who art thou' would be 'I am He (God)' or 'I am the Brahman'. One who has got this experience can be said to be a true 'Bhakta' (devotee) in the sense that he is not 'Vibhakta' (separate) from God or Brahman.

38. *Not longevity, but spirituality is the test of greatness.* (6. iv. 1-24)

The Hindu mythology speaks of four aeons as completing one cycle of 4320000 years. Considering this as the unit, they speak in terms of millions and millions of such units as constituting the life spans of the three great deities, namely, Brahmā, Viṣṇu and Maheśa, who are responsible for the creation, preservation and dissolution of this universe.

Naturally, those who worship these deities say with pride that a particular deity is the greatest of all. But from the view-point of the saint, the Ātman alone who is immanent in all the deities is the greatest of all. From a picture of an army painted on the canvas or seen in a dream, who indeed in his waking life can point out that a particular person is great ? As a matter of fact, none is either great or small. Only the imagination of the dreamer, or the brush of the painter makes it so. Even so, all the objects in the universe, including the various deities are ultimately no better than the painted pictures or moments of time, which vanish one after another. Therefore, just as the Ātman is great, even so the person who realizes the Ātman is great.

39. *Contrast between the Brahman and Māyā.*(6.*v*.1-26)

Brahman is formless, limitless, immovable, without any condition, invisible to the physical eye, indestructible, unborn, unaffected, non-phenomenal, one, the essence of all, without any impurity, too subtle to be comprehended, hidden, equal to all, the witness of all, homogeneous, without any break, tender at heart, and with all this it is also said to be beyond description. Māyā is just the opposite of this. And yet, the wonder of it is that in spite of the fact that the Brahman and the Māyā a e being mixed together, what is seen by the eye and understood by the mind and intellect is said to be the working of the Māyā alone. The saint alone knows the secret of making the distinction between the two, and so he contemplates upon the Brahman and leaves away the Māyā, just as the swan is reputed to be able to drink the milk and leave the water which is mixed with it. The Brahman is immanent in the world, but the saint knows how to keep the contact with the Brahman without being contaminated by the affairs of the world.

40. *Are gods many or one ?* (6. *vi.* 1-60; *vii.*1-45)

The Hindu mythology abounds in gods; but it speaks also of one God. Therefore the opinion of some scholars is that Hinduism is henotheistic in character, meaning thereby that some one among the several gods appears to be supreme for the time being, and that the other gods are subordinate to him. But this is not the whole truth. It will be seen that neither polytheism nor henotheism is incompatible with monotheism, if we remember that the first two forms of belief are only the two steps which are felt to be necessary for the formation of the belief in monotheism. The many gods then of the Hindus will not only be considered as having, turn by turn, the same status of the one supreme God, but also as having it simultaneously on account of the several view-points of the devotees of them all. Instead of being a part or an aspect of the whole of Reality, which we may call indifferently as the Ātman, or the Brahman or God, each one of the several deities, such as Rāma, Kṛṣṇa, Gaṇeśa, Viṣṇu, Kālī, Durgā, Lakṣmī and Sun has the whole of reality immanent within it, and can therefore be said to be the full representative of it. To be devoted to any one of them constitutes what is known as the worship of the Personal God (Saguṇa bhakti); to be devoted to the immanent and dynamic Reality in them all and to become one with it constitutes what is known as the worship of the Impersonal God (Nirguṇa bhakti).

Now, activity being the most essential feature of the nature of man, and devotion, so far as the vocal and ritualistic aspect of it is concerned, being also a kind of activity, it is natural that man should be drawn towards doing the worship of that aspect of Divinity, which, being personal, is dynamic and full of such qualities like compassion, forgiveness, grace, power, etc. as can be bestowed upon him. It will be only in the fullness of time that he will come to know that there is also the impersonal aspect of Divinity which can be worshipped without any kind of ritual, by means of silent and joyful meditation on the Name of God as well as by the silent and joyful contemplation on the beautiful visions of God. He will then come to know that the worship of the Personal God in the form of any of the images of the polytheistic faith of the Hindus is the right sort of basis for the beginners in the spiritual path; for, it will be on this basis afterwards that the structure of the worship of the impersonal God will be erected. Faith, reverence, love, awe, fear, joy and the feeling of dependence which will necessarily be involved in the worship of the image will increase all the more when the devotee will take up to the worship of the Impersonal, that is the worship of the immaculate Forms of light and beauty whether of his own body or of the idol which would manifest anywhere for being joyfully gazed at. It is this joyful gaze which constitutes the worship of the impersonal. He thus comes to know by his own experience that the Personal changes into the Impersonal and that the Impersonal is the Reality which is immanent in the Personal. In short, at the end of his entire career as the worshipper of God, he comes to discover that his own real Self, and the real Form of the idol he was worshipping are identical in value with each other, and that they are the Forms of the Absolute or the Brahman, which, in spite of its being formless, is capable of assuming any forms.

Considered thus, polytheism of the Hindus ceases to be the polytheism in the sense in which the critics are interested in condemning it, or the iconoclasts in destroying it; it becomes the bulwark of the highest kind of spiritual faith and experience which the mystics all over the world have enjoyed without distinction of caste, creed, nation, time or space. Polytheism gone, henotheism also has no place. There remains only the monotheism of the mystical type of religion which is one and the same for mankind as a whole. Worship then any deity, and you will then never dishonour any other deity; for you will experience that the one deity which you worship is the only one deity which is either immanent in all other deities or which assumes the forms of them all. Even so, worship any saint, you will be worshipping all the saints in the world.

It is however a misfortune that people go wrong in a double way. Thinking, on the one hand, that the worshipping a deity is a sign of ignorance or at best a relic of anthropomorphism, they deny for themselves the several virtues which are the *sine qua non* of spiritual life, namely faith, love, reverence, awe, fear, joy and the feeling of dependence on God. Or, on the other hand, they vainly speak about one God or one Brahman, without knowing in the least what He is, except by way of giving expression to some or other philosophical opinion. In this case, no doubt, some sort of intellectual joy they might get by riding over the sea-saw of speculative knowledge; but as there is no end to inference, intellectual opinions and disputations, they delude themselves by having sometimes a verbal victory over their opponents. In short, between an unknown and unknowable Brahman on the one hand, and a thorough-going disbelief in the worship of a saint or a deity, on the other, what these persons get is the hardening of their own ignorance, namely, the belief in the reality of the perceptible world, notwithstanding the short-lived and uncertain nature of it, and of their own life and pleasures of it. Add to this the various diseases, the miseries and the disappointments which they meet in life; and yet, the wonder is that they are conscious only of their bodies and bodily pleasures.

What all this comes to is that without wasting one's time in discussing whether there is one God or many gods, whether the worship of the Personal or the Impersonal aspect of God is superior to the other, one should begin with the worship of any of the great incarnations, prophets, saints or deities in whom he has full faith, or whom he has been asked by his spiritual teacher to worship. He should meditate on the Name of God and pray to him. And then, in course of time, he will come to know that though he is endowed with fame, glory and power, it is not he but God who is the real agent of his actions, that everything else is so short-lived that it is as good as naught, and that, his own self is identical with God. In short, he will experience that his own self is both the Personal and the Impersonal aspects of God. Therefore, so long as there is the constant danger of falling a victim to the temptations of the bodily pleasures, he will stick to his daily routine of devotional meditations and prayers to God. He will never raise the question as to why he should resort to the ritual of worship, when he knows that he never raises it if he behaves with great submission before a man who gives him his daily bread, and if he does all other duties in life without any complaint.

41. *The sensuously perceived is short-lived, the non-sensuously perceived is Real.* (6. *viii.* 1-50; *ix.* 1-34; *x.* 1-61)

It is a common-place knowledge to say that what is perceived ought to be real. But this is not always true. There is no water in a mirage which is perceived. The objects in a dream are not real. Horses made of clay and painted in beautiful colours do not run. Reflections of objects seen in water or in a mirror do not have independent existence of their own. Sensuous perception cannot therefore be said to be the sure test of reality.

As against this, those who possess spiritual knowledge say that God is real, though He is not perceived by the senses. A treasure which is concealed at the bottom of a lake is real, though what is seen is not the treasure but water only. A servant might not be able to discover the wealth of his master. But here also, one must not make the mistake of saying that unperceivability is the sure test of reality. For, the son of a barren woman, the horn of a hare are neither real nor perceivable. In view of the first set of examples, we conclude that the perceived something may or may not exist at all; or even if it has a kind of existence, it may be illusory, i.e., it may be the sign of something else which exists. The snake which is perceived on a rope does not really exist; but its illusory existence is the pointer to the existence of the rope. In view of the second set of examples, we conclude that what is considered as non-existent from the ordinary common-sense point of view and therefore unperceivable might exist, and might therefore be perceived in a non-sensuous manner. In other words, spiritual experiences like the visions of God can be said to have a non-temporal and non-spatial existence of their own, and that therefore they are perceivable in a non-sensuous manner, that is, by way of intuition.

Now, this intuitive faculty, which is dormant in every man, becomes active in a few only by living in the company of the saints and by the grace of any one amongst them who has the power to enable others to have the vision of God. This is not improbable. For to have a close contact with the king means to have an easy chance to become rich. Others who do not get this contact have to toil hard even for earning their bread. So, it is for anybody to choose between being entangled in the snares of the worldly pleasures throughout one's life, or to come in contact with a saint and to become liberated even while one is leading the life of a householder by seeing one's own Self and by realizing that he is identical with the highest Self or God who is both immanent and transcendent. To realize the condition of being disembodied even while one has his physical body, to live in the society and the world and do one's duties without being contaminated by the affairs of the world, is to have the cash value of all the spiritual activities one might carry on throughout his life. This is what is known as liberation while living as distinguished from liberation after death. But, one who merely goes on speculating and inferring about the ultimate destiny of man, and ceases to meditate on the Name of God will fall from the spiritual height even if he has attained it. Having no cash to his credit any longer, he just pulls on his life on borrowing, so to say, the short-lived objects of pleasure in life which he considers to be real, since like his own body they too are made up of Māyā. One has, therefore, to choose, as we have said above, between a life which is made up of short-lived, perceived objects of pleasure and meet with frustration at the end, or a life of unimaginable bliss by coming in contact with the saints, by meditation and by perceiving the Reality which otherwise remains concealed from the gaze of ordinary persons.

This unspeakable bliss is however capable of being received directly from the spiritual teacher, just as a person who does not understand what the sweetness of sugar means, in spite of his being told about it by analogy and comparison with other sweet objects, experiences it directly the moment some sugar is put in his mouth. In fact, all empirical experience also whether in the waking life or in dream tends to be more or less indivisible and unitary while it is experienced. When it afterwards becomes an object of thought for oneself who experiences it, or an object of description in language for the sake of communication with other persons, it is split up in three parts, namely, the subject who experiences it, the object which is experienced, and the relation between the subject and the object, which is expressed by means of an idea, an emotion or a will. It is this indivisible, unitary character of all experience which becomes more and more pronounced on the spiritual level. The identity of the self and God is a unitary experience no doubt; but when the meditator becomes conscious of himself as being identical with the vision of God which he sees before him, it is unconsciously assumed that experience of such an identity consists of a subject who is conscious, of an object of that experience, and of the relation between the subject and the object, namely, the identity itself. The conscious experience therefore of such an identity is not indivisible, though unitary. But if the same experience is lived with joy and peace, without being conscious of oneself as being different, it becomes at once one and indivisible.

One more point of importance. If the Sun who is the cause of making the difference between the day and night be not there at all, shall we not call it a state which is indescribable? If the wakefulness felt in a dream goes away, will not the dream also go away with it? It will then neither be described as wakefulness nor as dream. Even so, had the self and God been really different from each other, the experience of the two being identical afterwards would have been capable of being described. But if man, in being conscious of God, is becoming God, will it not be impossible for him to describe the bliss and peace? He will simply become blissful and silent about it. The words 'identity', 'non-difference', 'consciousness of identity' etc. are at best only attempts to describe to others an experience which is prior to the consciousness of identity, and which without implying any sense of duality is unique and indescribable. It is simply to be enjoyed silently and not spoken about.

42. *To describe the Brahman is to describe the experience of Brahman* (7. *i.* 1-61; *ii.* 1-55; *iii.* 1-53)

Just see how Rāmadāsa has dealt a crushing though convincing shock to many of the Vedāntins who have had unbaked opinions regarding the nature of Brahman. As usual, his motive in throwing overboard these false or partially true views is to arrive at his own correct and ultimate view that Brahman is indescribable by means of any mental or thought construction, but that it has to be simply experienced as joy and peace.

To begin with the most erroneous notions: (1) the ignorant man also speaks about the Brahman, but means nothing by it. For him Brahman is simply a word and nothing more. He uses it only to bewilder himself and others. (2) Next comes the man who says that Brahman is what is popularly known as the Akṣara (not transient) or the one-syllabled symbol of it, namely, the Aum. But what goes beyond both the transient and the symbolic representation of it can hardly be described by an arbitrary invention of an alphabet. (3) Following the Upaniṣadic statements, one might say that

Brahman is the same as the Ākāśa or the empty space. No doubt, space is as all-pervading as the Brahman, but it is just another name for the void or Śūnya which is nothing but ignorance. How can ignorance be a substitute for knowledge? Besides, Ākāśa, like the other four elements is jaḍa and not endowed with consciousness, as the Brahman is. (4) Following the Śruti again, one might be tempted to say that 'All this is Brahman'. What is meant by 'all' is the whole of the phenomenal world as produced out of the five elements of Prakṛti or Māyā. But Śruti itself says that whatever is produced and is perceivable by the senses (including the senses also) is bound to be dissolved. Where then will be the 'all' and the senses which will be aware of the 'all'? (5) Some one may improve upon this and say that Brahman is the Caitanya or the conscious Force which, being at the back of Māyā or Prakṛti, infuses its own energy into it and makes it move and produce everything else. This is indeed a useful inference and a postulate which will work in our speculative philosophy of the Vedānta. But what proof is there for believing in the continued existence of this inferred Caitanya when the short-lived creation of Māyā ceases to exist? Does the Caitanya also cease to exist when a living body becomes dead? Or, are we to rest satisfied with a sort of make-believe as if that it continues to exist? (6) That it does exist even after the cessation of the dance of Prakṛti might be the reply of some one, because he would say that the Caitanya which moves the Prakṛti belongs to Brahman and acts by the order of Brahman, so to say. But this implies that the conscious Force of Brahman is different from Brahman, and that the existence of Brahman or its 'sattā' is conceivable without itself being full of Caitanya. (7) A slight variation of the above view would be to hold that Brahman is the seer and not so much a Force or Consciousness. That which stands eternally as the 'Śākṣī' or the witness of even the Caitanya and is its support is the Brahman. But this also has no meaning unless there is some such entity as 'Sattā' which is different from Brahman. The 'Sākṣitva' or the seeing is possible if there is something different from the seer or the witness. (8) Brahman can be spoken of as Saguṇa also, since it has the quality of being the seer of all. But it is common knowledge that whatever is endowed with some or other quality is perishable in nature. (9) One may thus be driven to hold that Brahman is Nirguṇa or devoid of any quality. But what is the good of giving the non-dual Brahman a new name, 'Nirguṇa' and treat it as if it is confronted with something which is different from it, as is the case with Saguṇa Brahman ? If there exists no village, can there be any boundaries of that village ? Can Māyā be an entity, if it is described as a mirage ? Even so, in the absence of any guṇas, what meaning can be attached to the word 'Nirguṇa', except that it can simply be spoken as such ? (10) It is for this very reason that any name or any word which might be used for describing the nature of Brahman will simply be derogatory of it. Not only no description of Brahman will ever be a transcript of the life in Brahman, but it will not also enable anyone to have the experience of that life. (11 and 12) Perhaps, it is on this account that those who have realized the Brahman as 'Ānanda' describe it in that way. But as ānanda or joy indicates a state of mind, to describe the Brahman as Ānanda is to bring it on the level of the mind, and to make it dependent for its very existence on the experience of man. (13) In order to preclude these defects, one might say that to realize the Brahman is to become identified with it. Indeed this is excellent. It constitutes the real Nivṛtti or the total turning away from the Māyā which constitutes the Pravṛtti. But there can be no kind of description of the Brahman, at this stage. Therefore, it is that one passes imperceptibly into the final belief. (14) that the state of Brahman can only be silently enjoyed without trying to make any effort of defining the nature of Brahman.

It is at this stage that the devotee of God becomes one with God; he goes beyond puṇya and pāpa (merit and demerit) ;there remains no trace of his awareness as a separate individuality, namely, of the 'I', nor of the consciousness that he has now become the Brahman. Here is the complete surrender of the Self, known as the Ātma-nivedana; for the self as well as the entire phenomenal world vanishes into what remains as the only Reality, namely, the Brahman. This is the final resting place of joy and peace for all the saints and the yogis of the world.

43. *Contradictory characteristics of the Brahman* (7. *iv.* 1-52 ; *v.* 1-44)

Limitless and vast as the sky, the Brahman occupies all the space between the heaven and the earth, and envelopes all the innumerable worlds and every little thing or creature that exists. It is like the sky, the receptacle of all things and is not yet contaminated by any one of them, and remains forever far more spotless and pure than even the blue sky which becomes occasionally spotted with clouds. One might run as fast as he can ; he would not go beyond the sky. Even so, none can avoid being touched and surrounded by the Brahman, though it remains unknown, till he is made conscious of it by the grace of the Guru. There is nothing which can be said to compare with it. Though it is mixed up with the five elements, it is not contaminated by them, and though the Upaniṣads compare it with the sky, it has not the defect of being void as the sky (space) is. Nor like the sky does it possess the quality of sound which changes from moment to moment. For, continuously, without any break, might be heard the unstruck sound in which the Brahman would manifest itself. It penetrates the earth, and yet it is incomparably soft. Water is soft in the sense of being subtle, because it penetrates the earth. Fire is subtler than water, since a ray of light can pass through it. In the same way, wind and sky are subtler than fire and wind, respectively, since they possess the quality of penetration without being affected in any way. The Brahman however is the subtlest of all, since it is immanent in them all, and yet is not destroyed like the earth nor evaporated like water, nor burnt by fire, nor blown away by the wind, nor felt as being vacant like the sky or space. Not only it is immanent in the body of a man, it is also transcendent, and so can be visualized as being ever present in front of him. There is neither any empty space nor can there be a vacant mind ; everything is fully and always occupied by the Brahman, though it might strike as a wonder that it remains concealed and unseen.

Those however who have realized the Brahman say with authority that the Brahman is omnipresent to such an extent that it can be seen even through and across the words and the alphabet while we read a book. Seen on all sides while we walk, it comes so close to us that when we stretch our hand to fetch a thing, it is seen as intervening between us and that thing. This means that being the softest of all, it can exist in our eyes without causing any trouble to them ; it is heard as an unstruck sound even while we hear what others are speaking, or while we are mentally active in thinking or imagining. The moment, however, we begin to divert our attention to it our interest in attending to the other external things declines. Thus it is that we can tame our senses and bring them under control by employing them gradually more and more in realizing the Brahman, either by visualizing it, or by attending to the unstruck sound, or by feeling the touch of its presence and so on.

One may perhaps say that this way of attending to both the workings of Māyā and the Brahman is what is known as the fourth condition of being the witness of all that exists, since it is neither the wakeful condition in which one is aware only of the external things, nor of sleep or dream. But it should be remembered that even this condition of the division of attention is a state of the human mind, whereas the condition of visualizing the Brahman only is the supramental state known as 'Nivṛtti' or the retreat from the activities of the mind. This is the final condition of being one with Brahman, in which not only vanishes the ignorance, but also the egoism and the awareness in the form of 'I know the Brahman'. Here is the end of all imagination and of the awareness of the whole of the external world of things even while it exists from the practical point of view of the daily life. It is this supramental condition which will yield the eternal bliss of Brahman ; it is the condition of being constantly aware of Brahman, of remembering the Name of God without any break, and of fixing the gaze upon His visions to such an extent that one has no other experience of the world and of the empirical 'I' except the bliss and peace of Brahman.

If one were to call this constant remembering of the Name of God and seeing his Forms as itself a kind of 'idea' or imagination, we have no dispute with him. We only affirm that it is this pure and holy 'idea' or 'imagination,' which overtaking the mind and merging it completely in the Brahman, is able to put an end to all other ideas, imaginations and things of the world, just as the sun dispels the darkness of the night as soon as he rises in the heaven.

44. *Contemplation and Activity should alternate* (7 *vi.* 1-65).

It is a common experience of those who are novices on the spiritual path that while they listen to a sermon on the nature of God and the means and the method of realizing Him, they become full of enthusiasm and feel for the time being that they have a genuine love for God. But soon when they return home they find themselves engrossed with the affairs of the worldly life, and overcome by various desires, temptations and emotions like anger and others. This makes them as miserable and disappointed as an insect which is allowed to move forward, but is again prevented from doing so. The zest for God-realization carries the aspirant forward; his greed and attachment for the pleasures of life push him back into saṁsāra. His interest in life becomes lukewarm by his urge for God-realization; and his devotion for spiritual life becomes artificial and superficial by his deep-rooted attachment to the pleasures of life. This struggle on the see-saw of Brahman and Māyā becomes unbearable to them, and so out of despair they become inclined to give up one or the other of the two pursuits. What happens however usually is, they forsake God and indulge in pleasure.

The remedy for getting out of this predicament is to remember, in the first place, that neither God can be realized nor the attachment for the worldly life rooted out at one stroke. Both the ends will be fulfilled only gradually and in the course of time. As it is not possible for any one to be devoted to God for all the day and night, one should keep his hours of meditation and his hours of active worldly life fixed and alternating each other. That would maintain the balance between contemplation and activity and induce the person to become more and more devoted to the former than to the latter. Besides, if he cultivates the habit of remembering the Name of God, over and above his hours of meditation, even while he is engaged in doing the several duties and activities of life, such as eating, drinking, walking, etc., he would find that there is no incompatibility between meditation and activity, and that, therefore, they can be carried on with a considerable degree of attention simultaneously. Even the activities of reading spiritual literature, doing 'Bhajans' and delivering a sermon or listening to it can be carried on by dividing skilfully the attention between them and the meditation on the Name and contemplation on the vision of God.

A man need not be said spiritually great necessarily because he sits for meditation in a yogic posture and appears to others as an immovable statue; for this might perhaps indicate only the sound condition of his body, though people may be misled into believing that it is the condition of an equipoised mind (samādhi). The real samādhi means the undisturbed, unaffected and the uncontaminated, balanced condition of mind and intellect which occurs naturally as the result of constant meditation on the Name of God and undeviating gaze on the beautiful divine forms. To achieve this, what is required is love and regard for God and not so much a physical posture, though it is greatly useful for keeping the body fit and healthy and for increasing one's capacity for concentration. The great sage Śukācārya who moved unconcerned in the world, with his mind and eyes always fixed on the Name and the visions of God, has shown to the world that he could at the same time be very active by narrating the Bhāgavata Purāṇa to the King, Parīkṣit. He was a sage who was enjoying liberation even while he was living and could not be said a whit less than others who are supposed to get liberation after their death, since what is known as liberation or 'Mokṣa' consists in having 'Ātmajñāna', that is, the seeing of one's own Form (Self), as if in a mirror, always and everywhere. Such a person will have absolutely no doubt about having won his freedom and immortality.

45. *Mystical experiences as being beyond wishful thinking, but as dependent on Sādhanā.* (7. *vii.* 1-74)

The spiritual experience goes beyond the range of imagination and speculation. What is the good of imagining that the vision of God must have a particular form or colour, even though a novice may think that way during meditation? For, that would only mean putting a limitation on the infinite power of God to manifest in any form and complexion, and to exhibit any mood or quality which would generate in the mind of the on-looker emotions of fear, awe, reverence, love and dependence. One should never imagine the Brahman to be one way or the other, or attribute qualities or motives to it and say that it would behave this or that way. For, that would mean an attempt to rob its absolute independence and freedom over which man can never have any control. If one forgets to remember it, it will manifest before him and make him remember it, or it may suddenly disappear and make him forget it. One cannot avoid it being seen, nor can compel it to be seen. To try to understand it by thinking or imagining about it is to become bewildered all the more; but if one ceases to do so, it will suddenly reveal an aspect of its nature. In the very moment of seeing it as having a dark colour, it might be experienced as changing into white, blue, yellow or red. All these contradictions of spiritual experience arise because the nature of Brahman or God Who is the source and the possessor of all qualities, and Who is free to reveal any aspect of His nature as and when He likes, is neither limited by any qualities nor exhausted by them. He transcends them all, and may, therefore, be said as altogether lacking the qualities. Thus it is that the contradictions which appear in our spiritual experience arise on account of the independent, free and transcendental nature of God. The nature of our experience is a pointer to the nature of the object of our experience; the subjective is governed and moulded by the objective. Therefore, the rule and the caution for the meditator would be to allow the Brahman to reveal itself, and not to anticipate or imagine the nature of that revelation in one way or the other. He should remain content with what is given him to see, and be grateful to God, and not try to impose his will or desire upon Him.

This is the way of not only pleasing God but of becoming one with Him. To desist from cherishing any desire that God should appear before one in this or that form, to leave away all egoism, and to become more and more attached to the divine

Forms which he is fortunate to see, and to meditate on the Name of God with love and reverence is all that one should care for, if he wishes to be united with God. To bid good-bye to the doing of this sādhanā and to imagine or to indulge in make-believe that one is Brahman, is to give room to idleness and egoism, to become attached to bodily comforts, or to go into sleep under the guise of meditation. The mere verbal knowledge of 'I am the Brahman' might end in censuring the real devotees of God, and instead of being relieved from the fetters of saṁsāra, one may be bound all the more on account of his attachment to Godless things. One should never forget that the practice of spiritual discipline is a necessity so long as the body lasts; for there is always the likelihood of the consciousness of body and of the bodily pleasures of getting the upper hand over the spiritual consciousness and over the spiritual activities necessary to maintain that consciousness.

In short, in this game of Brahmanic hide and seek, one should always try to hide himself and his egoism, and seek to realize the Brahman by resorting to devotional meditation, and not to give it up at any moment even after one has realized the Brahman. Then alone there will be no chance of falling away from the uncontaminated condition of being lodged in Brahman.

46. *Listen to the Name of God as it is mentally uttered.* (7. *viii.* 1-50; *ix.* 1-60)

The real spiritual life is realistic, objective, universal and unique, and is known to very few. As such, it will be almost impossible for an ordinary man to have even an intellectual knowledge about it, unless he reads or hears about it. Much more impossible would it be for him to realize and live it unless it is imparted to him by means of a word or words by one who has already realized it. Hearing is the most essential means of understanding the meaning of what is being spoken or read either by others or by oneself. And having once understood the meaning of a word or words by means of hearing, one can become so attached and engrossed and united with it, that one would be able to say that the very meaning is all that he is aware of when the words are uttered. The words then, though absolutely necessary as vehicles of thought or as symbols, would in course of time, be felt as representatives or identical verbal images of the very content in them. There would then be hardly any difference between the Name and the named Entity or Person. Ordinarily, a name appears to be common or a general name, but when it is applied to a particular thing or person, it does not signify anything else. That is why the name of a great saint or that which is used as a symbol of God, would always indicate for a particular person or in a particular context, nothing else but that very saint or God. Supposing that the word or Name, Rāma or Kṛṣṇa or Jesus, is imparted by the spiritual teacher to his disciple as a symbol for God, what would happen in the course of silent meditation is that the disciple, instead of feeling that he is remembering a Name which is different from God, would come to know, in the first place, that his mind has become one with the sound of the Name, and that, in the second place, when God would manifest before him in some one or other form or as light, feel that he is identical with that divine vision itself.

Thus it is that when the Name is mentally uttered, it brings about the transformation of the mind of the devotee; first into the feeling of the identity with the content of the mind, and then into the identity with the concrete manifestation of that content into one or other immaculate forms of God which the devotee would see before him. The devotee becomes the Name of God, so to say, and then discovers that the Name is nothing else but God; and forthwith, the devotee as a separate entity, as a complex of body, mind and egoism, vanishes, and there remains God alone both as immanent and transcendent. All this will necessarily happen if the Name of God is heard mentally in the very moment of its being meditated upon silently and with full attention, love and respect. To achieve this final consummation of God-realization, one must devote considerable time to this kind of mental and silent meditation every day and without any break. He must do so, just as he must eat and drink every day to maintain his bodily nourishment. Then, as water finds its own way into the river or sea, even so one who has the intimations of God-realization would struggle all the more to be one with God.

Indeed, the beauty and the wonder of the real spiritual life is that the devotee leads the life of devotion with greater and greater zeal and loyalty, though he is being assimilated and identified more and more with the life divine. This is the Advaita kind of devotion in spite of the dualism between man and God.

With this will come in other virtues too. Dispassion and disgust for God-less things, purity of mind, firm faith and resolve, liking for the company of the good and the holy, cessation of doubts, desires, anger, jealousy, hatred and egoism, emergence of joy and peace, longing again and again to retreat in seclusion for the sake of meditation and for enjoying the love and glory of God,—all these and other moral virtues will come up of their own accord. Naturally, one who wishes to realize God will only read such literature or attend such lectures and sermons which will make his mind full of devotion of God.

47. *The Saint's estimate of his body.* (7. x.1-50)

Even a great saint does not look down with utter contempt on his own body. For he knows that a sound and healthy body is a very valuable instrument for carrying on his spiritual activities. But he also knows that the ultimate worth of the body in comparison with God-realization is almost nothing. With the experience of vision of God inside and outside, the saint ceases to be conscious of his body more or less, and becomes unconcerned to that extent to the pleasures and ailments of it. When the whole of the perceptible world becomes withdrawn from his ken, how can he be contaminated by anything which is bound by space and time? He becomes dead to the sensible world even while living, though he becomes immortal after death. This means that his mortal coil is of a very little worth to him at any time of his life. It is immaterial to him if it falls on a particular day or at any other time; whether on the bank of a holy river or in a forest. Let it be eaten by dogs or become rotten and full of germs. With God-realization he becomes so pure that he can confer purity on even the holy rivers and places of pilgrimage so that they should be able to purify the sinners. All this becomes possible for the saint, because throughout his life he utilizes his body for the service and attainment of God, and not for obtaining any other pleasures.

As opposed to this, the ignorant and the ordinary people of the world think that the body and the bodily pleasures are all in all. In no way do they become devoted to God, and as they fondle their body too much, they think erroneously that the death of a man without any previous disease or trouble is the sign of great merit in that man. Fools as they are, they do not understand that the condition of the body is no index of the spiritual worth of a man, which can be measured only in terms of moral virtues, devotion and realization of God. To them what is false is true, and what is true is false. And so, what is reserved for them is a life of degradation, sensuous pleasures, and ultimate frustration and despair.

48. *God is different from His creation.* (8.i.1-60)

Opinions regarding the nature of God are bound to differ since one among thousands of persons knows who the real God is. People who believe in many deities and worship them take pride in saying that a particular deity is the chiefest and the most powerful of all, because their own desires are fulfilled by worshipping that deity. Then they begin to preach their own faith and manner of worship with such great enthusiasm that they do not hesitate to fight among themselves. Most of them however believe that God is the creator of the world. Some of them say that God is immanent in the world, and, therefore, conclude that the world itself is nothing but God, and that therefore, the service of the humanity is the service of God.

This however is fallacious. They speak of creation as the work of God, but attribute it to a lesser deity which they worship. Neither do they understand that their desires are fulfilled not by the deity which they worship, but by the omnipresent God who is immanent in that deity, nor the simple fact that idol of stone representing that deity cannot have the power to create the universe. Besides, they do not understand that the relation of cause and effect is available in the phenomenal world only, and not between God and the phenomenal world.

And even supposing that it works equally between God and the world, they make the further mistake of forgetting that God as the cause must be prior to the world as effect, and that, therefore, God has a transcendental existence of His own, whether the world exists or not. And so, in a hurry, as if, instead of identifying the effect with the cause, they identify the cause with the effect and say that the world is the same as God. This helps them, in course of time, to dethrone God and worship the humanity in His place. What happens thereby is that they miss even the immanent God about whom they vainly speak so much ; the transcendent God, they have never seen.

Those, on the contrary, who have realized God, know that He exists in his own transcendental nature whether the world and the humanity exist or not; and as such, He can never be identified with either of the two, though He is immanent in them so long as they are not dissolved.

49. *Puzzles of Speculation and their solution.* (8. *ii*.1-55; *iii*.1-67; *iv*. 1-60; v.1-70)

It is not only the ordinary people who hold several opinions regarding the nature of God, but philosophers and other learned persons also create speculative puzzles which bewilder the intellect. This is especially so with reference to the hackneyed, though important, metaphysical problems regarding the nature and the mutual relations of Brahman, Māyā, the Impersonal and the Personal aspects of God, and regarding the problem how the world was created. Let us briefly see how Rāmadāsa deals with them all.

If Brahman is without any form or quality, whence has this world of names, forms and qualities come at all? To say that the nirguna Brahman desired to create the world is to say what is unthinkable, because the Brahman is by hypothesis, without any want. And, to say that it is the Māyā, which, as the power of Brahman, has the capacity to create the world, is to set up the dualism of Brahman and Māyā, as two entites. And, if Māyā is really all-powerful who indeed will be there to save us from the snares of Māyā, and what is the sense in saying that one should try to save himself ? Is there then any place or function left for devotion and for God who is reputed to be Compassionate and full of grace ? And if Māyā is not a false show but a reality how can it be removed at all by knowledge of God ? What indeed is meant by the distinction between the original Māyā or the Śakti, and Māyā as avidyā ? And what is meant by saying that the Māyā consists of the guṇas, and is the cause of the five elements in both their subtle and gross forms ? And finally, what is the distinction between the subtlest of the elements, namely, the ākāśa (empty space) and Brahman ?

The solution of these great problems will appear as dogmatic unless one comes in contact with the saints who have realized the Brahman, and knows as they do that the whole of Māyā and all that is created by Māyā is unreal in the sense of being perishable. The so-called created world is as good as not being created at all. It is an appearance, which looks like an entity which exists, but is either an illusion or a replica of something which is ultimately short-lived and perishable. We are only trying to know that which has no real existence of its own, though it has got the power to show something else as real and itself as unreal. A serpent which appears on a rope has no existence of its own, though it has got the power to show (if the light is brought in) the reality of the rope and the unreality of its own. To cite other examples, there are the waves, the mirage, the ornaments and the reflected images all of which are either illusions or modifications of things, and are either unreal or short-lived, and yet have the power to show that there are other real things such as water, the Sun, gold and a medium like a mirror which reflects. Even so, are the Māyā and the entire so-called created universe, which has its existence in space and time, unreal in the sense of being a temporary show which creates the illusion that it is real. But if the light of the realization of God is thrown on the deluded mind by some great saint, the same Māyā and the perceptible world have the power to show that God alone is real and that Māyā and the world are appearances.

One might contend that both the real and the apparent

things in the illustrations we have taken to point out the relation between Māyā (and its creation) and the Brahman are all from the perceptible world only, whereas the Brahman and Māyā are imperceptible, and the world as created by Māyā is actually perceived; and so, the analogical argument, it might be said, is not sound. But the objection holds no water, since there is no other way to understand somehow by means of language and reason that which is to be realized by means of devotional meditation as instructed by one who has realized the Real. The serpent will certainly be believed as real so long as the rope on which it appears is not seen. Similarly, the world will be real, creation will be real, and Māyā also will be considered as real so long as Brahman or God is not realized.

As for the genesis and dissolution of Māyā, it is like the stir of the wind or like a cloud in the vast Ākāśa. The wind becomes as still as the Ākāśa, the cloud comes and goes. Even so, the Brahman remains unconcerned and uncontaminated by the activity of Māyā, and its three guṇas, of its five elements and the created world of beings. Until all this is crossed, like the threshold of a temple, the real God will never be seen. Paradoxically, we may say that unless one goes by the way of the saints and attains to God-realization, one will never be able to discover that the whole of the phenomenal world, along with Māyā and its three guṇas, is as good as naught, an appearance only, and so unreal.

Another doubt which is sometimes raised is regarding this distinction between the ākāśa and Brahman. The other four elements which are seen or felt by the sense are obviously different from the Brahman which cannot be so perceived. The products of Earth, Water, Fire and Air are seen to be perishable; and the four elements also have qualities like softness, hardness, brightness, contraction and expansion, which are amenable to change. Brahman can neither change nor perish. The elements and their specific and general qualities mix with each other for the purpose of creating the universe; and when they separate, the universe also becomes dissolved. The Brahman remains the same whether the world comes or goes out of being. But so far as Ākāśa is concerned, it so resembles the Brahman and is so opposed in nature to the other four elements, that it looks arbitrary to some to consider the Ākāśa and the Brahman as distinct from each other. Like the Brahman, the Ākāśa also is all-pervading, imperceivable, spotlessly pure, changeless, eternal, one and uncontaminated by whatever happens within it. So, it is contended by some that Brahman and the Ākāśa are one and the same. This can be replied by saying that Ākāśa comes out of the Tamoguṇa of Māyā, which is just another name for ignorance, but which in its turn takes the forms of desires, anger, infatuation, fear, stupidity (śūnya) and grief. How can these occur in Brahman ? A superficial likeness should not make us believe that ākāśa and Brahman are the same, just as the supramental condition and the condition of sleep are not the same though to an external observer they might look as just the same. Besides, the most fundamental difference between the two is that whereas the ākāśa is neither self-existing nor self-conceiving, the Brahman exists by itself and is conceived by itself. And, further, to have the knowledge of Ākāśa one need not become the ākāśa, but one has to become Brahman in order to know the Brahman. In the one, the knower remains different from the known; in the other, the knower and the known become one only.

50. *Hindrance and aids to Spiritual Life.* (8. *vi.*1-54)

So far as the spiritual life is concerned, everyone is a friend or a foe unto himself. For, as observed in the previous section, if in order to know God one has to become God, then one must take great care not to give any room for idleness, sleep, procrastination and absent-mindedness. He must be alert, diligent, full of faith and intelligence, so that he can have the insight into the real nature of spiritual life. A mind which is vacant or inattentive can achieve nothing; neither the spiritual nor the worldly good. It will neither remember anything, nor possess any initiative or imagination. How can one who is absent-minded do any meditation or read and understand a page from some spiritual literature ? Sermons and advice will fall flat on his ears. The alternative to his absent-mindedness will be the state of sleep. He will eat a lot, go to bed and sleep soundly; and as soon as he becomes awake he will again fall in idleness. Thus his whole life will be a series of greed, over-eating, sleep, slothfulness, dullness and inattention. He will be worse than a stone. For even the most ordinary stone will be useful in some way or other, and if a chip is cut away from it, it will not stick to it again. But a man whose mind is never fixed and attentive even for a moment cannot be expected to have a firm resolve and to leave away his failings and vices. He will again and again be a slave of them.

On the contrary, one who is intelligent, assiduous and has a firm faith in his spiritual teacher, will leave his egoism and try to correct himself again and again. He will bring back his flying mind and fix it on the divine Name with fresh energy and joy. He will repeat nothing by rote, as if he is a parrot; but put his heart and soul in the spiritual passages which he will read and understand their meaning. To such an one the grace of God will come immediately; and he will be liberated from the turmoils of the worldly life as instantaneously as a drop of water becomes one with the ocean.

51. *One Ātman and one Liberation.* (8. *vii.* 1-66; *viii.* 1-70)

If then by the grace of the Guru and by dint of faith and diligence instantaneous liberation is possible in this very life, to pin one's hope that one would be born again as a human being and then begin to accumulate merit by means of giving away wealth and food in charity, is foolish indeed. Who knows one may be born as a beast or as a bird and shall have to die in ignorance, without getting a chance of realizing God? One should therefore remember with faith that liberation is achieved in the very moment in which he is initiated by the spiritual teacher; for what the teacher does is to unite the soul of the disciple with God. It is for the sake of realizing this permanently as a fact of experience that the disciple is asked to meditate on the divine Name. And while this is being realized, he comes to know that he is different from his body, senses, mind, intellect and egoism, and that there are no separate souls or things except the one, universal Ātman or God.

People however falsely believe that there are as many ātmans or liberated souls as there are embodied souls. This is like believing falsely that there are four kinds of ākāśa, on account of its being limited in three ways. Similarly, the many liberated and unliberated souls may be considered as if of four different kinds. But if we leave away the conditions or the environmental differences, we shall find that the Ātman who is joyful and uncontaminated is one only, just as the Ākāśa is one. The false belief that the Ātman or the ākāśa is more than one occurs thus: When the Ātman is embodied, that is when he is clothed as if by body, senses etc. he is known as the 'Jīvātman' (embodied soul); this corresponds to 'Ghaṭākāśa' (the ākāśa confined in a jar). When the Ātman is seen as pervading the universe, he is known as Śivātman (Siva=God); this corresponds to 'Maṭhākāśa (ākāśa confined in a house). The Ātman which transcends the universe is known as 'Paramātman' (the Supreme soul), just as the ākāśa which is outside the houses or other things is known as Mahadākāśa (mahad= great). And finally, when the same Ātman is seen without any limiting conditions, he is known as the 'Nirmalātman' (the Pure Ātman), just as the ākāśa without any condition is known as 'Cidākāśa' (as filled by the conscious bliss of the Ātman).

Now, it is at this highest stage of realizing the Ātman as the only one, blissful, universal Reality that one can be said to have attained true liberation. Here, occurs the complete surrender of the self to the Lord, the identification of the soul with God, the highest kind of devotion which knows no separation from God, and the concurrence of one's own spiritual experience of power, bliss and peace with similar experience of the Guru, and with what is narrated in the scriptures and the literature of the saints all over the world.

52. *Characteristics of a great Saint.* (8. *ix*.1-60)

Are there any signs of a realized soul, of one who has drunk deep the divine nectar and has become one with God? How does he behave with other men in the world, though in a way, his own body appears to him as if it is an object in a dream? However, before we proceed to narrate the virtues and the behaviour of such a perfect saint, we should remember as to what makes him a saint so that the several characteristics which make him out can be said to follow from what he mainly does in order to maintain his contact and identity with God. His external behaviour will then be an index of what he is internally, just as the lustre of his body will be said to be the effect of his having drunk the nectar-like juice of the divine Name. The first and the foremost occupation of the perfect saint which we may call as the crown of all other virtues is that he always looks on the vision of the Self, namely, his own immaculate Form. This is his constant internal state; and it constitutes his main spiritual discipline. But to maintain this condition unmitigated and always, what he does necessarily, and even when he is left to himself and alone, is that he meditates on the Name of God without entertaining any doubt. He lives in the world but does not belong to it, though he keeps himself busy in instructing others regarding the lore of the Self. Naturally, so far as he himself is concerned his mind is always steady on account of its being fixed on the Self, though his body might move here and there or be at rest.

In line with this, the other virtues which he exhibits and which come up in him naturally as the consequence of his being lodged in God are as follows. They are the model for the aspirant and constitute the way-up for him, though they are the way-down in the case of a great saint; and so, they should be practised in advance by the aspirant as far as it is possible. Being pent up with the vision of the Self inside, and seeing the same again externally, and on all sides, the saint is always full of bliss. He has no desires of his own, and therefore no cause for being angry in case they are not fulfilled. As there is for him nothing else beyond the Self, with whom should he have any dispute ? Why should he be jealous of anybody or why should he hate anyone ? For the same reason, he has no greed, no temptation, no regret, no arrogance, no hypocrisy and no fear; nor any anxiety regarding what might happen in future. He becomes indifferent to his environmental conditions, to his being respected or not, and to the pleasures and joys of the world, lest he might forget God. Like the immaculate divine vision before him, he too becomes spotlessly pure.

53. *The wise too fumble in their search for God.* (8. *x*. 1-82)

It is no wonder that people in general who know nothing

about spiritual life and who with blind credulity hold to the traditional notions about morality and religion which are mixed up with superstition, should tell us anything they like regarding what we should do and what we should not. But one becomes aghast when the learned and the wise tell us only half truths, since they too have not gone to the end of the spiritual life. Men of the so-called practical wisdom tell us that we should first try to make our worldly life a success, and then take to the devotion of God in old age. Others tell us that we should obey our parents and treat them as gods; do our duties according to the four stages in life, namely, those of celibacy and studentship, of an householder, of a dweller in the forest, and of one who has renounced the world; visit the holy places, salute the saints and worship the deities of the family and of the race. Some others tell us to cultivate the moral virtues and purify our mind first; we should not censure or hate anyone, avoid the evil company, feel compassion for others, and act according to what is laid down in the scriptures. And there are others still who advise us to practise the black art, and thereby secure wealth, position and power and be happy in life.

Those who are wise are serious no doubt about the spiritual life, but on account of their limited knowledge tell us some or other aspect of truth and not the whole of it. Some one thinks correctly that devotion is necessary for the realization of God, but does not understand the importance of works. Another emphasises the works only, as if that alone is sufficient to attain the liberation. A third says that one who wishes to be liberated should learn to be a witness only of all things which are, as objects of perception, quite different from the Self. Another wishes to correct him by saying that when all this is Brahman there would be no sense in differentiating the knower from the known. There is, however, in spite of this the difference between the perceptible world and the imperceptible Brahman, and so, it is necessary, says another, to eliminate the sensuous in order to realize the non-sensuous. No, this may not be possible, points out some one else; for even if the sensuous world be eliminated there is no certainty that the non-sensuous Brahman will be seen For, there is the realm of void between the two, and it is just possible that the seeker, after having given up his attachment and interest for the worldly things, might be thrown into the void, instead of being lodged in the Brahman. He might then think that the void or the vacant mind is itself the Reality, and thereby fall a victim to ignorance. This is like saluting a servant of the King, thinking him to be the King.

Thus it is that those who know the truth only partially mislead themselves and others by going into blind alleys. To realize the Brahman, one must not only go beyond the perceptible world but beyond the region of the void also. For, to realize the Brahman means to get oneself identified with it, without retaining the consciousness of the separate existence of the ego; whereas to be conscious of the void is to be conscious of the dualism and the separate existence of both the ego and the void, and therefore to be at a great distance from the state of the realization of Brahman.

CHAPTER III

IN THE HEART OF DĀSABODHA (*Contd.*)

Contents (*Sections* 54 *to* 93)

of Pervasiveness according to the degrees of Reality ; 91. The commanding qualities of the Ātman ; 92. Evolution of the cosmos and the involution of the Spirit ; 93. The author of Dāsabodha is God, says Rāmadāsa.

54. *The negative and the positive description of the Brahman.* (9.*i.* 1-29 ; *ii.* 1-41 ; *iii.* 1-45 ; *iv.* 1-44 ; *v.* 1-41)

First, let us see how Brahman is described negatively. It is formless, supportless, partless, spotless, without any limiting conditions, and incomparable ; it is desireless, without any quality or break, immovable, without defects or activity, unborn, unnameable, imperceptible, immeasurable, unimaginable, indestructible, infinite, and incapable of being cut, burnt, blown out or mixed with anything else.

To realize however the truth contained in this negative description of the Brahman, one must have the experience of it in some positive manner ; otherwise there would be no meaning of any negation. To see what Brahman is will alone enable one to say what Brahman is not. None will understand what light is if it is defined as absence of darkness. But one who has seen the light will be able to make that statement to some one else who is confused, so that the latter may be inquisitive to know what light is. And if, further, the light is shown to him, he too will then be able to make the same statement about light, namely, that it is not darkness. The expression of this statement before the light is seen is a mere verbal knowledge, which is neither a fact of actual experience nor a source of abiding satisfaction and mental peace. Brahman is therefore that which is to be experienced as the identification of oneself with it, without the feeling of egoism ; that which is seen as both within and outside of oneself ; as that which is all-pervading, and the source of constant joy and peace.

Notwithstanding however the description of Brahman in both the negative and positive ways, the experience of it is indescribable by means of words. One has to enjoy it silently, since to utter a word about it is to split that indivisible condition of joy into two, namely, the Brahman and the knower of Brahman. To say that 'I have observed silence' is to break it. Similarly, the attempt to make oneself aware that he has the Brahmanic consciousness even while he is enjoying it, by speaking to oneself in an inarticulate manner, that is, either by a slight movement of the tongue in the throat, or by means of mental speech or idea, namely, 'I am the Brahman', is as effective in breaking that unitive experience as it would be by expressing it in so many articulate words by the tongue. This means, in other words, that the unitive life of living in God which is said to be expressible by the formula 'I am the Brahman', can, as a matter of fact, never be expressed. The 'I' is required to be there in the sentence for the grammatical, logical and the social purposes of conveying one's thought to others. It will lose its own independent existence when it becomes merged in Brahman. What then exists is not the 'I' and the Brahman, but Brahman alone. The life in Brahman is not the transcription of 'I am the Brahman', though the latter is the most convenient mode of expressing that life as far as possible and approximately. The Brahmanic life is to be felt and lived ; it is incapable of being described.

Now, if there be such a God-intoxicated person, how can he be found out ? It is as difficult as it is to discover the Brahman. And if any one discovers it, he is himself lost in it. Even so, one who wishes to know what the saint is, must, in a way, become himself a saint by closely following into the footsteps of the saint. To look to the external side of the saint is to miss him and take him for an ignorant, ordinary man of the world.

55. From dogma to experience. (9. *vi.* 1-54 ; *vii.* 1-57 ; *viii.* 1-38 ; *ix.* 1-41)

We have had occasions during our discussions so far to deal with certain metaphysical dogmas the truth of which has mainly to be taken on trust. This is alright as a tentative measure. The real satisfaction however will come to us when we shall be able to turn the dogmas into facts of experience. For instance, it is not much difficult to understand that the soul is covered not only by one body, namely, the gross, physical body (sthūladeha), but also by three more bodies, one inside the other, namely, the subtle, the causal and the supra-causal (the Sūkṣmadeha, the Kāraṇadeha and the Mahākāraṇadeha). Of these three, the subtle is made up of the five senses of knowledge, the five of actions, the five prāṇas or vital breaths, and mind, intellect and egoism. The causal is made up of the complex of various desires, which gets itself mixed with the subtle and is said to migrate from one birth to another ; while the supra-causal body is said to exist when the soul becomes the witness of all. In short, while the first three bodies are known to all as being perceived and felt, or as made up of body, senses, mind and desires, the fourth one cannot be said to be totally unknowable, inasmuch as that can be experienced to some extent at least in an act of introspection, when one can look at his own anger or love as if, and know that he is angry or has the emotion of love. Therefore though it might appear at the outset that the statement that a man has got four bodies is dogmatic, it is the expression of the experience which all men have or will have with some imagination and effort. Even the statement that the causal body is responsible for the soul's migration from one birth to another, can be understood as meaning that it is his desires which make him what he essentially is.

Corresponding to the above four-fold scheme of bodies it is believed that in the cosmos too it is so on a larger scale. This is bound to appear as dogmatic, though we may have the verbal knowledge that the cosmos is the body of the great God, that He too has infinite hands, feet, etc., has a desire to produce this world, and is the witness of all that happens in space and time. As a matter of fact, what is the use of dogmatically being told and believed that there arose, like the movement of wind in the static ākāśa, the consciousness and the desire in Brahman in the form 'I am alone, let me be many', unless we see it to some extent reproduced within us as also the way of curbing it so that we realize the bliss of the unitive life in Brahman ? Māyā might have arisen in Brahman as the first gust of egoism, namely, 'I am alone ; let me be many'; this consciousness of oneself as being 'alone' and as pitted against the possible many, might have been the seed of activity (rajoguṇa), and from that again might have arisen the two tendencies of being good or bad (sattvaguṇa and tamoguṇa). These three in their turn might have been the cause of producing the five subtle and the five gross elements, as also the entire world of objects. All this knowledge about cosmogony might be useful for a student of Indian philosophy. But of what good is it for an aspirant, unless it is made serviceable for his spiritual discipline ? Not only will it appear to him as a useless jargon, but also as a metaphysical luxury which will simply become a hindrance in his practice of devotional meditation, and persuade him to become pedantic and hypocritic.

This will not however be the necessary conclusion, if the Vedāntic knowledge about Brahman and Māyā, and about the evolution of the world is properly used. Let the aspirant only retrace the steps in the reverse manner even by imagining that he has become larger than the universe, subtler than the elements, as transcending the three guṇas, as becoming co-extensive with Māyā or the power of God, and finally as becoming one with Him, without leaving behind a trace of his egoism and separate existence. This however can be the result of make-believe or auto-suggestion, and so may not prove to be abiding. It may be shattered into pieces the moment there arises some misgiving about it, or some counter suggestion or wrong belief.

There is however the sure method of transcending all the barriers during one's meditation as well as during the waking life by leading a morally good and virtuous life. Whatever may be the nature of the people round him, good, bad or indifferent, whatever the condition of the external Nature and the cosmos, and whatever may be the motives of Māyā, he will only try to befriend God by loving and adoring him by meditating on his Name, and thereby transcend the three guṇas, transcend the consideration of his body, transcend the influence of the five elements which have made up his body, and ultimately transcend the Māyā and become one with the visions of God and enjoy the peace and bliss of God.

56. *The path becomes the destination.* (9. *x.* 1-37)

There arises now a difficult question as to what should a traveller on the spiritual path do after he arrives at the end of the path, namely, the realization of God. Should he, or rather, can he continue to do his meditation or not ? If a poor man like a potter becomes a king, should he continue to keep the asses ? How can the supramental mind think at all on the mental plane ? How can the God-intoxicated be intoxicated in any other way ?

Apparently, what this means is that when the destination is reached there is no possibility of continuing the journey. But the implication is that the journey has no end, and that no one who is embodied can forever enjoy the condition of being disembodied.

None should therefore give up the (sādhanā) practice of meditation. One who does so runs the risk of being bound by the fetters of the temptations of the worldly life. And who knows that God does not contemplate upon himself? Besides, will not the continuity of meditation unto the last breath prevent a man from falling away from the high pedestal of God-realization, and teach others also not to give up the meditation at any time.

57. *The many as one* (10. *i.* 1-31 ; *ii.* 1-25 ; *iii.* 1-21 ; *iv.* 1-46 ; *v.* 1-28 ; *vi.* 1-40)

Ordinarily, it will be absurd to deny the plurality of things in this world. What is meant by saying that the One alone exists is that the Reality behind the transitory phenomena is one. Materialists have no difficulty in asserting that it is Matter in general ; some of the idealists also do not seem to have any difficulty in asserting the plurality of minds. Those however who have the mystical knowledge about Reality, that is, who have the direct, first-hand contact with it, as Professor R.D. Ranade likes to define the mystics, say, on the authority of their own experience as also of others, that it is of the nature of blissful consciousness and is one and one only. This presents a difficulty to understand not only for the ordinary people but also for the materialists, the pluralistic realists or idealists. If mind or consciousness were to be one, the joy and sorrows of one person, they would say, would have been felt as belonging to all other persons. Each person has his own hunger and thirst as also the subsequent satisfaction of eating and drinking. This means that there are as many minds or consciousnesses as there are persons in the world. What the mystic however means by saying that there is only one consciousness is not the blending of the several consciousnesses into one, nor an abstraction out of them, but the rejection of the many as illusory on account of their being bounded by several, incidental walls of bodies, senses, minds, intellect and egoism. It is these limitations which split the one consciousness as if into several others, just as the one ākāśa (empty space) appears as if it is split on account of the artificial walls of a jar or a house.

Just as, in order to get at the correct notion that there

is only one ākāśa, one must break the artificial walls of the jar and the house, even so, in order to realize that there is one consciousness only, one must know the secret of overcoming or forgetting the consciousness of oneself being identical with body, senses, mind, intellect and egoism. The consciousness, as understood by a realist or an idealist refers, to the consciousness of all these limitations (Upādhis) superimposed upon the real, but does not refer to the identity of the self with God ; while the consciousness of a great saint is the consciousness of God alone in which the consciousness in the form of egoism of the self and that of the body, senses, mind, and intellect is not only submerged but lost totally.

To have a concrete experience of this blissful consciousness, which we may call as God, one must make for himself the experiment of meditating on the Name of God along with his breaths, and with at least a provisional faith which is necessary to test a scientific hypothesis. It may appear, as dogmatic, no doubt, if it is said that out of the five elements wind is the only element which has, in the first place, the peculiarity of sustaining the life of beings; and secondly, the capacity of enabling the aspirant to visualize the Divinity which is immanent but concealed in it and in the universe. The first is the principle of activity, which belongs to Prakṛti, and the second constitutes the Puruṣa, or the very Lord of the Universe. The Wind, in short, has in it the combination of Puruṣa and Prakṛti or of Śiva and Śakti. Or, to speak in plain and simple language, it consists of the principle of activity and the source of that activity. Changing the terminology, again, we may say that it is the combination of Brahman and his Māyā. The individual soul knows only the domain of Prakṛti or Māyā ; but he allows the Puruṣa or God in him to remain concealed or dormant, till he becomes too old to realize Him. Instead, if he were to meet a great saint, get the Name of God sown in him, and water it day and night by his acts of prayer and meditation along with his breaths, he would soon find that God, who was dormant or sleeping in him as if, has awakened and come out like a sprout out of the pure soil of his heart and has manifested before him as a beautiful vision. The aspirant will then no longer remember, at least for the time being when he is lost in enjoying the beauty of the vision, that he has the consciousness of his body, senses, mind and intellect. He will be one with the Divine consciousness ; and with that the consciousness of the existence of the plural aspect of the world also will vanish. Thus, the dogma that there exists one God alone will be a fact of his experience.

This, we may call, constitutes the dissolution of the world in spite of its existence. In fact, no one can know when the world is going to be dissolved ; at best, it might be said to be dissolved with the death of the man himself, or when he is no longer conscious of it during his sleep. These are the only two ways in which the ordinary men of the world become aware of the non-existence of it, when as a matter of fact, it is they who themselves become either literally non-existent in their death, or figuratively so, during sleep. They become totally forgetful of the world as well as of themselves. In the case of a God-intoxicated man, on the other hand, it is the consciousness of God in which is dissolved the consciousness of the existence of the world and that of himself as made up of body, mind and senses. This might occur in his case daily during his wakeful condition also and not simply during his sleep or in death. Notwithstanding the physical existence of his body and of the world, he becomes forgetful of their existence on account of his all-absorbing and blissful consciousness of God. This alone is real to him ; and all else is as good as an illusion or a dream. Being conscious of the only reality of the identity of himself with God, he comes to know that even the very best consciousness of his being the devotee of God falls short of that reality, and is therefore to that extent illusory in kind. For, he then comes to know that to become conscious of the duality or the separateness between him and God, is to become conscious of what he is not in reality that is, of his body, senses, mind, intellect and egoism which are only too short-lived and which therefore do not differ essentially from dreams and illusions. In short, excepting the blissful experience of God-realization which alone is as eternally real as God, nothing else is real to him. The world and its creation ; man and his body and mind ; all his beliefs in his past and future lives ; his egoism about himself, his family and race ; his pride and arrogance for his knowledge, wealth, power, strength and his good and pious actions, are all more or less of the same value to him as are the dreams and illusions.

Yet, one thing is certain and real to him though it presents the pluralistic aspect. And that is the various forms of the visions in which God manifests before him, either during his meditation or after he comes out of it. They may appear as coming and going like other objects of the phenomenal world. But they are the immortal forms of God, which become invisible only to become visible again. They are the immaculate manifestations of God which are neither burnt by fire, nor cut by weapons ; they satisfy all the tests of Reality which can be applied to it.

58. *Miracles attributed to a saint are the work of God.* (10. *vii.* 1-31)

If, then, the survival of the soul and the belief in rebirth appear illusory when compared with the only reality of God-realization, the occurrence of miracles and the attribution of them to a saint who has passed away remain as an unsolved puzzle. That miracles should happen during the life-time of a saint is understandable to some extent. They might be said to be done due to the spiritual power which the saint has acquired. But that they should happen even after his death is something which is hard to explain. For, it can then neither be said that his personal wishes and interests are involved in the happening of the miracles, nor that he exerts his power for their occurrence.

As a step towards the solution of the problem, we should pose the question to ourselves in this connection as to why miracles should occur even during the life-time of a saint. Probably, as said above, the reply would be that the saint himself works them out by using his spiritual power. But on several occasions, the miracles occur in a place far away from where the saint lives, and the saint comes to know them after he is told about them. And yet, they are attributed to him because they happen exactly in the manner in which they were seen happening in a dream along with the presence of the saint, or as the saint had foretold the devotee. Here, also, it cannot be said that the saint is directly responsible for bringing out the miracles. He might be interested in the happenings of events in a particular way ; he might have acquired spiritual power too ; but there is no direct evidence to show that he consciously and deliberately uses it for producing a miracle. For, on many occasions, with all his pleasure and delight over the occurrence of events according to his wishes, he too becomes surprised that they have occurred in that way. Neither does he enter mentally in the dreams of other people, nor could it be possible for him to appear at a far distant place where the miracle is happening. In short, whether a miracle occurs during the life-time of a saint or after his death, he has very little to do with it, except that in certain cases his personal wishes might also be involved.

If however a saint is asked to give his own opinion in this matter, he would say that miracles occur on account of the combination of the force of the implicit faith and devotion of the devotees themselves and of the power of the grace of God. Does this mean that the saint does not come in the picture at all ? No, not so. The saint does come in the picture ; he is connected on one side with his disciples and other devotees who have faith in him, and on the other, with God. He acts as an intermediary between them and God. Naturally, to the extent to which he is interested in their well-being, God too gets himself interested ; and though the saint might not do anything to fulfil the desires of the devotees, God comes forward and does it for the sake of the saint. This then is the explanation that miracles happen primarily as the work of God, and secondarily, as the result of the faith and devotion of the people themselves who are attached to the saints, and through them therefore attached to God also.

Therefore, it follows that disinterested love and service of the Guru and of God coupled with the grace of them will be so powerful, that it would fulfil the desires of the devotees, even by working out miracles not only during the life time of the saints but also after their death. There ought to be no wonder if the spiritual power, accrued on account of devout meditation on the divine Name and contemplation on the visions of God, should also remain behind the bodily death of the saints since they become as immortal as God on account of their immaculate forms. The saint is the Personal aspect of God on account of his being embodied ; and so the devotion shown to him or to the Guru becomes as powerful as that which is shown to the vision of God. One must therefore be as fixed in his devotion to his Guru as to the immaculate Form of God. This constitutes the highest Sādhanā and the end-in-itself. The devotee also will then become so powerful that there will be no obstacle which he will not be able to overcome. His disinterested love for God will of itself achieve any desire that comes in his mind. The fulfilment of a desire is too trifling a thing before the power of God. Let not the devotee therefore thwart the power and grace of God by bringing between him and God the tiny desires of his mind and think of them only. God knows what his devotee wants and has the power to fulfil his desires of His own accord.

59. *Criteria of God-realization.* (10. *viii.* 1-34 ; *ix.* 1-30 ; *x.* 1-68.)

When can any one say that he has realized God ? What are the tests which he can apply to his own experience of God and see how far he has advanced in the infinite process of the realization of God ? In the first place, being graced by God through an intermediary who has realized God, the aspirant makes the discovery during his daily exercise of devotional meditation that there is not only correspondence or similarity but absolute identity between his self and God. He comes to know that the metaphysical dogma of his having four bodies corresponding to the four bodies, as if, of God becomes a fact of experiential reality. With a little of introspection, he comes to know that at the back of his physical body, there exists the subtle body which is made up mainly of the five senses, mind, intellect, and the wind he breathes; that behind the subtle, there exists the causal body, a complex of several desires ; and that finally, at the back of all, there exists the subtlest body known as the Mahākāraṇa-body, that is, his own egoism which owns all the three above-mentioned bodies.

There is however another dogma that God too has four cosmic bodies, namely, the physical universe as the gross body ; the five essences of the elements as the subtle body ; the desire to create as the causal body ; and the egoism that 'I am one' along with the will to produce, as the subtler one than the causal body. These four are respectively known as the Virāṭa, the Hiraṇyagarbha, the Avyākṛta and the original Prakṛti or Māyā. Excepting however the verbal knowledge, none can have any knowledge of these by the ordinary methods of observation and introspection.

But, it is by the method of devotional meditation that one comes to see that the two sets of four bodies correspond exactly to each other, and are therefore all to be rejected in order to discover the identity between the self and God. To see that the vision of the Ātman within is the same as the vision of the Ātman (i.e. God or Brahman) outside, in spite of the existence of the complex of body, mind etc., is the first and the foremost test of God-realization. But lo, there are now no two entities, the self and God ; but only one, namely, God. So the second test is that there must be complete surrender or annihilation of the self on the altar of God. And then, with the emergence of the experience of the omnipresence of God, and with the experience of all the things and beings as forms of God, the devotee would further come to know that God is the only stuff out of which the world has been produced, just as the spider produces the thread out of its own body, or just as the ornaments are made out of gold. Further still, he comes to know the omniscience of God, and thereby knows the plans and the purposes for which God has created the world. This insight into the omnipresence, omnipotence and omniscience of God constitutes another very important test of the realization of God. And, when God becomes all in all, the object of meditation, and of direct vision and love, and as a consequence of this, when all the moral virtues flow into the devotee naturally and with ease, can there remain any sin or blemish in the person who has identified himself with God ? The consciousness of being sinless and meritorious is the further test of God-realization. God alone is merit (Puṇya) ; all else is sin (pāpa), he will then say. And if God is without birth and death, the devotee will also say the same about himself. So, not to have any fear of death, nor any desire or repugnance for prolongation of life or rebirth, will therefore be the further tests of having realized God. The only end, the only mission and the perfection of life being God-realization, all other works will culminate in God and lose their power of producing good or bad effects. Not only the sins will be burnt in the fire of God-realization, good works too like charity and self-sacrifice will cease to produce their effects. Even incomplete works will be to God as complete and perfect as they ought to be. Works also will be considered as powerful means of realizing God. That will be a sure criterion of one's own moral and spiritual worth, if one comes to know that it is the enhancement of sattvaguṇa and the overcoming of rajas and tamas and of all desires that would make him realize that God is both the protector and saviour of the world. And finally, the experience that God manifests before him in various forms, and as light, as flaming fire, and as immanent and blissful presence in him, is undoubtedly a criterion of which the mystic himself is the judge.

Such an one will always be cautious not to become in the slightest measure self-conceited and indifferent to his Guru or to God ; for he knows that, if he is not to be lost spiritually, he must always be humble, though he be exalted by the grace of his Guru to be in the company of God.

60. *Brahman at the apex of changeable gods.* (11. *i.* 1-44 ; *ii.* 1-40.)

Just as the cosmogonical account of the origination of the universe tells us that there first arose in the mind of Brahman an idea to create the universe, even so it is said that desire is the cause of the birth of a man. Whatever may be the truth of these metaphysical dogmas, the fact for us to note is that different people have different desires and that these are fulfilled by propitiating a particular deity. People therefore stick to the worship of that deity only and say with pride that their deity is the best of all. Along with this, we have to note that there are four kinds of gods, three of which are changeable, and one, the unchangeable Brahman. There are people who worship images made of clay, metal or stone ; people who worship the incarnations of God such as Rāma and Kṛṣṇa and meditate upon them ; and people who worship the inner Self who is said to be the on-looker and the intelligent being of all. But when the so-called 'all' or the entire phenomenal world of Prakṛti becomes dissolved, and there remains nothing to look upon nor anything which is inner or outer, gone then will be the idols and the images, gone the memories of the incarnations of God, and gone too the so-called inner Spectator ; what would remain then as the Real is the immaculate changeless Brahman.

Neither therefore those who worship the idols, nor those who live upon the memories of the glory of the divine incarnations, nor those who keep themselves close to the changeable nature of the inner Self, shall be finally released. Those, on the other hand, who understand that active and constant meditation on the unchangeable God, and the actual participation in the nature of God is far superior to the hearing of the glories of God, become themselves as immaculate, as changeless and as eternal as God is. It is they who in experiencing the identity of the inner Self with God forget the self and enjoy the bliss of God.

61. *How the spiritually-minded should behave.* (11. *iii.* 1-30 ; *iv.* 1-30 ; *v.* 1-27 ; *vi.* 1-19.)

The spiritually-minded might live the life of a house-holder. Then he will look not only to the good of his soul, but also to the happiness of his family members and of those who come in contact with him in his worldly affairs. Know he will, first of all, that the maximum span of life generally available to man is one hundred years, out of which more than half is spent in sleep, childhood, and indulgence in sensuous pleasures. Out of what remains, a considerable part might unfortunately be wasted in disease, old age and anxieties of various kinds. His first concern then ought to be to make haste to save his soul, when all around he sees that people and his own kith and kin are dying in numbers without achieving any spiritual good. Who indeed would sit idle when the neighbour's house is on fire ?

He should then, make a firm resolve to bid goodbye to idleness. After getting up early in the morning, the first thing he should do is to silently meditate on God as far long as it is possible, in a place which is solitary but not fearful or uninviting. He should do all his duties in life most conscientiously, please the people by sweet words and benevolent actions, but at the same time, read a lot of spiritual literature and learn to renounce all that would bind him to the consciousness of his bodily comforts and belongings. Not to waste a single moment ought to be his motto, whether he is engaged in doing the duties of his worldly life, or in carrying on his spiritual activities. Works, devotion and the realization of God should be three-fold aim of his entire life.

In order to achieve this, his whole life must be regulated by adopting various moral and spiritual virtues. Just as the same routine of works is to be done again and again, even so the same kind of thoughts about the spiritual life and meditation should be resorted to again and again; the same prayers should be offered and the same sermons preached, so that people might become more and more devoted to the worship of God, and there would come into existence an assembly of saints. One must be just to all ; and yet forgive their faults, cover their defects with compassion, and bear the burden of their anxieties. One might enlarge his field of contacts and activities, but should be cautious not to get entangled by them. He should be quick enough to know his enemies as well as the wicked persons in general, but should be prudent not to give them all the same treatment. Some, he should forgive and oblige; some, he should keep at a distance and observe how they behave ; and some, he should deal with as they deserve. All this requires courage, strength, discretion, and a capacity to bear hardships and face the risks. Thereby one will be able to collect friends and do spiritual Good to others which would be abiding.

And, if he wants to be spiritually great, he should be the prime mover and the centre of all other activities, and yet remain hidden and uncontaminated, just as God is the mover of all without being himself moved. Then alone will he be the instructor, the support and the saviour of others; and then will he be justified in expecting that others also would be as wise and spiritually great as he is. Then will come to meet in him, devotion, realization and dispassion, and he will be an ideal saint.

62. *Dive deep in order to find out the Ganges of Spiritual knowledge.* (11. *vii.* 1-22.)

Rapid is the stream of this worldly existence. Yet, deep below the surface flows calmly and peacefully the holy river, the Gaṅgā of spiritual knowledge. Alas, those who cannot dive deep into it are swept away by the furious current and are either crushed in the crevices, lost in the whirling waters, or cut into pieces by being dashed against the rocks which are lying concealed in it. But those who dive deep, and from below swim courageously against the current reach the very source of this mysterious river, which we may call the original Māyā or Prakṛti of God. They will then be struck with wonder to discover that there in the original Māyā reside the incarnations of Brahmā, Viṣṇu and Maheśa, that is the Creator, the Preserver and the Destroyer of the universe, and that the water at that place is the sweetest and the holiest of all. They will find that the great and the mighty river is flowing eternally in all the directions and has enveloped all the worlds and all the space below and above them all. The river enters into all beings and things ; but none will understand the mysterious power of its water, unless he becomes one with it. For it gives equally life and energy to all things whether good or bad. Simultaneously does it make one thing as sweet or bitter, another as poisonous or life-giving, and a third one as beautiful or ugly. It gives equal freedom to all to become what they wish to be. Even the great among the meritorious and the morally great live by its support and energy.

There are still a few who, being graced by God, do not stop at the source of the river, but go beyond it. And when from that transcendental, supramental state of peace and joy, they look back towards the river of Māyā, they are amazed to find that the water in it is dried up and that there is left no trace of the river itself. Rāmadāsa exhorts us to follow in the footsteps of these very few who live in the peace of the supramental realm.

It appears to us that the metaphor of the river is used by Rāmadāsa to convince us of the utility of meditating on the divine Name along with our breaths, so that the spiritual energy generated by the meditation at the lowest plexus, known as the 'Mulādhāracakra' should rise step by step through the different plexuses, known as 'Svādhiṣṭhāna, Anāhata, Viśuddha and Ājñā, till it reaches the Sahasrāra' at the top of the brain. The other plexuses, beginning with the Mulādhāra are located near about the anus, the naval, the heart, the throat, and in the portion of the forehead between the two eye-brows. Alternatively, the energy is said to rise from the bottom of the spinal chord, and through it, it goes up and meets the Ājñācakra, and then passes on further to the Sahasrāra. In the case of ordinary people' all the energy necessary for the cognitive, affective, and conative functions comes down from the brain through the nervous system and becomes useful for the life as a whole. Most of this energy is however exhausted in the acts of various enjoyments including the sexual one. But, in order that the energy should be conserved and made use of for the yogic and spiritual purposes, self-control and meditation are recommended. When the divine Name would spring up from within and create vibrations which would reach the brain, the soul would begin to have spiritual experiences like visions, voices etc., and it will become one with God, nay, by the force of meditation it can go even beyond the brain and meet the transcendental Being.

63. *Reach the Self, reach the Lord, and reach the Brahman.* (11. *viii.* 1-25 ; *ix.* 1-25.)

If a man lives in a house and does not know who owns it, or if he has not seen or heard the name of the king of the land where he stays for a long time, will he not be treated as a suspect? Similarly, is it not strange that even the so-called learned and the wise do not ever think as to what must be the cause which gives support to their bodies and sustains their life? In vain do they say without experiencing that it must be God who is immanent in the world and without whose power and will nothing will take place, not even the movement of a leaf of a tree. One must go by the way of the saints in order to know the truth of this, and learn to meditate on the divine Name, so that God who is hidden in him and in the world would someday reveal Himself to him. And then, after seeing and knowing who the immanent God is, the devotee should continue to worship him just as one must first know who his master is before he should salute him.

It will not therefore be enough to experience the presence of God within oneself ; one must have the experience of the same God outside himself, as also immanent in the whole world. Pantheism is more important than theism, transcendence more important than immanence. God who fills the whole world is naturally of far greater importance than God who fills the body. Naturally, also, one who attains the experience of the immanence of God in the world becomes himself immanent in the world, and so transcends his earlier experience of having seen himself as filled with God. The earlier experience is of immanence of God in one's own body only ; the later one consists of the vision of God as transcending the body, but at the same time, as immanent or filling the entire world. Therefore the experience of God as being both transcendent and immanent is of far greater importance than that of his being merely immanent or merely transcendent.

There will however be one more and final experience of God. Now what is that thing which God should transcend or God should fill ? One might reply that it is the body of the devotee which should be filled or transcended by God, or it is the world which should be filled by God. But what shall we call that experience, when on account of his deep and joyful absorption in the contemplation of the vision of God, the devotee becomes completely oblivious of his own body and of the whole world ? Is he now experiencing the immanence or the transcendence of God ? Or, is he himself consciously experiencing any of these two states, though he has transcended both the consciousness of his body and of the world ? There being nothing beyond God at any time, the words immanence and transcendence have no meaning with reference to God. And there being equally nothing except the vision of God during the ecstatic condition of the devotee, the words immanence and transcendence have lost their meanings with reference to the devotee also. His self (Antarātman) has become already merged in God who might now be called as transcending the body of the devotee (Bahirātman), as well as immanent (Antarātman) in the world. But when the merging or the surrender of the self in God (Ātmanivedana) becomes so complete as to make him forget the existence of the world also, we may call it as the condition of the joyful and peaceful existence of Brahman only, inasmuch as Brahman is considered as God so long as there is the separate existence of the devotee of God. It is this blissful experience of Brahman that constitutes the apex of spiritual life.

It is at this stage that creation, preservation and destruction of the world cease to have any special significance ; there will be no talk about the individual or the cosmos as having four bodies; about there being three states, the wakeful, the sleeping and the dreaming ; neither about the mind and its states, nor about intellect, will or egoism. Here verbal knowledge turns into direct insight ; the several incarnations of God appear as existing in their eternal immaculate forms, but as manifestations of the One, central Light ; there is devotion without division ; and the realization without the realizer as a separate entity.

True it is that the finite will never know the Infinite of this kind. But it is within the reach of the finite to worship the Infinite daily with love and regard, and then being graced by God and the Guru, lose its finitude and become the Infinite, gradually and approximately.

64. *The activity of a saint is without any self-interest.* (11. *x.* 1-25.)

As the main function of a saint is to keep himself close to God and to lead people to the service of God, so that they too should be saints like him, he takes utmost care not to waste a single moment without meditation or doing some other service to God. Cultivating in himself several good qualities, he teaches them afterwards to the people. Though his fame spreads far and wide, he does not easily allow any one to know what he really is. People might test him in several ways ; but he emerges always as a man having no personal desire of any kind. He mixes with the people mainly for the purpose of carrying along with them spiritual activities like meditation, singing in chorus the Name and qualities of God, and the offering of prayers and praises to God. Otherwise, he lives in solitude, and does not care much to live with any body, or to look or to speak with any one. He has his own way of testing the worth of people ; and according as he finds them, he allows them to come near him, or else keeps them at a distance. He has to collect men, no doubt, in order that they should be useful for spreading the knowledge of God; but he does this in secret. With this end in view, he always moves from place to place and finds out new and new men, but does not allow them to flock around him, or to know or infer about his plans, or the places which he intends to visit. His motive in doing this all secretly and cautiously is that people selected by him should not make a show of devotion, but do their duty heartily and loyally. Rāmadāsa tells us that only when the saint behaves in an utterly disinterested manner, people become convinced and submit themselves to him and do as he wishes.

65. *Lead the worldly life after being Spiritual at heart.* (12. *i.* 1-20; *ii.* 1-30.)

To live the worldly life and to live the life of the spirit are not incompatible. In fact, to live in the world and yet not to be of the world is an art which can be practised only by living in the world. If in the search for God, one leaves the world altogether, it is likely he might not get sometimes even food to eat. And, if being totally indifferent to the spiritual quest, one were to plunge headlong in enjoying the pleasures of the world, he would very often than not, ultimately end his life in miseries, frustration, and despair. One becomes virtuous, wise, respected and happy by coming in contact with others in the world, and can make others also so by setting an example of his own. Even the behaviour of a saint cannot be understood, appreciated and followed unless he exerts himself for showing what saintliness consists in. How can a sandle tree be differentiated from other trees, unless a piece of it is shown to produce fragrance out of it by its being rubbed with pressure and friction ? If one who is wise does not forgive others who go wrong on account of ignorance, will he not be considered as only one among them ? It is very difficult to win the approbation of the people at large ; even so, it is very difficult to discover the presence of God in the world. But one has to show his moral and spiritual worth only in a society, if he really wishes that others also should be great morally and spiritually.

So, ultimately, it depends upon oneself how to knit together the ethico-spiritual good of the society with his own personal good. For this, he must teach himself rather than others, knowing full well that example is better than precept. For, surely, good or bad words are echoed back to us. The wise man therefore should try to please all by entering into their hearts by sweet words; and he should hasten to do so, knowing full well that he has to die some day. Notwithstanding however his efforts to do good to the people, and his kindness on several occasions in forgiving them, if he would still find that the wicked are not a whit better, he should leave the place in silence.

66. *Disgust for God-less objects, the sine-qua-non of real devotion.* (12. *iii.* 1-33 ; *iv.* 1-20.)

One may find a great treasure ; but what is the use of it to him if he is miserly ? Similarly, what is the use of having been initiated by the spiritual teacher, if one never sits for meditation, or of his detestation for pleasure, if he has no discrimination and no love for realization of God ? One might become so agitated and harassed by quarrels, disputes, and innumerable worries and miseries in life that he might renounce everything, go in a forest and think that he has become free. But if he is thoughtless and has no control over his mind, he would go astray and become all the more deluded and caught in the snare of the temptations and the sensual pleasures of life. He would be cut away from the worldly as well as from the spiritual life, and become more miserable than before. One who speaks out at random mere verbal knowledge without having the least realization of it is like a person who is imprisoned but speaks about his bravery, or like a chained dog which continues to bark. What he possesses is no knowledge about God, but mere greed, egoism and pretence. Neither will a mere show of dislike for pleasures and objects of sense, nor that of mere bookish knowledge, be of any value if there is no thoughtfulness and real love for God.

On the contrary, one who has realized God to some extent at least would enjoy real freedom both internally and externally. He will not only be not contaminated internally by his being busy in joyfully singing the Name and the glories of God, but externally also he will have absolutely no desire even if he were to get the kingdom of the world. He will never give expression to mere idle and tall talk about spiritual knowledge, but speak out only that much which he has experienced as true and real. He will win the hearts of the people by his upright and virtuous conduct and thereby win the favour of God too, who is always immanent in all. Such a man alone will go beyond all limitations, all distinctions between 'mine and thine', between the devotees and God, and beyond the rounds of birth and death, cause and effect, and beyond all sins and impurities of mind. Such a man, alone, says Rāmadāsa, becomes supramental in nature ; and being a loyal servant of God, he alone will be capable of saving the people and bringing them on the path of God. To such a person alone one should surrender, and learn from him the way and the method of realizing God.

67. *Four varieties of Self-surrender, and four of Meditation on the Name of God.* (12.v.1-22)

Complete self-surrender to God means complete annihilation of the self by the process of meditation and absorption in God. It is the total destruction of egoism by being merged in the consciousness of God and in nothing else but God; so that, what ultimately remains as Reality is God-realization in the form of bliss and peace which is unutterable and therefore is simply to be experienced in complete silence. But before this final stage of self-surrender is attained, there are other three stages which must first be attained through the different stages of meditation, which we shall first mention.

There are four kinds of speech, and corresponding to them, meditation can be carried on in four different ways. It becomes more and more powerful as the speech becomes less and less articulate and subtle. There is first the spoken word which is uttered by tongue and is audible. So, the first way of meditation would be to utter the divine Name loudly, so that it can clearly be heard and attended to. But as the tongue might get tired after a while, meditation also might not last long. To overcome this defect one is advised to utter the Name in the throat. But this is more difficult to do, requiring as it does more energy and attention to observe that it is really uttered distinctly and clearly, though inarticulately, and that it is also heard from inside. In a sense, the difference between the two kinds of speech is a difference of degree only, so far as the articulation of the words and the audibility of the sound are concerned. But one great advantage of meditating on the divine Name in one's throat is that the mind and the soul of the meditator are to a great extent cut off from the objects of the external world, since the attention is diverted and fixed on the utterance and the hearing of the Name. This means that the mind of the meditator is gradually being assimilated with the meaning of the Name and begins to feel more and more interest and joy in doing the meditation.

All this happens to a greater degree still, when along with the meditation, the Name descends deeper still to the region of the heart which is believed by some as the seat of the mind, though not of the soul. Here, there is no attempt at articulation; even the vibrations of the sound and the unconscious movement of the tongue in uttering the Name in the throat are silenced. The mind is at its full liberty to observe that the Name is being meditated upon and also heard clearly and distinctly as before; but as there is no physical connection of either the muscles in the throat or of the tongue, the entire process is done by the mind only. The meditator, the meditation and the hearing of it are all mental in character. The understanding of the meaning of the Name, the focussing of attention and energy on it, the identification of the mind with the Name as it becomes more and more absorbed in meditation, the consequent joy of it, and the more and more forgetfulness of one's own body and the objects of the external world are due to the activity of the mind only. This whole process resembles that of reading and understanding a book mentally. The man only sees the words and sentences as if mentally while reading; but the seeing itself sums up the whole story. Even so, the seeing by the mind sums up the entire process of meditation at this stage. But what happens miraculously here is that the mind loses its own character of being unsteady and of flying away from one object to another, and becomes almost merged in the Name. This we may call as the threshold of the supramental stage of meditation, which is the fourth and the final stage of the soul's being identified with the Divine.

Now, the mind being almost absent, the question arises as to who is the meditator, and who the listener. The answer is that it must be God on whose Name or symbol meditation was till then going on, and in whom the mind had got itself joyfully absorbed. There is no longer the division between the meditator and God as the object of meditation. The subject becomes its own object by the process of meditation; or, we may say that the object bifurcates itself into its own subject and so meditation is continued with utmost joy and peace. This is how paradoxically, Bhakti which is dualistic occurs in Advaita which is the only non-dual Reality. This is how God contemplates upon himself; this is how the God-intoxicated mystic ejaculates in raptures the name of God which reverberates with music, and throws open as if the doors of the kingdom of God for all to enter in it.

In the light of this, what shall we say about the process of self-surrender ? To begin with, there occurs the conscious and the deliberate surrender or dedication of all things to God. All the objects of the senses, the pleasures, the sorrows, and other events, the mind and the speech are all dedicated to God. Then, by the power of meditation, they are felt as belonging to God. This we may call as the physical or the 'gross' surrender, by conscious and deliberate effort. The second is the refined and the mental surrender, which occurs naturally and without much effort, as the result of constantly thinking that there is none else but God who is responsible for all that is created, and for all that happens and changes. As meditation gathers momentum and force by being mental and silent in character, the surrender also of all that is amenable to change and destruction, whether in the external world of objects or in the internal world of emotions and desires, becomes automatic, sincere, and full of love and regard for God. The next stage of surrender almost comes in the wake of this, when as the result of the mind being fixed and identified with God in the process of meditation, the self too with all its belongings becomes merged in God, but is conscious and proud of being fortunate to become one with God. And, finally there comes the last stage of surrender when the self becomes bereft of its egoism and its feeling of being separate from God. It is at this stage that self-surrender becomes just a synonym for the indivisible unity and oneness of Godhead, for the Pure consciousness of Existence, Power, Bliss, and Peace, all packed together in one indistinguishable whole.

68. *God-realization impossible without renunciation.* (12. *vi.* 1-31; *vii.* 1-31)

We have observed in an earlier section that to live the spiritual and the worldly life simultaneously is not incompatible. But this does not mean that a man can remain equally interested in both of them to the end of his life. What will mostly happen is that the hold of the temptations and the pleasures in the worldly life will be far greater than that of the spiritual one, unless there is the deliberate effort to detach the mind gradually away from them and to train it to get itself fixed in the meditation of God. No doubt, there are saints who live the double life of the sense and the spirit in a harmonious manner; they do their personal and social duties very well, and they are devoted to the worship of God equally well. This is quite understandable if the hours of duty and the hours of worship are kept apart. But this need not be the case always. If one would look deeper into the life of a great saint like Ekanātha, he would find that notwithstanding the division of hours of duty and of devotion, every moment of the saint's life was a moment given to the service of God. The whole of the worldly life, with all its pleasures and sorrows and with all its contents, becomes a series of sacrifices or offerings for the worship of God. But as the worship and service of God become more and more internal, and there is no need of any external offerings, there comes about inevitably the renunciation of them all. Though of utmost use in the beginning as means for the service of God, they are ultimately cast away as useless superfluities, or even as hindrances in the way of the devotional meditation on the Name of God.

How else can a man rise from polytheistic beliefs and worship of the images to the deep and silent meditation on God; from the mixed and transitory joys and sorrows of the worldly life to the unmixed constant bliss and peace of living with God; from the ritualistic cult of sacrifices to the surrender of the self in God; and from the thraldom of the five elements and the three guṇas of sattva, raja and tama of the Māyā or the Prakṛti to the supra-sāttvika condition of the freedom of the Brahmanic life, if he is always immersed in social customs and social visits and activities like games, entertainment, hobbies, tours, picnics etc. and in the innumerable worries and problems of the worldly life; and in looking to the comforts of his body and the sensuous well-being of himself and of his family and of his kith and kin? Where will be time for meditation, if from morning till late in the night, there is no breathing space between one activity and another? Spiritual life is not like catching the leaves of trees casually while one is riding on a camel. One has to toil every day, continuously and regularly at fixed hours and for a long time, before one can expect to have a glimpse of the beautiful visions of God. But to do this means to give up many of our activities of social life as also to cut down the hours of our sleep.

And as the spiritual exercise of meditation on the divine Name and of contemplation on the visions of God would increase in yielding more and more of joy and peace, and as a consequence of this and of absorption in meditation more energetically than before, forgetfulness of one's own body and environment will be so natural that renunciation too of all that exists except the vision of God will be natural with the devotee. Even the various miraculous powers which such a great devotee might be endowed with will be discarded by him as obstac les on the path of becoming one with God. So, the only lesson one should have from this is to learn to renounce the world and the ego, little by little even at the beginning of his spiritual pilgrimage.

69. *In this temporal fair, the vision of God is the only gain.* (12. *viii.* 1-34)

Our consciousness of time is nothing but the consciousness of change in our environment. Had there been no change or movement of the Sun, or no change in external things or in our internal states of mind, there would have been no consciousness of time. What we call morning, evening and noon are only the divisions of time as determined by the changing positions of the Sun in the heavens; and it is this change which makes the periods of time as irreversible in nature. The moment of death also is therefore irreversible ; that is, it cannot be averted or postponed even if hundreds of thousands of rupees are given as the price for avoiding death. What we can however do so long as death is away is to become aware of something which does not change and which therefore confers its own timelessness upon us. To become conscious of this homogeneous, changeless and blissful something, namely, the vision of God, is to have immortality as the greatest gain in life. But to attain this, we must, even while we are doing our daily duties in life, train ourselves and be prepared to renounce in advance all our attachment to the evanescent things in life. One who can do this is a wise man ; one who does not is as good as a beast which comes into being and goes out of being for no purpose.

70. *The routine of a wise man.* (12. *ix.* 1-30 ; *x.* 1-43)

First of all, he should bid goodbye to idleness and get up early in the morning before sun-rise, and should daily and without any exception meditate on the Name of God, and after reading spiritual literature for a while, think over it. He should make his meditation so intense, prolonged and absorbing that he should himself be convinced that he is moving from devotion to devotion, from illumination to illumination, and from dispassion to dispassion. Then, taking his stand on his own experience, he should preach to others what he has himself practised, in such an easy and convincing manner as will not frighten them in the least, but will persuade them to go by the same path towards Godhead. And as they become more and more interested in treading the path of God, he should all the more proclaim the glory of God to such an extent that it will fill even the heavens with joy.

One should eat, no doubt, to his heart's content, but should never waste the food if it is left over. Himself being satisfied by the knowledge of God, he should distribute the same to all. Should not the swimmer save others from being drowned ? Even so, one who has realized God should teach others how to become devoted to God and thereby form assemblies of saints. To win the hearts of the people and to lead them towards God-realization requires great skill and kindness of heart. Himself remaining undisturbed and calm in spite of provocation, and bearing up with courage the abuses, the insults and the ill-treatment at the hands of the wicked and the vile, he should be ever prepared to forgive them, if they are likely to be improved and converted to the life of the Spirit. But, instead, if he becomes impatient and gives them up as lost, he would lose the opportunity of spreading the gospel of God. And, certainly, who can have the access to the knowledge of God, if the man who has realized God were to die suddenly ? The realized soul ought to think therefore that it is his life-long duty to turn the minds of the sinful and the ignorant towards the service and devotion of God.

Himself, however, he should make the firm resolve not to beg anything from anyone of his disciples. Rāmadāsa tells us that so far as he is concerned, he asks of them only one thing, namely, that even after his death they should worship God.

71. *The Self is the barometer of the Real and the unreal.* (13. *i. to x.* 1-300.)

Who is the self in the first place ? He is the principle of life known as the Ātman. He lives in the bodies of all the beings of the world and is the chief cause of all the movements and the conditions of the good and the bad qualities of mind, of the achievements and the failures, and of the emotions, the cognitions, the will and the pleasures and sorrows of life. In short, without the Ātman the body will be a corpse, whether the body is gross or subtle, causal or the primeval, or as belonging to the individual or the cosmic soul. The body is short-lived, the Ātman is eternal. And yet, as it moves from the avidyā (unreality) to the Vidyā (Reality) and vice versa, and partakes in the qualities of both as occasions arise, one has to be very careful not to allow the Ātman to slide down to the level of the voluptuous, the mean and the sinful. If one talks always about delicious food, or is interested in describing the beauty of women, the Ātman (mind) of that man degenerates to that extent. If, on the other hand, one were to talk and read and discuss about God and all other spiritual matters, his mind would be elevated to that extent, and enable him to dissolve the perceptible world of Māyā in his meditative love of God, and get himself assimilated with Him. He will then discover that his Ātman is no longer amenable to change and that it is nothing else but the uncontaminated Brahman. Though staying in and with the body, which becomes subject to various influences, the Ātman then will never forget its real nature, and say with infatuation that he is the same as body, mind, senses, intellect and the ego. Whether it is the course of worldly life (Pravṛtti) or the condition of spiritual illumination (Nivṛtti), the saint will never miss his real Ātman or God. He will find the Lord as immanent in the whole universe, in the perceptible world of the five elements and the three guṇas of the Prakṛti, as also transcendent of it, and as the creator, the sustainer and the destroyer of it.

This is not however the final destination of the Ātman. The saint's meditation on the Name and his close contemplation on the vision of the Ātman will enable him further to identify it with the transcendent Brahman itself. For, it is that very vision of the Ātman which he will see always before him, as having the same characteristics of Brahman, namely, that which will not be burnt by fire, or moistened by water, or blown away by the wind, or cut by the weapons. In short, by breaking the artificial walls of body, senses, mind, intellect and egoism of Prakṛti which were superimposed upon the Ātman, he would discover, in the first place, that it is not merely a reflection of the Brahman, but the Brahman itself. And, secondly, by breaking the walls of the five elements and the three guṇas of Prakṛti, he would discover that even the attributes of immanence and transcendence of Brahman have ultimately a relative significance only. And, thirdly, when there would be no difference between the Ātman and the Brahman, how will he be able to speak about that blissful condition which passes beyond all thought and speech ?

From all the discussion done so far, there emerges one important point. It is that great caution must be taken not to turn this theoretical knowledge about the Ātman or the Brahman into a false Vedānta. True it is that the Ātman is immanent in all the good and the bad, the animate and the inanimate things of the world. But this need not make us blind to the obvious differences that we notice among things and things, and equate them so far as our behaviour is concerned. Will any one be satisfied if he is given sand, when what he wants is sugar, on the plea that sugar and sand are ultimately two forms of one and the same earth ? One never drinks dirty water thinking that it is the holy water of the river Gaṅgā. In the same way, notwithstanding the immanence of the Ātman and its being the source of all, there is all the difference between the sinner and the meritorious, the coward and the brave, the vicious and the virtuous and the morally good and the bad. In fact, it is the existence of the differences between one thing and another and between one quality and another, and the necessity of making the transition from bad to good, and from sin to holiness, that will justify the struggle for the moral and the spiritual progress. What one should do is that he should pray to the impartial Ātman who is residing in him to help him to move from darkness to light, from ignorance to knowledge and from what is bad to what is good. The Ātman should be befriended because He is the source of all that is Good, Beautiful and Holy.

72. *The key to happiness is to have no expectation.* (14. *i.* 1-80.)

What should a man do in order to be virtuous, wise, happy and contented ? Let him bring in practice the following advice in all the details and on all occasions. (1) He should think well before he resolves not to entertain any desire nor expect to have anything from anybody. But if he once makes the resolve, let it not be known to others; for if it is not kept he will have no face to show to those before whom he has spoken about his resolve. (2) He should not look with an evil eye upon the wealth and women of others ; for it will be very difficult to withhold the temptation of possessing them. And then, too, he will have no courage to move freely in the society. (3) Even if some one offers him wealth, he should not accept it ; for that might make him greedy and unnecessarily obliged to his donor. (4) To decline such offers will be possible, if he has really no desire for enjoying the comforts and pleasures of life. (5) He should neither allow his spiritual activity to be slackened nor his courage to be lost. (6) Without being ashamed of the people, he should loudly and with great love sing the Name and the praises of God. (7) He should take great care not to get himself associated with the mean and the wicked; otherwise, he would fall away from the path of God, and would get himself engrossed so much with the sensuous pleasures that he would not hesitate to employ any foul means to achieve them. (8) The preaching of sermons, the narration of the glorious deeds of God, and the singing of the praises and of the Name of God, or the doing of worship or any other spiritual service should never be used as means of livelihood or of amassing wealth. He should go by the golden rule and avoid extremes in all things. (9) Even if he moves from place to place for spreading the gospel of God, he should neither mix with the people for all time, nor be always away from them. For there is the double risk of meeting the sceptics and the wicked, as well as of losing the chance of meeting the saints. Besides, it is very necessary that he should have his own time to meditate silently and in a solitary place. Hence, it follows that he should neither resort to a forest always nor visit the busy market place or a factory very often. (10) He should not be too talkative; neither should he shut his mouth always. For unless he talks, how can he satisfy the inquisitiveness of others ? (11) Neither should he be a glutton, nor abstain from taking food. For both the conditions are not congenial for the practice of meditation. (12) Even so, too much or too little sleep is neither wholesome for the health of the body; nor for the equanimous condition of the mind. And, when both the mind and the body are not in a fit condition, how can meditation be carried on ? (13) Rituals and external forms of worship need not be rooted out altogether, inasmuch as being the traditional modes of expressing and conserving the religious emotions, they would be useful to some extent and to some people at least in the beginning of their spiritual life. Besides, there being no substitute for the rituals, there would only be general scepticism. They should however be very few in number. (14) Sympathy and compassion to all who are in search of spiritual life should be there no doubt but there should be no worldly and emotional attachment to any one. (15) Regarding the spiritual experience also, he should enjoy it without being aware that the experience is different from him. (16) Notwithstanding the transcendence of spiritual experience beyond mind and intellect, the mind must be fixed on it, and the intellect must be firm and resolute (17) Though the perceptible world of sense ought not to be made the object of constant interest and attention, the non-sensuous perceptible visions of divine forms should be seen again and again. The names and forms of the sensuous world, in other words, should not only be not recalled, but forgotten in the efforts to remember the Name of God and in seeing his beautiful Forms. (18) For when it is said that the names and forms are illusory and short-lived, they must be understood as belonging to the world of Prakṛti or Māyā, but not of the imperceptible divine world. (19) All this is done by him in order to increase the faith and devotion of men to God, though he himself remains hidden and unknown.

73. *Be even a mendicant for obtaining the knowledge of God.* (14. ii, 1-22)

If God-realization is the prize to be had, why should one be ashamed if he is required even to lead the life of a mendicant? One should not however stick to one place and become a burden to a few persons only. On the other hand, if he moves from place to place, he might meet a great saint here and there, learn from him some new facts and aspects of spiritual life, and feel that he is not at all in strange waters. Mendicancy will also give him a sort of independence and freedom from care, as well as opportunities to spread the gospel of God.

74. *The poetry of the God-intoxicated*, (14. iii, 1-54; iv. 1-35; *v.* 1-41).

What makes a man intoxicated with the love of God, how unconsciously and naturally he produces out of himself words of praise and immortal wisdom, and how with these again as means he worships God, are all unique and marvellous. Love with reference to God is not an empty word, nor an emotion which has its ebb and flow. It connotes a frame of mind or disposition which comprises several qualities, emotions and attitudes towards life as a whole. Negatively, we can say that a person of this disposition looks upon the pleasures of wealth, prosperity and sex as nothing but vomit, and is bereft of sin, vice, egoism, anger and arrogance. Positively considered, he is a person who has his heart fixed on the meditation on the Name of God, and who, with increasingl ove andr everence, looks upon the beautiful forms of God. He does not allow a single moment of his life without being conscious of God; and so, he becomes more and more forgetful of his bodily consciousness and of the joys and sorrows attached to it. His mind, intellect and heart are deeply coloured in one hue only, namely, the undying and the unswerving love of God. As such, seeing he does not see the people around him; and being perfectly shameless as if, he dances with joy and sings as loudly as he can the praises and the glories of God. Why should he fear anyone, since he sees everywhere nothing else but God? Instead of saying that his heart is set on God, we may as well say that God himself has come to reside in his heart. Naturally, then, he becomes as unperturbed, joyful and calm as God himself.

Rare indeed is the person who is learned but never disputes; who has realized God and yet is a devotee; and who sings and describes the qualities of God but does not charge anything for it. When there is an image of God which is worshipped by many, he does not disturb their faith by preaching that God has no form; for he knows that God is both personal and impersonal, and that by worshipping the Personal one comes to realize the Impersonal. On the contrary, he too joins them in their loud chanting of hymns and prayers, worships the deity as they do, and claps his hands and prostrates before it with great devotion. When, however, there is the select audience of those who have advanced in spiritual life, and when there is no image before them, he speaks like a philosopher-mystic and preaches that God transcends all images, forms, qualities and names, and yet is capable of manifesting in all of them.

Will such a great saint ever bring in sexual imagery in his narration of the glorious deeds and qualities of God ? He knows full well that to indulge in such things is to rouse at once the sexual emotion of the audience also, and to divert their attention from God to women. So, neither will he speak nor write anything which will not be useful for increasing their faith in God, but which will simply be a source of entertainment and fun. Those who merely write for the sake of entertainment write either for gaining cheap popularity or for obtaining wealth. Therefore, they borrow some material from others, add something of their own by way of imagination, and imitating other writers and poets write in some such pattern as will please the readers and bring money for themselves. They write in order to flatter the kings and the rich so that they may secure big gifts from them, and so turn their back against God. The philosopher-saint, on the contrary, never writes a word which is not inspired by the grace of God or which is not intended to increase the faith, the devotion and the knowledge of God. Whether it is prose or poetry, it aims at producing in the minds of the readers and listeners the emotions of awe, reverence, love and gratitude for the greatness and goodness of God, and at teaching them to understand and to appreciate what is at once beautiful, frightful, sublime and majestic, whether in the Nature outside or in the human creation. In short, the ultimate aim of his writings is to intimate the reader of the infinite divine manifestations of light, colour, form and musical sound. The divine poetry has its source in divine madness and aims at reproducing it in others. It rises at the confluence of the love of the saint and the grace of God, and is therefore simple, sweet, forceful and appealing. It is the spontaneous outburst of utterings and ejaculations out of the depth of meditation on the divine Name and of the blissful contemplation on the visions of God. It is the word of God, not of man. It is God who sends forth the poem through the mouthpiece of his best devotees. It is grace incarnate.

If one is fortunate to attend to its meaning and to sing it with the help of music, it will lead him to Godhead. But, if unfortunately, one is inattentive to the meaning and is carried away by the melody of the musical notes, he goes away from God. For music is both good and bad; a friend and a foe. If it is subordinated to devotion, it will be an excellent help for God-realization, but if it dominates, devotion will soon slip away, and there will remain only the entertainment of the mind. Music ought to be a means and not an end in itself. The saint takes very willingly the help of music, but soon goes beyond its melody in order to merge himself in the unstruck divine music.

75. *Combine devotion with practical wisdom* (14. *vi*, 1-33; *vii* 1-40)

A devotee of God also has to cultivate certain virtues if he wishes to live in society. Natural defects will be excused, but not those which can be removed by education and training. How can one be blamed for innate deafness or blindness? None can change the complexion of the skin. But if one does not know how to behave he cannot be excused. All the more, a devotee of God has a duty to perform. He has to make the people spiritually-minded and to lead them on the path of God. He would come across with all sorts of people, and with all of them he has to behave with patience, courage, tact and goodness. In the first place, he must be a true devotee of God; that is, he must find joy in contemplating on the vision of God, or on the vision of his own immaculate form, or must be absorbed in deep and silent meditation on the Name of God. To him there must not be anything greater than or even equal to God. As such, he must feel utter disgust for all things other than God. It does not then make any difference whether he stays in his house as a responsible member of his family, or leaves it in due course for the sake of saving the souls of other people in the world. It should be remembered that one who leaves his house and family in a fit of anger makes himself and others miserable in all ways. Himself being as ignorant as his teacher, he makes others also like him.

Therefore, in the second place, he must know that his highest duty, next to the realization of God, is to make the same easily attainable to all. But this he will not be able to achieve unless by his own amiable behaviour he makes others believe that he is a true friend to them all. He must adorn his heart and soul with virtues like compassion, fellow-feeling, forgiveness and capacity to toil hard for the spiritual good of others. He should enter into the hearts of others, suffer with their sufferings, and try his utmost to make them free from them. Gradually, he should instruct them the way and the means of realizing God, and save them morally and spiritually by remaining in their company for some time and making them attached to God by meditation, worship and prayers. Thus it is that he should make himself happy by making the people happy.

76. *Meditation, the only way to go beyond Māyā,* (14. *viii.* 1-49 ; *ix.* 1-31 ; *x.* 1-21.)

There are people who have a genuine desire to realize God; but not knowing the method of meditation they resort to false methods ; and so, instead of reaching the Brahman they wander again in the domain of Māyā. As we have observed more than once that to know God is to become God, it is very necessary to become acquainted with the true method of meditation which will make one more and more identified with Him. And once God is seen as both the innermost and the transcendent Reality beyond all phenomenal existence, there will be then no mistake of identifying Him with any other illusory or short-lived things of Māyā. In vain do the people think that the perceptible world of space and time is real, though the common experience is that everything is changing and that nothing is permanent. In vain do they feel that Brahman which is without any form or quality might not exist, because it is not seen by their physical eyes. This might be a good way of making the distinction between the real and the unreal from the every-day, practical view-point of the worldly life. But it is thoroughly misleading from the spiritual point of view. The infinite and the omnipresent Brahman can never be cognized or measured by any phenomenal instrument. Firstly, it has to be seen as the Ātman who resides in the hearts of all, and then realized as bereft of the qualities of the changeable Ātman also. One who has identified his self with Brahman will alone be able to go beyond Māyā; he alone will be able to say that the experience of the Personal aspect of God leads one to the experience of the Impersonal aspect of him, and that, therefore, it is wrong to consider God as possessing a body.

Let us then first describe the false method of meditation and notice the flaws in it ; and then, we shall mention the true method by resorting to which the saints have attained the Brahman. People, in general, never possess the fixity of mind, since their interests in life are also various and short-lived. Their mind is broken, so to say, but with great effort they try to make it one, and visualize by means of imagination an image of their liking and worship it with material gathered in their mind. This sort of mental worship of an image of God which also is mentally produced might be very useful in the beginning to increase one's faith and devotional attitude; but, in the end, this itself becomes an hindrance in the way of directly seeing the visions and the immaculate forms of God. One might, for instance, create in his mind an image of God of a certain height and mentally put a crown upon the head of that image. He might then worship the image in several ways, such as waving the lights mentally, applying the sandle-paste mentally, and so on. One such act of homage might be to put a garland of mentally produced flowers round the neck of the image. But in doing so, the devotee might, on one occasion, find that the crown on the head of the image has become higher than usual, and that therefore the garland could not be thrown over it. Naturally, he becomes discomforted, and asks his Guru as to what he should do.

The Guru tells him to remove the crown and place the garland round the neck of the image.

Aptly does Rāmadāsa observe that both the disciple and his teacher are fools. Was it difficult for the teacher to tell his disciple to increase mentally the length of the garland of the mentally produced flowers, and then to put it round the neck of the image, without removing the crown on the head ? This is the danger of all mental worship that the mind should create something which it ought not to create, or not create something which it should. Besides, after the worship is over, everything vanishes along with the image of God ! After all, this is only a make-believe, a thing of imagination, and not at all a reality. Will God disappear altogether, if once he is seen as being the same inside and outside of mind ? The real God is ever visible in all the conditions of life ; and so, the real meditation consists in remembering His Name unceasingly and with such concentration and joy, that there remains no distinction between the devotee who meditates and God who is meditated upon. Even so, there would afterwards be no distinction between the self who sees God and God who is seen. The devotee becomes the Brahman (God).

77. *A saint will be free from desire and yet be active.* (15. *i.* 1-35 ; *ii.* 1-30 ; *iii.* 1-30; *vi.* 1-30.)

People are generally active in order to obtain the objects of their desires ; but a great saint would be active even in spite of himself. He might wish to be useful to others in making them realize the spiritual good, and so become intensely active in quite a disinterested manner. In fact, who else but a saint can spread the knowledge of God, if he too were to remain self-satisfied and inactive. Already there are the ignorant and the fools who call themselves wise and quarrel among themselves saying that they alone know the truth. No body knows what God is; and yet worshippers of Śaṅkara and Viṣṇu fight against each other saying that their deity is the only supreme God. Others follow suit, and say the same thing about other deities, because their desires are fulfilled by worshipping them. Add to this the opinions of the philosophers who do nothing but merely speculate about the nature of the Reality which goes beyond intellect and logic. In fact, no body wants God ; almost everyone cares for his own belly and struggles to increase his material gain. And, generally speaking, what goes on in the temples, for instance, singing the Name of God (Hari-Kirtana) is also far removed from the real method of having the direct contact and experience of God. When such is the state of affairs, and when there is none to give the right sort of advice or prevent people from going morally astray, there should be no wonder if people change their faith and their language and become easily converted to another faith either through pressure or through temptations of worldly gains, and if there reigns then complete selfishness, greed, power-politics and confusion.

In these trying circumstances, it is the saint, as said above, who alone can come forward and change the order of things. With his deep insight into spiritual knowledge, his high moral rectitude and sense of justice, and his practical wisdom, he first sorts out the people, and selecting the chief amongst them brings them round to his way of thinking. And then, through their help he enters into the hearts of the masses, and makes them change their trodden paths of scepticism, wrong beliefs, sensuous pleasures, greed and jealousy. He makes his residence in the mountain valleys which are not easily accessible to people and meditates there for the good of all. And whenever there is the need, he comes down from there, gives them a few pointed words of advice, and retiring again to an unknown place, exerts his influence from there silently and secretly. On occasions, he mixes with people for spiritual activities and turns their minds to the service of God. Externally, he looks like a beggar, but is a limitless source of success, power and fame. People may be intimately acquainted with him ; but he keeps them away from him if they are doggedly indifferent to spiritual life. On the other hand, he keeps on moving from place to place in order to find out ever new groups of people who would follow his advice and join the spiritual fold. He thus strives hard to knit the hearts of the people by the common bond of spiritual knowledge, so that the blessed Name of God might be glorified by being sung loudly and that they should also lead a morally good and social life.

This is what Rāmadāsa tells us as a piece of autobiography and says that the saint must be old inspiritual knowledge and not old in age. His greatness is measured by the greatness of his spiritual illumination, by the fullness of the awakening of the Divinity in him, by his being proud of having lived the life of Truth and Reality, by his indefatigable efforts in spreading that knowledge to others, and by his immense capacity to endure the insults and the ill-treatment at the hands of the wicked and the jealous, while executing the noble task. Without in any way engaging himself in verbal disputations as to whose opinion and path are correct, he listens to all, but does what he thinks to be right. If the occasion demands, he would even pretend that he is accepting a defeat, but would soon prove that he alone is in the right and that all others are wrong. Under the guise of being a mendicant, he would visit several towns and villages and make a searching investigation of the varying nature of individual persons by visiting their houses, and try to win their hearts by teaching them gradually the details of what is morally and spiritually good. In short, it becomes the active mission of a great saint not only to wipe out his own, unseen Fate, which is generally considered as the result of the actions in the previous births, but also to help others in wiping out their unseen Fate by increasing their own spiritual worth. His is the mission of conquering the world in order to change it into the Kingdom of God by the triple means of works, devotion and spiritual illumination.

78. *The descent and the ascent of the changeable world.* (15. *iv.* 1-31 ; *v.* 1-32 ; *vii.* 1-42 ; *viii.* 1-40.)

Logicians and metaphysicians differ in their views regarding the concepts of change and permanence. Some say that they are relative terms and so according to them they both are the characteristics of the Real. Some others say that change implies permanence no doubt; but they think that change is more real than permanence ; while there are some who say that what is permanent can never change, and that change is only apparent and not real. This last view is the view of the Advaita Vedāntin, and is the expression in language of an experience which never changes. This is the experience of the blissful Brahman.

From the spiritual point of view the cosmological account that the world is produced out of the five elements of Prakṛti or

Māyā which in its turn belongs to Brahman as its power appears more as a dogma than as a fact of experience. The descent of the phenomenal, changeable world from Brahman is almost taken for granted. The changing nature of the world as it exists and the short life of man with his joys and sorrows in it are empirical facts which can never be denied. The important problem which awaits solution from the spiritual point of view is to know how to convert the changeable into the unchangeable so far as the destiny of man is concerned. When and in what manner the whole of the phenomenal world is going to merge back into the original Brahman has for him only a speculative interest. Yet, it affords a clue to determine the way in which man can advance spiritually. In fact, neither the evolution or the dissolution of the world, nor the descent or the ascent of it, is of much practical interest for man. Nor can man do anything to change the course of either the evolution or the dissolution of the world. But, there is one thing he can do, and this is to bring about even while he is living the dissolution of his own empirical and sensuous nature into the transcendental, supra-sensuous nature of God. He can verily work out his spiritual ascent into the unchangeable, blissful Brahman.

Now, as the ascent is generally known to be the opposite of the descent, the spiritual ascent also consists in reversing the process of descent, namely, of asserting the body and all its material and psychical belongings as owned by the ego. The law of the physical universe is that everything is dissolved in that from which it has been produced. For instance, all that exists on earth is dissolved into earth; the earth is dissolved into water, water into fire, fire into air, air into ākāśa, and ākāśa into the threefold Prakṛti or Māyā, and Māyā into the Brahman. Even so, the law for the ethico-spiritual ascent is that everything lower is to be dissolved into what is next higher to it. But this is to be done during meditation far more on the psychological level than on the physical or the physiological one. A certain amount of help could indeed be taken by means of the yogic postures ; but the main task is to be accomplished by devotional meditation on the Name of God and contemplation on the Forms of the visions of God. If the meditation is carried on along with the breath, both the mind and the breaths come under control ; and as concentration would increase on the Name and Form of God, and as the soul becomes fixed in the vision, there would result excessive joy and peace out of that unitive life, as also the forgetfulness of body, senses, mind, intellect and egoism. This means that there would occur naturally and step by step, the dissolution or the elimination of the consciousness of oneself being identical with any one of the above-mentioned products of the Prakṛti, or of being of the nature of any one of the three guṇas of Māyā.

When the soul ascends to this supraphysical, supramental, supraconscious state of ever-wakefulness which goes beyond the waking, the sleeping and the dreaming conditions of the ordinary life, as well as beyond the three guṇas of sattva, raja and tama, the consciousness of even the great statements, 'I am the Brahman,' 'All this is Branman,' also goes away. For, after all, these statements, instead of suggesting the division between the 'I' or the 'All' on the one hand, and the Brahman, on the other, suggest the undifferentiated, indivisible identity of the 'I' and of the 'all' with the Brahman. What remains then at the apex of the ascent, is the blissful Brahman conscious of itself, and not at all the individual soul with its consciousness of the 'I' or of the 'all'. This does not mean that the external world as such ceases to exist at the supramental level ; it only means that its existence does not create any discordant note in the consciousness of the identity of the self and the Brahman. Therefore it is that in being conscious of the material world, the saint becomes conscious of the principle of activity which lies behind it as its source ; and similarly, in being conscious of that principle, which we may call as the Prakṛti or Māyā, he becomes conscious of the Personality of God who possesses the Māyā as his power. Even so, in being conscious of the Person of God as possessing the various attributes, he becomes conscious of the one transcendental Impersonal Absolute or Brahman, which being without any quality or form is still the source and support of all the qualities and of all the forms, and of all that exists. And, finally, the difference between the knower and the known becomes so negligible that the saint as the knower while he knows or realizes the known, is so completely lost in the known, that is, the Brahman that what remains is simply to be experienced as a blissful condition which defies any description by word of mouth.

79. *Devotion leads one to the vision of the Omnipresence of God.* (15. *ix.* 1-34 ; *x.* 1-33.)

How then can one have the vision of this omnipresent Brahman or God ? The reply is that it is only through unswerving devotion to Him. For it is the loving attachment to God that makes the soul more and more co-extensive with God and ultimately enables it to merge in Him. One who has no such love falls away from God ; and this is the greatest sin. It makes him bound with the bodily consciousness and with the various desires for sensuous pleasures. The thoughtful, on the contrary, knows that his love for God will neither be on the increase nor be free from the alloy of pretence, till he becomes free from desires and egoism. He therefore not only reduces his desires but gives them up altogether, or burns them, so to say, so that like the burnt seed they would never raise their head again. In rooting out them all he acts like a true sannyāsin. And with his heart and soul intent upon the realization of God, he takes to meditation throughout the day and night, and awakens the potential divine energy in him. In course of time, he finds that the very Prakṛti, which used to act upon him as an alien power, has become friendly and helpful to him. His body becomes accustomed to the postures he takes while he sits for meditation ; his mind does not fly away from object to object, but becomes steady and attends to the uttering and the hearing of the Name of God ; his intellect being free from doubts and misgivings, becomes firm in its resolve ; and his egoism drops down on account of his prayerful surrender. God manifests before him; forthwith his ignorance and fear leave him. He becomes all the more devoted and steadfast in God ; his egoism for having seen God also drops down, and he reaches the supramental state of the consciousness of bliss and peace. Finally, he becomes merged in God.

80. *Even the place of meditation of a saint like Vālmīki becomes purifying.* (16. *i.* 1-21.)

Vālmīki, the famous author of Rāmāyaṇa was in his early life a very sinful and murderous person. But remorse and repentance wiped away his sins, and being graced by God he began to meditate on the divine Name so intensely and incessantly that mountains of his sins broke into pieces, and the merit that accumulated became limitless. The Name of God which he was meditating upon began to surge up from within, and he became so unconscious of his body that an ant-hill grew up around it. God became so pleased with his devotion and with his extraordinary meditation that Vālmīki became endowed with prophetic insight and inspiration to compose poetry. The whole of the Rāmāyaṇa came out of his mouth long before Rāma was born as an incarnation of God on earth. No wonder then that the place where Vālmīki meditated became so holy that people who visited it became purified of their sins, and that dried-up trees began to put forth new foliage. Verily, had there been no God-intoxicated saint like Vālmīki, we would have been deprived of the purifying story of Rāma. It is on account of the very great service which the sage Vālmīki has done to humanity by composing the Rāmāyaṇa that it has become possible for us, says Rāmadāsa, to get ourselves devoted to the worship of Rāma.

81. *Even the physical elements function well owing to the immanent force of God.* (16. *ii* to *x*. 1-281)

It is God as the inner Self of all who not only protects the entire universe but compels all the beings in it to do and to discharge their functions and duties properly. None can disobey his command and remain without doing good to the world at large. The Sun cannot cease to shine and become even a whit cold, since the power of the eyes to see and the whole of the intelligence of men are dependent on the light of the Sun. The earth cannot lose its virtue of forbearance and forgiveness, though all sorts of sins, atrocities, dirty and ugly deeds are being done daily on its surface. How else can there be an example of tolerance and forgiveness for men to follow ? Another lesson too from the element of water. It goes down in humility and gets itself lost in vapour. And while it mixes with the vegetable and the animal kingdom of the world, it gives equal support to all. Sweet, bitter or poisonous, whatever may be the nature of things, all are equally dependent on water as their very sap of life. Fire, like the sun, is the principle on which depends health, longevity and the very life itself. Wind, as everybody knows, is equally required to sustain the life through breathing. Even the great yogins know the very important role which the wind plays in the process of Prāṇāyāma, and in having control over the mind. All the movements and strength of the body, involving contraction, expansion and suspension, are due to the wind alone. Greater and larger than the wind is the inner Self, who being the subtlest and the fastest of all, is at the back of all, and is responsible for all the cognitions, the affections, the wills, the emotions and the actions. Though one and the same in all the beings, it appears as being many on account of the several bodies it assumes. And finally, greater than the Self or the Ātman is the Brahman who remains eternally one and the same and without any change, even though times without number, the worlds come into existence and go out of existence. It is formless and qualityless, though it contains within it all the forms and qualities, and is capable of manifesting at any moment any other form and as being endowed with any other quality. It might manifest as an unstruck sound, as light, as at once an aweful and delightful presence, as conscious force, or even as one's own immaculate form. It is the soul of the individual, the immanent Ātman in all the beings, as well as the transcendent and the hidden Godhead in all.

All this however would be realized only when one would meditate on God. Devotional meditation is a very great support; without it there would be no abiding success in anything that one might do even if he puts forth great efforts. One who is not backed and favoured by God might be put down and defeated by any unknown and unforseeable power. Therefore, it is desirable that whoever wishes to know the plans, the purposes and the workings of God should immediately resort to the meditation on the Name of God. The power of the divine Name, especially of the Name, 'Rāma', is so great that the meditator not only becomes capable of visualizing the visions of God as endowed with more and more lustre and beauty, as he gazes at them with more and more concentration, but he also becomes himself endowed with a like lustre which would attract the onlookers towards him. To possess this, an unshakeable faith in doing the meditation is required, says Rāmadāsa.

82. *Knowledge of God can be spread by those alone who have realized God.* (17.*i*.1-30; *ii.i*-34; *iv.* 1-31; *vi.* 1-32; *vii.*1-30; *x.*1-30)

There exists world-wide difference between one who is indissolubly attached to God on account of his constant meditation on Him and one who has merely a verbal, Vedāntic knowledge about the Brahman. The former is always in search of the company of the good and the holy; he gives himself up to the reading of spiritual literature and to the listening of the sermons and the singing of the Name of God. He compares the meaning of what he reads with his own experience, knows the difference between the Ātman and the Brahman, on the one hand, and the Māyā, on the other, and understands the necessity and significance of the human body in which God would manifest and reside as if in a temple. His own experience becomes a guide to him in learning a divine secret that man should fear God and should always be prepared to offer to him with love and reverence all the objects of his desires and the pleasures of his five senses. He also comes to know another secret of divine life that not to meditate and serve God and not to offer in homage all that he possesses is to invite the wrath of God and His punishment in the form of various diseases and miseries.

Naturally, such a person alone knows that God as the internal Self or the Ātman is the conscious Force (Caitanya) which springs out of the quality-less (Nirguṇa) Brahman and becomes known under various names, such as the original Māyā, the triple Goddess of the three guṇas, the deity having half the body of a woman and half that of a man, known as the Śiva-śakti, the Prakṛti-Puruṣa, the knower (Kśetrajña), the Seer, the Immutable (Kūṭastha), the Witness, the Lord of the guṇas and powers, and that which transcends the guṇas, namely the Śuddha-sattva. The Ātman, being capable of infinite change and being associated with the physical body and with all the things in the universe, is the cause of all the phenomenal changes in nature, of all events in space and time, of all the bodily and mental states, and of all the human motives, and of his pleasures and pains. That in the blissful Brahmanic condition there is no difference, but that in the empirical world of the practical, daily life, there exist infinite distinctions and differences, is therefore, recognized by that person alone who has realized the nature of the Ātman fully well. For it is the Ātman alone who has the double capacity of exhibiting change and changelessness, of encompassing the phenomenal world of Māyā and its five elements and three guṇas, as well as showing its face as Sat-cit-ānanda of the Brahman. Such a person alone can think of bringing realization of the Ātman at the doors of others, by showing them the way of meditation and surrender to God. Whatever is said about the Ātman can with greater and greater approximation be said about the person who has realized the Ātman. Like the Ātman, he too can wield the power of Māyā for establishing the Kingdom of God, since he has become, so to say, a part of God. And then, like God, that is, like the Brahman, he too can be said to have gone beyond all dualities, all distinctions and all differences. However, so far as his actual behaviour in the world is concerned, he does not make any confusion between right and wrong, merit and demerit, and good and bad. For it is only by negating the wrong, the evil and the sinful, and by doing what is right, good and virtuous, that he can at all rise above others morally and spiritually.

As opposed to this, in vain does a man talk Vedānta who does not know anything of the spiritual life and who is never amenable to the rigorous discipline of it. All is Brahman, says he, and equates a sannyāsin who has renounced everything for the sake of God with a voluptuous person who indulges indiscriminately in all sorts of pleasures. Merit and demerit, sinlessness and sinfulness, right and wrong are to him the same. The reason perhaps is that he wants to behave as he likes without any hindrance. But how can he do away with all the natural differences? He does not put his food in his nose. He supposes himself to be as uncontaminated as the Ātman is, till he does not become subject to the diseases and the miseries of old age and the unbearable consequences of his own conduct.

What is then required even as a preliminary to the beginning of the spiritual life is intellectual clarification and morally good conduct. Coupled with this, there must be the company of the good and the holy, meditation on the Name of God, and surrender unto Him. And then, after having gone beyond the power and the guṇas of Māyā, and being backed by the grace of God, he should, as the last stage of his spiritual experience, silently, and without a word of mouth, enjoy the supramental, undifferentiated unity with Brahman, which indeed is the unmixed bliss.

83. *Effortless meditation known as Ajapā, and the mental hearing of the Name.* (17. *iii.* 1-30 ; *v.* 1-24.)

Meditation on the Name of God is considered as the direct way to realize God. Without it, to have the experience of the subtlest Being which not only goes beyond the two elements of wind and Ākāśa, but also beyond the most active principle, namely, the original Māyā is almost impossible. But it is this original, conscious Force of the qualityless (Nirguṇa) Brahman and God or Ātman as the Saguṇa Brahman, which we have to realize by means of our meditation (upāsanā) and by the grace of God.

Rāmadāsa tells us that though it is impossible to negate the world by destroying it, we can do so by cutting ourselves away from it even while it exists. We shall begin to meditate on the Name of God along with the wind we breathe and see what lies beyond it, namely, the Ākāśa which is the subtlest of the five elements and which is very close to the Brahman. As meditation grows in intensity, love and surrender, Brahman manifests all of a sudden in one or more of its infinite, immaculate forms; and then the Prakṛti along with the whole of the phenomenal world will vanish from our consciousness altogether. In course of time, meditation which is already going on silently along with our breathing, and without the Name being uttered loudly by the tongue, is felt as going deeper and deeper from the tongue to the throat, from the throat to the region of the heart, and from there to the region near the navel. Here it is that one utters the Name spontaneously, or rather, it is being uttered spontaneously, and can be heard at the same time clearly and distinctly. The Name comes up of its own accord, and is being uttered and heard simultaneously by the sādhaka. He might be described as breathing the Name and not so much the wind. And as the breaths amount to twentyone thousand and six hundred during twentyfour hours, meditation which goes on in this silent and subtlest form can be said to be natural and effortless, or the 'A-japā' type of meditation, that is, one in which no effort at counting the number is made. When this will be achieved by long practice, it will constitute the most natural and the highest kind of the worship of God. Thus it is that by holding God fast in the heart, one can enjoy the bliss of being disembodied even while possessing the body.

84. *The four bodies and the eighty-two principles.* (17. *viii.* 1-34; *ix*, 1-22).

(1) First, there is the Antaḥkaraṇa-Pañcaka consisting of the five aspects, namely, the inner sense which is simply aware of something; of the Mind which always thinks in different ways and is unsteady; of Buddhi which determines the course of action; of Citta, the capacity to attend; and of Egoism which creates the feeling of ownership. (2) Then, there are five kinds of wind known as Prāṇa-pañcaka, namely, Vyāna which occupies all the limbs of the body; Samāna which resides in the navel; Udāna in the throat; Apāna in the anus; and Prāṇa in the mouth and the nostrils. Then comes (3) Jñāna-pañcaka, (five organs of knowledge) consisting of ears, skin, eyes, tongue and nose; (4) The Karmendriya-pañcaka (five organs of action), namely, tongue, hands, feet, the generating organ and anus; and finally, (5) Viṣaya-pañcaka, (five objects of knowledge), namely, sound, touch, form, flavour and smell. These twenty-five factors or guṇas make what is known as the subtle-body (Sūkṣma-deha).

This subtle body can be better described by considering five different combinations of the above-mentioned guṇas according to the five elements. The inner sense, Vyāna, hearing, speech and sound belong to the element of Ākāśa. Mind, Samāna, skin, hands and touch are the guṇas which belong to the element, Wind. Buddhi, Udāna, eyes, feet, and form (Rūpa) belong to Fire. Attention, Apāna, tongue, the generating organ and flavour belong to Water. And, egoism, Prāna, nose, anus and smell belong to Earth.

Regarding the gross body, similarly, the five elements which make it possess the guṇas are in this manner :—Desire, anger, grief, infatuation and fear characterise the element of Ākāśa.

Motion, turning one way or the other, expansion, contraction, and cessation are the characteristics of the Wind. Hunger, thirst, idleness, sleep and sexual intercourse are due to the element of Fire. Semen (Śuklita), blood (Śoṇita), saliva, urine, and sweat are the varieties of Water. Bones, flesh, skin, veins, and hair are due to the Earth.

The third and the fourth bodies are known as Kāraṇa and Mahākāraṇa, and are made up of desires and ignorance (ajñāna), and of knowledge (jñāna) respectively. But what is known as Vijñāna, or the realization of Parabrahma can be attained only after the four bodies and egoism are completely destroyed. The Self will then be merged in Brahman; there will be no more birth and death. All this, however, will be had only by being devoted to God; but this, in its turn, can be genuine and secure after one surrenders himself at the feet of a saint.

In addition to the four bodies and the fifty guṇas or principles with reference to them and the elements, there are thirty-two more. They are the four states of wakefulness, sleep, dream and that which transcends these three; four presiding deities over these, namely, Viśva, Taijasa, Prājña and Pratyagātmā; four places where they reside, namely, the eye, the throat, the heart and the head; four kinds of enjoyment which they have, namely the gross enjoyment, the secluded joy of pleasures, the Ānanda and the egoism due to Ānanda ; a, u, m, and the moraless sign known as Mātras and as belonging to the four bodies ; tamas, rajas, sattva and śuddhasattva as varieties of the guṇas; and the four powers of action, substance, wish and knowledge. On the cosmic level, there are two more bodies known as Virāṭa and Hiraṇyagarbha, which also must be eliminated by realizing the Ātman.

85. *The hierarchy of gods.* (18. *i.* 1-24; *viii.* 1-25.)

The general polytheistic worship of idols is due to the belief that such worship of them is being done in the places of pilgrimage. These idols are mostly made of stones or metals. The origin of these kinds of gods however will be further found in the belief that God incarnates from time to time in the forms which correspond to these idols. But the incarnations whose memory is preserved in images of stones are themselves as short-lived as the latter are. Even the so-called higher gods, Brahmā, Viṣṇu and Maheśa, who are credited with having the powers to create, to protect and to destroy the universe, respectively, are not supreme. For above them is the Ātman who is immanent in all the objects and beings of the universe and has got all the powers of creation and so on. But being wrongly informed, people miss to see the Ātman who resides in their hearts and go in search of God to the places of pilgrimage, only to find there nothing but water and stones. It is then that being disappointed some of them come in contact with the saints, and being instructed by them make a real search for God. They then come to know that the highest and the only God whom they ought to worship is the inner Self who is the creator, the sustainer and the destroyer of all things. They however do not stop with the discovery and the worship of the Ātman; they go beyond it and reach the Brahman, which unlike the Ātman, is qualityless (Nirguṇa) and changeless. It is at this stage that they become completely sinless, and being one with Brahman, they become as uncontaminated and free as Brahman is.

86. *With all alertness have the contact with the God-realised.* (18. *ii.* 1-30; *iii.* 1-20; *iv.* 1-40; *v.* 1-33; *vii.* 1-20; *ix.* 1-24; *x.* 1-50)

Rāmadāsa tells us that with all the waste which one might have made during a considerable portion of his life on account of idleness, excessive sleep, useless talk or sinfulness and greed, one must take the earliest opportunity of mending his behaviour by having contact with the good and the holy. For, it will be almost impossible to reach the God-head, if one were to disregard the company of a God-realized person out of indifference or a sort of veiled contempt for him. The contact of the body and the Ātman is so intimate that to please or displease an embodied, living person who has realized God is to please or displease God himself. Even the incarnations of God are worshipped because they once possessed a physical body. So, the first thing that one must do is to find out a person who has realized God, and after being in his company observe him how he speaks, how he behaves, how he meditates and how he displays his various virtues on different occasions, so that one might be able to follow in his footsteps and become as uncontaminated and free as he is. He should not only revere a God-realized person but also serve and adore him as he would serve and adore God; but at the same time, he should be careful not to extend the same service and adoration to all other God-less people under the supposition that God is immanent in all beings. It would be enough if he only takes care not to hurt anyone, or in a general way, tries to please them as far as possible.

The second thing one must do is to leave away all idleness, excessive sleep and bad company, and resort to a secluded place, where he should perforce train his mind to meditate on the Name of God with great concentration, love and regard. Without being tired and without allowing any break in his daily spiritual exercise he should toil and toil for a very long period of time, so that gradually and slowly the truth of the great statements, 'I am the Brahman' and 'All this is the Brahman' would dawn on him. God would manifest in some form or other inside and outside of him; and he would come to know that the Real Being is the subtlest of all. This is a matter of experience and not of expression by means of words. In course of time, meditation on the Name would be more and more mental in character and the immaculate Form of God would then be simultaneously present; and with that the sādhaka would discover that his own self or the Ātman is identical with Brahman.

When one would rise to this stage of spiritual experience his tongue will be reluctant to speak a word, his eyes will be busy in gazing at the immaculate, divine vision before him, and his mind and ears in attending to the uttering and the hearing of the divine Name. Will it then be possible for a God-realized person like this to come under the influence of sleep or of any baser emotions like sex ? Will he unnecessarily ruminate over a thing of the past or wander with imagination for nothing ? Being even unmindful of hunger and thirst, he would like to carry on his meditation and contemplation with greater and greater zeal, joy and peace.

87. *A blessing and a piece of advice to Chatrapati Śivāji.* (18. *vi.* 1-22).

God is proud of his devotees like you, O Śivāji, and that the goddess Tulajā Bhavāni whom you worship is pleased with you. Yet, you should be always on the alert, and be aware of the danger which might come on account of the Muslims who have been the cause of oppression since long. You have to show to the world that you are the rarest amongst men, as you have been accepted by God as His own, and as you have received several gifts from Him. God is the doer of all things, no doubt; yet, he intends them to be done through you. Therefore, as you adorn your body with beautiful dress and ornaments, you have to adore your soul also with the qualities of a statesman and a warrior. They are the divine gifts to you. Examine the hearts of others and see what intentions are hoarded in them, so that you will be able to act with justice and courage. As multitudes of people are depending on you for protection and livelihood, you have to relieve them from their anxieties. Extraordinary indeed is your task; but you have to do it with very great efforts. You have to bear the miseries of all, but relieve them soon by your prowess, wisdom and tact. Then alone you will be able to raise the banner of your success and fame, and thereby re-establish the Kingdom of God. All these virtues and powers will come to you as gifts from God, and you will be remembered verily as an incarnation of God.

88. *The behaviour of an active Saint.* (19. *iv.* 1-31; *vi.* 1-30; *vii.* 1-30; *viii.* 1-30; *ix.* 1-31 ; *x.* 1-30)

There are saints who prefer to remain unknown and hidden, for they are temperamentally more contemplative than active. All their activity can be said to be internal only and is utilized in making their meditation intense and prolonged. They are necessarily introverts and of a retiring disposition, and they believe that whatever good they are capable of doing to the society or even to mankind can be done, though invisibly, by the power of their meditation only. On the other hand, there are saints who also are very particular and keen in doing their meditation silently, regularly and intensely, but they occasionally do mix with people with a view to bring them gradually on the pathway to God by their own example as well as by precept. They too are introverts and of a retiring disposition essentially, since they too go in seclusion for concentrated meditation on the divine Name and contemplation on the visions of God. But they have also to perform the divine mission of turning the minds of men towards God. And, indeed who else is competent to do this most difficult and the most important task except the saints who have realized God ? That is why Rāmadāsa tells us how such a saint ought to behave when he moves among people with the intention of doing the work of God.

Look to his spiritual status first. By his constant meditation and contemplation he has become one with God and one with the Brahman. Thereby he holds in his hand the key to the divine knowledge, glory and power. He has become as pure as the Sun, and as uncontaminated and undisturbed as the Brahman. He has no desire of his own, and looks down upon everything except God as useless. Notwithstanding this, he strives every nerve for the upliftment of the humanity from the abyss of sensuality to the heights of the spiritual life. How he achieves this with great tact and wisdom without losing the balance or the equanimity of his mind which is so essential in maintaining the Brahmanic condition, is worth being carefully kept in mind.

In the first place, he does not allow the balance to be tilted in favour of mere social service, because he knows when exactly he should go into seclusion and do his meditation. Intense meditation followed by intense activity alternate so harmoniously in his case that both become more and more fruitful and helpful to each other. The self-same activity, instead of being monotonous, becomes a source of new joy every day; and the self-same meditation makes his mind courageous, strong, and peaceful. The social activity thus becomes for the active saint a source of help to him and to the society at large, and not at all a hindrance or a set-back to him. Besides, it is the fulfilment in some measure of the divine purpose which the saint has to do. This he will not be able to do, unless, in the second place, he feels pained by the miseries and joyful by the happiness of others, and unless he is determined to confer obligations on others continuously, though in doing this he has many a time to bear the insults at the hands of the wicked and the sceptics. In course of time, however, these very people would flock to him and support him when they come to know that their faults have been forgotten and forgiven by him. He is then loved by all and wanted by all. Like the head of a family, his love for others and his concern for the spiritual good of them all is so genuine that, in the third place, whenever they are in great difficulty and are eagerly waiting for him in order to get redress, he comes all of a sudden and relieves them, or brings consolation to them by the power of his grace even from a distance. This he does in order to teach them that when the feeling of dependence on God and the love and faith in Him are genuine and absolute, God will not linger even for a minute, but will jump in the midst of calamities and save his devotees. So, in the fourth place, the active saint will have only one business, namely, to fill the world with God. He would, on that account, so narrate the exploits and the glory of God, and so proclaim the divine Name loudly and dance with joy, that people around him and in his company would also be tempted to do likewise and attain to Godhood. And, finally, as more and more people begin to come into the spiritual fold, the saint keeps the reins in his hand and gets the things done by others.

Sometimes, as a tactful measure, he would even show that he has greater trust in those who are untrustworthy than what he has in his own trustworthy and devout followers. This is like making a thief an officer of the treasury. But the saint does this deliberately, so that the thief being responsible for his charge would be prevented from robbing, and prevent other thieves also from doing the same. As a thief knows the ways of the thieves, it is indeed a good contrivance to set a thief to catch a thief, just as to draw out a thorn which is stuck into the body a thorn is to be used. Instead of naming a person openly as a fool or arrogant, and making him thereby an enemy, is it not better silently to set another fool or an arrogant person to meet him? This will put an end to the trouble and the way will be clear for all; and yet, the hand of the saint will remain unseen.

The saint however should take the greatest precaution to see that he is first securely and permanently lodged in the spiritual life, before he begins to help others in saving their souls. What is the good of trying to save the people from being drowned, if one cannot swim well and save oneself ? It is better to remain unknown and meditate for oneself than to make oneself known as a spiritual helper and then make spiritual wrecks of himself and of others. To be useful to others as an active saint requires the toughness and the courage of a warrior. To saddle an unruly horse and ride it is not a joke. Even so, one who cannot control and tide over the changing situations and environmental conditions in life (upādhis), should better remain content with the bliss of meditation on the Ātman. There he will get all the rest and the peace of mind; and if his devotion would increase day by day, he would get the strength and courage to help others also in their spiritual efforts. In this way, without going out and without moving from place to place as an active saint is expected to do, he too can be of immense help to all those who would visit his place and seek his guidance in spiritual matters. What is of the utmost importance for the saint to remember is that whatever he wishes to preach should be the direct outcome of what he himself has gained spiritually. What he will therefore ask the people to do is only one thing, namely, to meditate upon God with faith and devotion; he will not demand anything else from them. And supposing some of them become indifferent to what he says, he would not mind it much, thinking that it was by a chance that he met them, and that again is a chance that they might go away from him. His is a disinterested service to them. It is in this spirit that he moves from place to place, and himself being full of ecstasy, he preaches and spreads the gospel of God.

Being unmindful to this all, there are pseudo-saints, or saints of far less calibre, who create disciples after disciples without knowing their capacity or willingness to have spiritual knowledge. Naturally, when the disciples run after various objects of desires, the teachers also run after them and try to please them in some or other way, with the result that they fall in disrepute and become unhappy along with their disciples.

89. *Advice to the traveller on the Spiritual path.* (19. *i.* 1-20; *ii.* 1-23; *iii.* 1-30; *v.* 1-30)

Long before one is initiated in the spiritual life, what one should better do is to introspect within himself and remove all the defects which he might possess and which are harmful for the growth of the spiritual life. He should start with the belief that all the miserable and wretched conditions in life are due to sinfulness, and that sinfulness might grow in abundance on account of the miseries in life. Therefore, in order to stop this vicious circle, he should first of all leave away idleness, excessive sleep, jealousy and greed. Then, leaving away all egoism and arrogance, as well as the company of the wicked and the sinful, he should, with all humility put his faith in whatever is being told by the wise, the good and the holy. As the spiritual life has to be commenced with the reading and the hearing of sermons and other spiritual literature, he should visit the places where this might be going on and hear attentively what is being preached. He should then think over what he has heard and do accordingly, and get his doubts resolved by persons who have already realized the end of their spiritual life. Then he should only speak that much which he has come to know, and strive again for knowing something more, and thus rise step by step on the spiritual ladder. He should not straight away say that there are no supernatural beings, gods and deities without knowing, or that there is one Brahman only, and therefore cease to worship and do the various rituals in connection with it, such as applying the sandal-paste, and the offerings of flowers and fruits and so on. He would find that these are useful in their own way for enabling him to realize the higher and higher truths of the spiritual life.

Thus will he rise from the worship of the idols and the images to that of the incarnations of God, and from the worship of those who are dead and gone to the worship of Brahmā, Viṣṇu and Maheśa who are respectively supposed to be the creator, the protector and the destroyer of the universe; and finally, from the worship of these to the contemplation of the Brahman who transcends the three guṇas. It is this real, the imperishable and the highest God who can be seen and realized after being graced by the spiritual teacher. And, after having realized this for oneself, it can be imparted to others as well; but for that one must first win their hearts by sweet and truthful words, suffer with them in their woes, and strive very hard to lift them up.

90. *Degrees of Pervasiveness according to the degrees of Reality.* (20. *i.* 1-30)

The greater the degree of Reality a thing possesses, the greater is its capacity to pervade all other things which fall short of that degree; and conversely, the greater the degree of pervasiveness of a thing, the greater is its degree of reality. Applying this twofold criterion to several entities we can say which thing is more pervasive and on that account more real also. We have however to keep in mind in this connection that pervasiveness is only one of the three characteristics of reality, the other two being self-existence and self-conception. Pervasiveness is different from what is known in the Vedānta philosophy as the quintuple mixture of the five elements. The latter is a theory connected with the Vedāntic view about cosmogony. It states that each of the five elements, namely, earth, water, fire, wind and ākāśa, is composed of one half of itself and one-eighth of each of the remaining four elements. This might perhaps lead one to believe that this is an illustration of pervasion, since each element pervades to some extent in the very constitution of the other elements. But this is no pervasion, it is only a mixture. Pervasion has got a spatial significance in the context in which we are going to speak about it. It has also the sense of being subtle, prior and independent; and as such, one thing can interpenetrate another without being mixed or compounded with it.

A mountain or a river on the earth can be said to be more pervading than another in volume or expanse, that is, as occupying more space. Functionally also, a man may be more busy than another. The earth itself is infinitely more pervading than a tiny portion of it. Water is prior and subtler than earth because it penetrates the latter. Fire is prior to and subtler than water. Fire or light is seen to penetrate water, and is said to exist independently on account of its prior existence and its being the cause of water and earth. Air or wind is more pervasive than earth, water and fire. And finally, ākāśa is considered as the most pervading of all, since it is the first among the elements which has come to exist, the cause of them all, and the subtlest of all, as it occupies more space than anyone of the other four. It is the limitless, empty space which can exist independently even when all other products of it are dissolved. What is necessarily associated thus with pervasiveness, and what therefore becomes the chief characteristic of reality is the independent existence of a thing, even when everything else is dissolved. From this point of view, ākāśa or empty space is the only entity which is all-pervasive and which can exist alone and independently, when everything else along with the four elements is destroyed. Ākāśa then is the only element which can be said to have some claim to reality.

In considering the question about the reality of the elements, we have considered it with reference to the five parts of Māyā or the eight-fold Prakṛti. There remain the three parts of it known as the three guṇas, sattva, rajas and tamas. But they are overcome by one another; and all of them also can be transcended. So, they too are not real. The element of ākāśa also is not ultimately real, because though it is all-pervasive, it has sound as its quality, and is of the nature of tamas (ignorance). It cannot conceive itself, though it can be said in a sense to be self-existing, because none has got any idea regarding the manner in which it is destroyed. Besides, it is a part of Māyā which itself is dependent on the Brahman, and is after all a product and not the first cause.

When we consider the higher categories of mind and the Ātman, the first impression we get of them is that both of them are real. Mind is no doubt a part of the Ātman, and can fly in no time to any place or object and pervade it altogether. But as it flies and attends one object, it is absent in other places and becomes oblivious of other objects. Mind too, therefore, is not real. It is only an instrument, a means only, and it is not at all pervasive as it is supposed to be. The Ātman is the reality behind all the phenomena. But he is, at the same time, designated as the seer, the witness, the internal self and the individual as well as the cosmic soul. As such the Ātman too, even the cosmic one, known as the 'Śivātmā' becomes subject to the rounds of birth and death, as is clear from what the Lord Kṛṣṇa himself tells in the Bhagavadgītā that he has to take births again and again for establishing the kingdom of God. One who realizes the Ātman becomes the Ātman himself, the knowledge incarnate. But there is still in him a tinge of egoism, in that he knows that he knows, and is conscious that he creates, protects and destroys the universe. Knowledge is a relative term, and derives its meaning from its correlative, namely, ignorance. But it must give place to a unitive experience, before the Ātman can be said to become the Brahman to which, in the absence of the 'all', the term 'all-pervasive' also cannot be applied. Brahman as the disembodied state of bliss and peace is only to be silently enjoyed and is not at all capable of being expressed by means of word. The all-pervasiveness of the ākāśa and of the Ātman exists only to culminate in the Brahman.

91. *The commanding qualities of the Ātman.* (20. *vi.* 1-30)

The Ātman alone is the support of consciousness and of all motion and change. Due to him is the power of the mind or the inner sense to think in all possible ways and to attend, to resolve, and to be conscious of being the owner of things. The three guṇas of sattva, raja and tama belong to the Ātman, as also the nine-fold devotion and the fourfold liberation. The effortless, uncontaminated state of the mind is due to the Ātman, who is always the seer, the witness, the knowledge incarnate, and the consciousness which includes both the parts of meditation, namely the mental uttering and hearing the Name of God. The triads of the seer, the seen and the seeing, of the knower, the known and the knowledge, and of the meditator, the object meditated upon and the meditation, are all nothing but the Ātman. The meaning of all the Vedas, the Purāṇas and the sciences; the secret path of the spiritual life, and the omniscient being are all the Ātman itself. The distinctions between man and man, namely, the bound, the aspirant, the sādhaka and the perfected saint; the intellectual clarification and the spiritual illumination; the waking, the sleeping and the dreaming states, as well as the fourth state which goes beyond the three states; the Prakṛti, the Puruṣa and the original Māyā; the eight kinds of bodies of the individual and the cosmos; gods and goddesses; the original Power known as Śiva-śakti or Mūlamāyā, are all due to the Ātman. The creation and sustenance of the world; the vocal and the instrumental music; all the disciplines of knowledge, as also ignorance, illusion and delusion, and the good and the bad propensities of the mind are due to the Ātman. The different kinds of meditation, the elimination of the elements as not constituting the reality, and the consequent surrender of the self, are due to the Ātman. The innumerable gods and goddesses, sages, and suprahuman beings, the sun, the moon, the stars and the zodiac signs and planets etc. owe their existence to the Ātman. In short, the Ātman abounds in qualities; while the Brahman is without any form or quality. Yet, the worship of the Ātman will undoubtedly lead one to the Immutable Brahman, as the Ātman is nothing but the Saguṇa Brahman.

92. *Evolution of the cosmos and the Involution of the spirit.* (20. *ii to v and vii to ix.* 1-211)

Evolution and involution, creation and dissolution, or what is the same thing as Pravṛtti and Nivṛtti, are the two opposite processes of descent and ascent of the same Spirit. Neither in the one nor in the other is the Spirit, or what we may call as the Absolute or the Nirguṇa Brahman, disturbed or contaminated in any way. Notwithstanding its immanence in all the created things or evolutes, the Brahman is as independently real as it would be when all the creation is dissolved. The blissful peace (Ānanda and Śānti) of Brahman remains ever unsullied, full, and without the smallest ripple of happiness or misery of the mundane life. As the evolution courses its way from the subtlest to its grossest form, from the Īśvara or the Ātman to the formation of the eightfold Prakṛti or Māyā consisting of the five elements and the three guṇas, and from this to the various animate and inanimate things and beings of this world including the man, the downward force of the Spirit means more and more forgetfulness on their part about their real nature, that is, of their being non-different from the Brahman, and the wrongful, illusory assumption of their being of the nature of body, senses, mind, intellect and egoism. Thus, during the descent, the One *appears* to become the many, on account of the various layers of the self-projected elements and guṇas of Prakṛti, and there arise the various distinctions and differences of things and beings, as well as the various pulls and pushes of aspirations, emotions, will and egoism. Along with this, comes about the decrease in the original bliss and peace of the Brahman, and the corresponding increase in the misery and the mental worries of man. It then remains for him to be content either by being a slave to Prakṛti and by being bound by the effects of his good and bad actions, or to become free from the fetters of both Prakṛti and Karma, by his devotional acts of surrender to God and meditation on His Name.

The evolution or the descent of the Spirit is a process dealing with the creation of the cosmos. It was decreed by the Brahman and has already been accomplished to the extent to which we are seeing it at present. It is a fact which has to be accepted. Whether the actual process of the evolution was exactly like what is described in the Upaniṣadas, whether all the evolutes came into existence successively or simultaneously, whether the whole account is merely a guess-work, an intellectual exercise, or the description of what actually took place is beyond the ability of any man to say. Perhaps, it might have been thought as a replica in the reverse order of what takes place in the process of the ascent of the Spirit which is left for man to work out during the course of his meditation and contemplation on God. For, it is the ascent which alone is important to the man, and is to be achieved within the short span of his life. The intermediary stages which he would come across by reversing his steps ought to be just the same, as are dogmatically asserted to be in the course of the evolution or the descent. We shall therefore be content by describing the spiritual ascent which is verifiable in experience by adopting the intellectual and the ethico-spiritual life of moral virtues and of devotion and meditation.

As man is essentially a rational being, much can be comprehended by the intellect and accepted as true in fact long before, or even without any direct experience about it. For instance, that all the vegetable kingdom and the creatures and the human beings in the world would perish in course of time, but that the earth would remain as it is, is a truism which will be accepted by all. With a similar exercise of the intellect, it will not be much difficult to acquiesce that the earth too like the other three elements of water, fire and air is bound to perish some time in the distant future, on account of its being physical in nature, though not quite certainly in a fixed order. And when the physical body dies, it goes without saying that all the organs of action and knowledge along with mind, intellect and egoism also will cease to function. But this is not the end we expect. Not death but life must be there in order to enjoy the spiritual good. And it is exactly here that mere intellect will be of no use to us, and that we shall have to get ourselves yoked to the spiritual discipline of meditation. Physiologically, no doubt, we all are living; but while we shall live spiritually, it shall be our death to whatever is material, empirical and sensual in nature. This will be our spiritual ascent, or the ascent of the Spirit in us to its original status of the one, non-dual reality of the Brahman.

How this is achieved, beyond what the intellect has already grasped we shall explain in brief. Soon after one sits in a comfortable posture in a quiet and secluded place and begins to meditate on the divine Name imparted to him by his spiritual teacher, first along with the breaths which he inhales and exhales, and then uttering it and hearing it also mentally, what will happen as the immediate effect of this is, that the whole of the external perceptible world would vanish from his consciousness. Even his breathing would become slow and soft; it might even automatically be suspended for a while, as it happens in the condition of a kind of 'Kumbhaka', (a process in Prāṇāyāma) when both the inhaling and the exhaling of the air stops. This means that for him who has come to this stage of meditation, and at least during the period of meditation, the whole of the physical, external world consisting of the four elements of earth, water, fire, and air, including his own body, his five organs of sense, and five of action, has vanished from his consciousness. Here too, it is not necessary that they should vanish in a particular, fixed order,—an order which is just the reverse of that of the cosmological evolution as described in the Sāṁkhya and the Vedānta systems of philosophy. It is significant that they vanish, and that the meditator is left alone, as if he is identical with the element of ākāśa or the empty space. What might then exist for his consciousness is his own mind and its desires and imaginings and the various memory images which could be recalled. Along with these, there might be also several emotions, prejudices, likes, hatreds and egoism which must be creating a huge mental world for the meditator to wander away from his meditation. For, the mind is the fastest, the subtlest, the most unsteady and the most creative of all, and consequently it is most difficult to have control over it and to make it steady and calm. But here also the remedy is the same, namely meditation. With greater concentration upon the mental uttering and the mental hearing of the divine Name, the mind will not only be pacified but also stopped in doing its function of recalling the memory images or imagining about possible alternatives. With the vanishing of the mind will vanish all the emotional and the volitional appendages of the mind, as also the intellect and the threefold colouring of these by the qualities (guṇas) of sattva, raja and tama of Māyā. And with these again will vanish, though last of all, the inveterate foe of the spiritual life, namely, the egoism of being actively good and obliging, sinless and spiritual.

What now remains at this stage of meditation in the consciousness of the sādhaka is the presence of the immaculate vision of the deity upon whom he contemplates, and on whose Name he had been meditating till then. It is this God, the object of his meditation and contemplation, that is, his own inner Self as having an immaculate, bodily form, who is now to him the creator, the protector and the destroyer of the universe. This constitutes his realization of the Saguṇa Brahman, the originator of all forms and qualities and of all that exists in space and time. He is the knower of all, the immanent presence in all, and the source and the power behind all change and motion. There remains however one stage further to which the sādhaka is necessarily led on account of his very contemplation on the

Saguṇa Brahman. And that is when his Self becomes identified and merged in the Brahman; when his consciousness of being different from the Brahman goes away; when he becomes aware of nothing else but the changeless bliss and peace of Brahman; when, in short, there exists nothing but the Nirguṇa Brahman; and when in the absence of the 'I' or the 'all', even the various epithets of God or the all-doer Ātman, such as, the witness and the knower of all, the immanent presence in all, the transcendent Being of all, the Creator, the Preserver and the Destroyer of all, and so on, appear as derogatory of the everlasting and unique experience of perfect calm and bliss, of a consciousness which is simply to be enjoyed and is incapable of being expressed in words.

Where is now the ākāśa or the empty space ? It is the plentitude of the being of Brahman. What has become of the consciousness of the lapse of time ? There being no change or break in the homogeneous, blissful experience of Brahman, the divisions of time into past, present, and future have no meaning. It is a perpetual presence. How can there be any sense of direction, of up or down, right or left, east or west, etc., when simultaneously, inside and outside, in front of and behind oneself, there is nothing else but Brahman ? Images of gods can be made, worshipped and thrown away; Brahman can neither be caught hold of nor is capable of being cast away, if it is once seen. To realize it, one need not travel to distant places of pilgrimage; one has only to meditate and gaze at it with attachment. That constitutes its worship; and therein lies the final and real consolation and rest for even the greatest of the saints and of the gods. Therefore, one must go by the way of the saints who have realized the Brahman, and not get deluded by doing what the ignorant people do. This is Brahman which is not contaminated by mud, which is not carried away by floods, not burnt by fire, but which is seen as remaining still and unshaken in the mud, in the floods and in the fire. Stand or run away as fast as you can, it will be your constant companion. Look wherever you like, it will be first there before you see anything else. It will be seen as touching and enveloping all things, without being touched or enveloped by anything. None can go beyond it just as a bird cannot fly beyond the sky. So pure and immaculate it is that the bliss of contemplation on it is ineffable indeed.

93. *The author of Dāsabodha is God, says Rāmadāsa.* (20. *x.* 1-37)

If God is the All-doer, and the beginning and the end of all, will it not be a lie, asks Rāmadāsa, to say that he is the author of Dāsabodha ? In fact, whatever has been said in it is due only to the grace of my Lord, Śrī Rāma, who is always proud of his devotees. I have no delusion regarding the permanence of my body; for it is made up of the five elements which will ultimately be destroyed. I have reached the Impersonal Brahman; I have measured the extent of Māyā and its elements; the dream of the phenomenal world has vanished, the moment I was awakened to spiritual consciousness, and I began to enjoy the ineffable bliss; I have gone beyond the rounds of birth and death.

Why should I then praise the Dāsabodha ? Whoever will ponder carefully over the work which is divided into twenty groups (daśakas) of ten sections (samāsas) will gradually come to know the whole of the spiritual life. He will realize the Ātman who resides in his body and will come to know directly that the Ātman alone is the All-doer.

Chapter IV

THE UNFADING PEARLS IN DĀSABGDHA

[The first figure indicates the number of the Daśaka (Chapter), the second Roman figure indicates the number of Samāsa (Section), and the last figure or figures indicate the number of verses as we find them in the Dāsabodha of Rāmadāsa.]

1. i. 4. Devotion is the surest way to realize God.

1. ii. 7. With the sight of the vision of God, the mind loses its power to attend to other objects.

1. iv. 6. God, though beyond Māyā, has necessarily to be described by the help of Māyā.

1. v. 26. The saint alone can reveal the knowledge of God.

1. vi 7. Be as pure as fire by seeing the vision of God.

1. vi. 9. Nothing is beyond the ken of a God-realized person.

1.viii. 3. God resides where his devotees sing his Name.

1. ix. 3. Realization of Brahman is as concrete as the cash-value of a thing.

1. ix. 26. Without God everything else is weariness of the flesh.

1. x. 50. Treat even the longest life as if it is for a couple of days.

2. i. 39-40. Fool is he who thinks that his family life and wealth are all in all.

2. ii. 32, 39. Do not be ashamed to surrender to the Spiritual teacher and to meditate on God.

2. vii. 38, 58. Know him to be endowed with Sattvaguṇa (the drive for purity and spiritual illumination) who has given up all his desires, pleasures and egoism for the sake of God.

2. vii. 83. Know him to be endowed with Sattvaguṇa who becomes afflicted with the afflictions of others, and who does not become jealous when others are joyful.

2. ix. 18. Increase your devout meditation to such a pitch that even the wicked who used to scoff at you will begin to admire the path of devotion.

2. x. 23. One who talks about the knowledge of Brahman without realization is a learned fool.

3. ix. 5, 59. Death levels down all except those who have realized the Ātman.
3. x. 13. God behaves with us as we behave with Him.
3. x. 27. 37. A sound body and a long span of life are the greatest assets for spiritual life.
4. iii. 3, 14. Meditate on the Name of God at fixed hours and remember Him always.
4. iv. 14, 17. Be identified with that which you will visualize as the result of meditation.
4. v. 29, 33. Whatever you possess and whatever you like best, offer that to God.
4. vi. 7, 9, 16. Make salutations over salutations to God and to the saints.
4. vii. 2, 28. Serve in all respects the Guru and God, both mentally and physically.
4. viii. 6, 23, 31, 32. If you wish to be befriended by God, leave all pleasures and confide your secrets to God and the Guru with absolute faith and love.
4. ix. 10, 11, 15. Who is this thief of an 'I' (ego) who wants to remain as a separate entity besides the blissful Ātman, when even the Māyā or the Prakṛti itself vanishes ?
4. x. 30. Liberation consists in the indivisible union with God which can be had by transcending the realm of qualities.
5. i. 23. Realization of the Brahman is impossible without the grace of a realized soul.
5. ii. 22, 28, 38. Rare is the saint who has no desire and who insists upon having control over the senses and meditation on the Name of God.
5. ii. 52. Rare is the saint who even after realizing God resorts to meditation.
5. iii. 8-10. A pure heart as the soil, the potent divine Name received from a great realized soul as the seed, watering the plant by constant meditation and fencing it by virtues, are the pre-requisites of an excellent spiritual harvest.
5. v. 3. 36. To know the past and the future, or to read the thoughts in the minds of others, is in no sense the knowledge of God.
5. vi. 1-5. Ātma-jñāna means the seeing of the Ātman by the

Ātman. It goes beyond the range of the senses, the mind and the intellect.

5. vi. 13-14 There will be no spiritual gain by repeating the statement 'I am the Brahman'.

5. vi. 50 In the blazing fire of the realization of the Brahman, the straw of the perceptible world and the false notion of the 'I' will be completely burnt.

5, vi. 58-59 Form the daily habit of sitting in a secluded place and of listening to the divine Name as it is being meditated upon, so that you will be soon disgusted with all Godless objects.

5. vi. 73 To cease to meditate on the divine Name after the realization of God is to become bound again.

5.vii. 39 Know him to be a bound person who is after wealth and woman.

5. viii. 6, 24 One who repents over his misdeeds has still a chance to save himself if he comes in contact with a saint.

5. ix. 4 Acceptance by the Guru is the first step towards realizing God.

6. i. 14. 15, 31 Verily, fallen is the person who has not realized God; but if he wishes to save himself, he should come in contact with a saint and be initiated by him.

6. ii. 42 With the realization of Brahman, the saint becomes unconcerned with what might happen to his body.

6. iii. 5 Face to face must be seen the eternal vision of the Brahman.

6. iii. 24, 32, 35 Surrender of the Self will be complete when all the distinctions vanish.

6. iv. 24 One who realizes the Brahman is a Brāhmaṇa.

6. v. 21 Māyā is that which is devoured by time; Brahman is that which devours time.

6. vi. 30 Disputations have no end; turn them into such fruitful conversation as will culminate in the bliss of Brahman.

6. vi. 55 Though the worship of the Saguṇa aspect of God is not the final end of devotion, it is the indispensable support of the endeavour to attain the Nirguṇa Brahman.

6. vii. 10, 22 To do as the Guru asks you to do and to serve him are the foremost conditions of having any spiritual gain.

6. vii. 24 There will be no greater misfortune than to fall away from the esteem of the Guru.

6. vii. 33-36 Frustration and misery will be the end of the egoistic feeling that man is the doer, while success, fame and spiritual power will be the fruits of the experience that Rāma is the doer.

6. vii. 43 The world is as good as unreal to him who is absorbed in the meditation on the Name of 'Rāma'; and then with the vision of Rāma, the whole of the phenomenal world will appear as a dream.

6. viii. 38-43 The perceptible world of the senses is believed to be real, because both the world and the senses are the products of Avidyā (Māyā). Hence, the Brahman remains unknown.

6. ix. 1, 3, 16 Penetrating through the perceptible world, the saint sees the hidden treasure of the divine knowledge; while those who seek philosophical opinions only are no better than the fillers of their belly.

6. ix, 19-20 God is hidden no doubt; but He can be found out in the company of the saints.

6. ix. 26-27 The difference between the direct and the immediate vision of God and the imaginative, mental visualization of the image of God, is as wide as between the cash and the credit values of things.

6. ix. 29 One can meet and be permanently united with God in this very life.

6. x. 10 The imparting of the Spiritual experience by a great realized saint is like giving sugar to a person who does not know what sweetness means.

6. x. 14-15, 30, 42 To say that the Ātman is the witness of all is not the expression of the whole and the final truth. In fact, it is the Ātman who sees the Ātman only.

7. i. 18 Let the mind make salutations to the Lord when it would become impossible to salute Him by the help of the body, for instance, during the conditions of deep meditation or of contemplation.

7. i. 20-21 The whole of the worldly life is itself a great dream, during which man groans under the weight of

greed and grief; and yet, he says with ignorance that wealth, wife, sons, daughters and so on belong to him.

7. i. 28, 46 Words of silent meditation can be heard if the meditator has his ears spread all over his body and mind.

7. ii. 10, 17-18 To apprehend the Brahman is, no doubt, impossible for the speech, the mind and the intellect. But what this really means is that it can be realized without their aid, and that its bliss can be enjoyed without there being any prior want or desire.

7. ii. 31 Great saints are different physically but non-different spiritually.

7. ii. 38-41 Notwithstanding the pull and the push of the bodily pleasures and egoism, the sādhaka should, with courage and devout meditation, get himself assimilated gradually with the Brahmanic joy and peace.

7. ii. 47 Now as sound, now as light, now as the feeling of the on-rush of energy, now as a delightful presence, and now as power and so on, will be the various forms and modes in which the Brahman might manifest itself.

7. iii. 44, 49 To meditate on the pure idea, that is, on the Name of God, is to put an end to all other God-less ideas. This is the supramental, natural, and the most joyful, peaceful and equipoised condition (Samādhi) of a great saint.

7. iv. 16, 20 Brahman is immanent in the world; but being also transcedent, it can exist by itself with or without the world.

7. iv. 27-37 Brahman penetrates the earth and the adamant, but is not hard like them; on the contrary, it is subtler and softer than the sky. Incapable of being destroyed by the elements, it fully pervades even the so-called vacuum or void. It cannot be intercepted by anything, nor can it be avoided to be seen if it becomes manifest face to face.

7. vi. 54 Liberation means complete annihilation of the sense of egoism.

7. vii. 52, 53 Get over egoism by first finding it out; and meditate and enjoy the bliss of Brahman by realizing the Brahman.

7. vii. 56, 61, 63 Do meditate on God, but avoid the spiritual egoism, that you are a great devotee of God. Then alone you can enjoy the disembodied condition even while you have a body.

7. vii. 64-66 Do not leave meditation on the Name even after you realize the Brahman. Or else, you will become idle, and developing your bodily consciousness you will falsely think that you are liberated. Thereby you might indulge in doing sins only, or waste your time in sleep and disputations which will bear no fruit.

7. vii. 70-71 Do not be ashamed of the people who, out of ignorance, might scoff at you and say, 'O, here is a credulous person who has given himself to meditation.' The moment even a perfected saint leaves away his practice of sādhanā, he might fall down from his high pedestal and become no better than one who is bound by the fetters of Māyā.

7. viii. 9, 38, 47 Śravaṇa or the hearing of the scriptural passages, especially that of the divine Name by the mental ears, if resorted to again and again like food and water, has got the power of making one united with the meaning of it, namely, God himself.

7. x. 1 Oh, the power of Māyā, on account of which what is real appears as unreal, and the unreal as real.

7. x. 10-15, 32 Places of pilgrimage and holy waters become themselves purified when the saints look at them with grace. Hence it is that whatever may be the place where the dead body of the saint falls, it becomes a place of pilgrimage. And hence again, those who worship such a saint are also purified and saved.

8. i. 40-41 Fools are they who say that the world is the same as God on account of His being immanent in it; for, like the potter of the jars, God is the transcendent cause of the world.

8. ii. 46 One must not forget that gold alone is real, and not the names and forms of the ornaments which are made out of it.

8. iii. 1, 2, 38 A rope is a rope with or without the apparent serpent on it. The serpent does not exist; but it appears

on the rope and lasts so long as its cause, namely, the ignorance of the rope lasts. Even so, the world appears on account of Māyā and lasts so long as its cause, namely, the ignorance of Brahman lasts. With the knowledge of the rope, the illusory serpent goes away; even so, with the realization of Brahman, the world becomes as good as non-existent.

8. iv. 58 If you wish to see God, you must cross the front gate in the form of this phenomenal world.

8. v. 66 Awareness of ākāśa implies that it is different from the seer; but in becoming aware of one's own Form, he becomes identical with it.

8. vi. 36 Sleep, idleness and absent-mindedness are the characteristics of the fool and the ignorant.

8. vi. 46-48 Faith and intelligence are both required to shed one's egoism and to become united with God.

8. vii. 11, 29, 30 Even acts of philanthrophy and charity, if done with egoism, become the cause of new births and new bondage.

8. vii. 59 To become initiated into spiritual life by a great saint is itself the promise of liberation.

8. viii. 21, 22 A river does not return after it has once gone into the sea. Even so, the devotee is not separated after he is united with God.

8. viii. 43, 46 Who will bother to kill the illusory serpent after one has seen the rope on which it had once appeared and caused fear ? Even so, what realized soul will fly away from the world after knowing that it is short-lived and is like a dream ?

8. ix. 1 If some one drinks ambrosia, his body also is bound to shine with divine lustre.

8. ix. 9 The chief characteristic of a saint is that he is always intent in looking at the vision of God, whatever may be his condition or activity while he is in society.

8. ix. 26, 29, 39, 46 He becomes as fearless as Brahman and devoid of blemishes like anger, jealousy, sensuous desires and so on.

8. x. 70-72 One might be able to cross the phenomenal world; but it is very likely he may make the blunder of consider-

ing that the void which is caused thereby is the Brahman. The void itself will then be a new object for him, instead of the objects of the phenomenal world. Therefore, avoiding the void also, he should continue his meditation and realize the Brahman, and then realize himself as non-different from Brahman.

9. ii. 23-25, 34-35 The two views about the Brahman, namely, that 'all this is Brahman', and that 'what transcends all this world of Māyā is Brahman', can be the subject-matter of argumentation and therefore of speech only, though this might yield intellectual pleasure. In the case of the direct experience of Brahman, however, which goes beyond speech and beyond the 'all' of Māyā, there is no scope for either of the two views. Hence it is that the Vedas and the saints prefer to be silent about their experience of Brahman.

10. vii. 10. 11 Never think that the realized saint will be born again. But when it is seen that his power lingers behind him and works out miracles, it should be remembered that this is due to his having lived a highly meritorious life, namely, of living in the company of God.

10. vii. 14 If one remains in a solitary place and fixes his soul on the vision of God with all attention and will, he will surely be endowed with divine power.

10. vii. 20-22 God is the giver of fruits, no doubt. But if you worship Him in order that your desires should be fulfilled, you will get the fruits only and not God. On the other hand, if you be devoted to God and meditate upon Him, you will not only meet God, but without your asking you might get the desired fruits also.

10. viii. 20 If, being puffed up with pride, you desert the company of the saints, then it should be upto you to think as to who would be the loser. The ignorant and the unholy will not be able to save you.

10. viii. 21-24 If you are not absolutely convinced that you have become sinless and have gone beyond birth and death, by experiencing that you are identical with God, and that God is the only doer and creator of the universe, then remember that whatever you might have done by

way of meditation and contemplation is not as yet sufficient.

10. ix. 24. There will be no realization of the Ātman without the grace of the Guru, and no end to karma and its effects without the realization of the Ātman.

10. x. 52-56 Can there be disturbance of any kind in the supramental condition of God-realization ? The vision of a Form of God is the vision of the real form of the Self as Brahman. This is the only truth, and the only great merit which can be had by the grace of God. All else is falsehood and sin.

11. i. 9 The will of God is known as the original (Mūlā) Māyā with its eightfold distinctions of the five elements and the three guṇas. The same is also known as Guṇa-Māyā on account of its three guṇas. And then when it takes the form of this universe, it is known as Avidyā or the inert (jaḍa) matter.

11. ii. 40 Let your external behaviour appear as being guided by Prakṛti; but let your mind be fixed on the reality, namely, the Brahman.

11, iii. 3, 4, 6,7 Where is the time left to have contact with God, if the childhood is lost in ignorance, youth in the enjoyment of pleasures, and old age in disease and infirmity ? And when will you be awake to spiritual life, when on all hands, people and your own kith and kin are dying, and your own house is on fire ?

11. vi. 14 Like the immanent but invisible Ātman, the realized soul also should be at the back of all good works, but remain unnoticed.

11. vii. 1, 10, 21, 22 In the ever-flowing river of Prakṛti, there is also the invisible current of the river Gaṅgā in the form of divine presence, which purifies and saves the world. One should therefore take the help of this divine current and swim against the flow of Prakṛti and reach its very source, namely, the Brahman, even the sight of which would purify him. And then, if he looks back on the stream of Prakṛti he would find that the water in it has dried up, and that he alone remains being united with Brahman.

12. i. 2, 3 One who does not discharge his worldly duties properly would hardly be able to act according to the rules of spiritual discipline. On the other hand, one who is averse to spiritual life would be miserable in his old age. Therefore, one should give up idleness and be honest and conscientious in doing his duty as well as in being devoted to God.

12. ii. 18, 19, 24. Toil hard, but win the hearts of others by exhibiting your virtues, especially of forbearance and forgiveness. And, if it becomes too difficult for you to forgive and hold up courage, quit the place in silence.

12. iv. 12, 20 What is very essential in spiritual life is the combination of the realization of Brahman and the renunciation of all other things. Without any disgust for God-less things, there will only be a verbal knowledge about God, and the growth of God-realization will be much hampered. And without God-realization, renunciation will only be a pretence. One must therefore make himself free internally as well as externally.

12. viii. 3, 4 The sense of the passage of the time depends on the awareness of changes in the external phenomena and in the internal conditions of mind. In the absence of any such change, there will be no consciousness of time also.

12. viii. 19, 23, 30, 34 What are known as Pravṛtti and Nivṛtti are respectively the tendencies of man towards having worldly pleasures or the spiritual joy of living in the presence of God. Thus will people be divided in two camps, in a general way. A rare among them, however, lives in both the worlds. In this mortal fair, there is no gain greater than God.

12. ix. 26 A great saint alone is able to carry the glory of God beyond all that is phenomenal in him and in the world.

12. x. 1, 2 Be yourself first perfectly satisfied by partaking of the spiritual food; but whatever remains after you have dined, you should distribute it among others, and not allow it to be wasted. One who is very strong and can swim well should try to save others from being drowned.

12. x. 13, 34 Remember that death is certain; therefore make haste to meet God and enable others also to do so.

As for me, says Rāmadāsa, I have made the vow of not asking my disciples to give me anything except their promise that they would meditate on God even after I pass away.

13. ii. 8, 9 Devotion to God will not remain different from the knowledge of God; for, it is devotion which first enables one to see God and then to become united with Him.

13. ii. 27, 28, 30 The process of the unison with God is one of rising higher and higher not only from falsehood to truth, or from the unreal to the real, but also from what is partially real to what is wholly real. Thus, the transition is to be made from the vision of one's own static Self, to the vision of the mutable, dynamic caitanya, and from that to the experience of the identity of the Self with the Immutable and uncontaminable Brahman. At this stage, the devotional language about liberation will also have no meaning; for it will be the condition of ecstatic unison with the Nirguṇa, the unspeakable Brahman.

13. vii. 13, 14, 26, 29 The mind has a peculiarity of its own. It gets itself assimilated with the meanings of words as well as with various objects. The soul should therefore be fixed on the divine Name so that it would rise along with the mind to the Saguṇa and the Nirguṇa nature of God.

14. iii. 23, 30 Love for God should so increase day by day that the devotee should not feel ashamed of the people around him, while he dances with joy and sings the Name and the glories of God.

14. v. 3, 4 An extraordinary phenomenon would it be if gold should emit fragrance, or the sugar-cane should bear fruit. Equally uncommon is the saint who is free from any desire and has both learning and realization of God.

14. v. 9, 10, 12, 25 He is a learned fool who, instead of narrating with love and emotion the glorious deeds of the Lord while he is standing before an image of God, preaches unto others that the Nirguṇa aspect of God alone is real. Equally foolish is he who goes out of the way and is lost

in describing the beauty of women, though they might be the residents of the heaven. In fact, such an one is a loser in both ways. His faith in the saguṇa aspect of God is destroyed by his verbal knowledge about the Nirguṇa Brahman; and there being no realization of God as Nirguṇa, he gets himself plunged in doubts and temptations only.

14. v. 33-35 In a similar way, the musician also who sings and praises the glories of God is carried away from God, if he becomes mindful of the tune and the melody of the song only.

14. viii. 24, 36, 43 True meditation of God consists in meditation on His Name, and not upon any image of God. What good can be achieved by the meditation of a broken mind on an object which might be equally broken? The sign of true meditation is that the mind of the meditator should neither be disturbed by imagination nor by any doubt. A garland made of imaginary flowers may prove to be too short for being placed round the neck of an imagined deity which might suddenly become too tall.

14. ix. 26 One who has known the King will not make any mistake regarding who the King is. Even so, one who has seen God will not make any mistake about Him.

15. i. 10, 11 Alas, the mean-minded person resorts to black art and witch-craft in order to ruin others. He does not know that he would thereby displease the Lord of the Universe who is immanent in the hearts of all.

15. i. 21-22 If one takes pride in sticking to what is true, just and real, then it is no egoism.

15. i. 26, 30, 31, 34 Let people take you to be a simpleton by looking to your dress and external appearance. You should be wise enough to meet all, but select only the prominent and the efficient from them as your comrades, because they would help you to further the cause of upholding the virtuous and the spiritual life. Then the commoners also will join and help you.

15. ii. 18, 21-23 The active saint speaks only a few pointed words, but attracts the hearts of all. He might look as a

beggar and live in the valleys of the mountains, but caring for the good of all, he carries on his meditation regularly, so that people should also come to know the direct way of devotion to reach God.

15. ix. 18, 29 Sinful is he who has gone away from the Ātman. On the other hand, for him who is whole-heartedly devoted to God, there would be nothing which is wanting. Even Prakṛti would change her nature and be helpful to him in leading him beyond the phenomenal world, as it did, says Rāmadāsa, in his own life.

16. ix. 4, 16 What is known as Nirguṇa is but another name for that which contains in it infinite qualities and which lasts for ever.

16. x. 30, 31 Whatever is not supported by the grace of God is bound to be destroyed sooner or later; and this may happen all of a sudden. Therefore, one should make haste to meditate on God with faith and love.

17. i. 6, 9, 13 Body is the temple in which God resides. Therefore, if one wishes to be free from disease and infirmity he should fear Him always and offer Him the fivefold pleasures which arise from the five senses, and meditate upon Him in order to have His grace.

17. i. 23, 29 One who is always in contact with God should alone be called as a 'Yogī', as the root 'yuj' meaning 'to join' suggests.

17. iii. 17 Taking the help of wind (one's own breaths) one who meditates and goes beyond it, will find that God is very close to him.

17. iii. 24-25 Greater than the eightfold yoga or the philosophic knowledge is the devotional way of meditation and contemplation.

17. iv. 25-26 One should never equate merit and sin, the saint and the voluptuous, under the pretext that all this is Brahman.

17. v. 1, 2, 6-8 The number of a man's breaths during twenty-four hours is twentyone thousand and six hundred. If he were to repeat the divine Name along with each breath, that will be his most natural meditation known as

'Ajapā', that is, meditation done without counting the number by means of a rosary.

17. vi. 18 The experience of Brahman will ever be the only unmixed joy and peace.

18. i. 22-23 Rāre is the person who observes the activities of the Ātman. Even a little of this knowledge will burn his sins.

18. ii. 28-29 One should meditate on God to such an extent that one should feel that whatever he speaks is due to the grace of God.

18. iv. 34, 36, 37 One might worship even the bodily form of a saint who has realized God; for, that may perhaps please God. But what is the use of worshipping the bodies of other persons who are as stupid and as away from God as an ass is.

18. viii. 11-12 People go in search of God and visit places of pilgrimage, not knowing that He lives in their heart. And, then, what they find in all those places is water and stone only.

18. viii. 20-21 Whatever works are done by people out of ignorance become only a source of fresh hindrance for them. In fact, why should anyone be attached to God, if he will not become free from the bondage of works?

18. viii. 22-23 Worship first the Saguṇa God, and then being graced by him, know his Nirguṇa aspect also, and become one with it.

18. x. 3-4 Do not expect that every time you meditate upon God, you must receive a fresh reward from Him. But meditate and wait for His grace; God is sure to bless you.

18. x. 49-50 One who becomes joyful while meditating silently on God will be the foremost among the seekers to receive the grace of God and to know the secret of the divine will and plan.

19. iv. 9-10 A great saint is as pure as fire; his purpose of life is to confer moral and spiritual good on all.

19. viii. 29 To contemplate for some time and then to be active for some time ought to be the rule for a sādhaka.

19. ix. 23-24 Know ye well as to who is bad and wicked, but do not expose him. On the contrary, treat him as you

would treat the good and the gentle. Otherwise he would be a difficult problem for you.

19. x. 8 With devotion to God as your shield, do whatever you think to be right and good.

19. x. 22 To lead an active, spiritual and moral life requires courage, strength and intelligence. How can a weak and a coward cope up with the task ?

20. iii. 14 Unhidden is flowing the banner of the Lord, Rāma, and is proclaiming to the world that He is the omnipresent Ātman of all. One who is fortunate will know Him.

20. iii. 25-27 Among the multitudes of men, there are few who are good, and among the good there are very few who are saints. But among several saints, rare is the saint who has realized God. One must find out such a saint and get himself benefited by his company.

20. iv. 26, 28 Works are necessary to execute a plan successfully. But they must be supported by the grace of God. Then will a man know that God is the real doer, and the giver and the enjoyer of all, and that man is nothing.

20. vii. 24 When saints who have realized God meet together, they verily enjoy a seclusion which is unique.

20. x. 16, 19, 36 Brahman is that which can at once be experienced as being the same, homogeneous Being on all the sides of a man, above his head, and as filling the whole of the space. All is rest and peace then; and there remains no consciousness of the whole of the phenomenal world nor of one's own body.

20. x. 30-35 How can I then say, asks Rāmadāsa, that 'Dāsabodha' is my work and not of God ? I shall be dishonest if I say that God is not the sole author of it.

Chapter V

SELECTIONS FROM OTHER WORKS

A. Verses Addressed to the Mind

1 I make salutations to the Lord, Gaṇeśa, and to Śāradā, the Goddess of Learning, in order that I should be able by their grace to realize the Infinite God who is at once both Saguṇa and Nirguṇa.

2 Bhakti (devotion) is the only means by which God will reveal Himself; but one must also lead his life in a moral and upright way, and avoid what is considered as blameworthy.

3 Blessed is he who is morally good, and being devoted to God (Rāma), meditates upon him in the early hours of the morning.

4 Do not harbour any evil or sinful thought; let your mind be fixed on what is essential and lasting, namely, morality and the Name of God.

5 Leave away all thoughts about the sensuous life, and stick to what is eternally True.

6 If you become angry, you will only repent afterwards; leave away also the hydra-headed monster of desire; nor should you have any pretentiousness and jealousy.

7 With extraordinary courage, bear the insults hurled at you; but so far as you are concerned, speak only sweet words, and that too with humility so that people may be pleased with you.

8 Act in such a way that people will speak well about you even after you pass away. Never mind, if like a piece of sandlewood, you have to toil hard in doing good to others. The saints will be pleased with you.

9 Do not have a greedy eye on the wealth of others; you will thereby incur sin only, the effects of which you shall have to experience. Besides, you will be unhappy when you do not get that wealth.

10 Forget the pleasures of your body and fix your affection on Rāma only ; you will thereby know that even the bodily pains will not be able to distract you from the experience of divine bliss.

11 None is there in this world who is happy in every way. Search, and you will find that every one will reap what he has sown.

12 Do not lend your mind to sorrows and anxiety. Think not of the body and its considerations ; and you will be able to enjoy the bliss of liberation even while you are living.

13 Make haste to leave all the crookedness of the mind; for death is approaching you every moment. Such a great potentate as Rāvaṇa had suddenly to lose his kingdom on account of his sinful deed.

14 Whatever may be the karma due to which men are born in this world, they all, whether great or small, must go into the jaws of death.

15 Due to egoism and ignorance it is that man thinks about his own greatness, but never about his death. Alas, he has to leave all and to die one day. For after all, this is a mortal world.

16 One dies, and another mourns for him; but . 'no dies soon afterwards. It is the greed of man whic keeps him perpetually miserable and so becomes the cause of his rebirth.

17 Vain is the anxiety of man; for whatever is to happen does happen as the unseen result of his previous actions. Not knowing man mourns over the separation or loss of things.

18 Why do you sing the glory of a man ? Sing instead praises unto the Lord, Rāma, who has been extolled by the Vedas and the Purāṇas. For, this alone will bring about your well-being.

19 Do not leave the path of Truth and take to that of the untruth. Speak the truth and truth alone, and never tell a lie. For, once a lie, it is always a lie.

20 How I wish my mind should be free from desires, and especially from those concerning wealth and women; for, then alone there will be a chance for me to realize God and put an end to the rounds of birth and death.

21 Every hour, death is approaching you nearer and nearer.

There will be none except God who will relieve you at the time of death. Utter therefore constantly the Name of Rāma. All other talk will yield you no good.

22 Why should you waste your life and grieve like the common run of people ? Let the Name of God be on your tongue at all times; and let not sin-begetting egoism touch you in the least.

23 Do not feel yourself bored by listening to me. Is there any guarantee that you would be able to have the vision of Rāma at some future time, or of happiness following happiness ? Be sure, everything except God and His Name will come to nothingness.

24 Try your utmost to protect the body; death will ultimately take it away. Get yourself devoted to Rāma, and cease to be anxious about what would happen to your worldly life.

25 Coward that thou art, thou art afraid of this worldly life. Take courage, and leave away fear. For, over thy head is the protection of the Lord Rāma. He will never forsake thee even though Yama, the God of death, is full of wrath.

26 Hold fast in your mind what I say as the truth. Rāma is merciful and proud of his devotees, and so will never forsake them. He has taken a bow in his hand; seeing him the god of death is filled with horror.

27 Can there be any one in the whole world, who would dare to look even askance with suspicion or anger at the servants of Rāma who is proud of his devotees and who would never forget to protect them ?

28 Indifference to devotees is foreign to the nature of Rāma. The Purāṇas describe him as one who has made a vow to bear all the burden of his devotees on his own head. But, alas, man is lacking in faith.

29 With what attitude God behaves with man depends on with what attitude man behaves with him. Not only does Rāma not neglect his devotees, but he protects them also if they put their faith in him.

30 How can Rāma be indifferent to his devotees when he is bliss incarnate and their saviour ? He is always very

close to them; but he only wishes that they should show a little courage when difficulties or dangers crop up.

31 Instead of being indifferent to his devotees, he jumps as if from above and saves them from calamities. He is like the rising Sun who removes the pangs of separation of the Chakravāka birds during night. Let therefore the drums be beaten in honour of the devotion to God.

32 I pray to you, O my mind, to have your lodgement in Rāma and look at him with wonder and joy.

33 Reside in Rāma whom the Vedas and the Purāṇas have extolled; and be ever content by offering all your fickleness at His feet.

34 Reside in Rāma and look at him intently and with all reverence. You will be able thereby to banish all your evil thoughts and to experience all the divine joy.

35 Wander not from place to place; you will be simply tired thereby and will not derive any joy or benefit. Instead, make your lodgement in Rāma only.

36 Mind only one thing then; befriend yourself to God, Rāma, to such an extent that you can be said to be living in Him. You will then be able to hear the musical sound of his anklets, which will as if proclaim that He is your saviour.

37 Achieve what is spiritually good by constantly meditating mentally upon the Name, Rāma, and by not uttering a word which does not refer to His glory.

38 Be dumb with the people, but celebrate the Name of Rāma with great respect. Leave away that house where the Name cannot be meditated upon, and go straight into a forest where you can do so with joy.

39 Alas, what an attachment people feel for those in whose company Rāma cannot be meditated upon. This will simply produce egoism and put an end to all spiritual joy.

40 Whoever is alert and thoughtful will gaze at the vision of Rāma with all attention. For, he knows that whatever time is spent without the company of Rāma

would be a great loss to him, and would bring nothing but weariness to him.

41 Blessed is he among the servants of Rāma, who sees by his physical eyes the same vision of Rāma which he sees within him, and who keeps on glorifying the qualities of Rāma.

42 Blessed is the servant of Rāma who does not spare his body while promoting the cause of God. Whatever duties fall to his lot, he does them faithfully, while the Name of Rāma remains on his tongue.

43 Blessed is the servant of Rāma who behaves as he speaks, who sees and worships only one supreme God even though he is looking at other several deities, and who entertains no doubt about this.

44 Blessed is that servant of Rāma who is not overtaken by lust and other desires, who leads a life of celibacy, who is equally unconcerned with pleasures and pains, who has not a tinge of ignorance in him, and who has become perfectly tranquil in mind.

45 Blessed is that servant of Rāma, who having left away jealousy, arrogance and selfishness, is not entangled by the attachments of worldly life, but who speaks with humility and with a sweet tongue.

46 Blessed is that servant of Rāma who passes his time in contemplation, and in joyful conversation with people with a view to arrive at the truth regarding the nature of the ultimate Reality and the source of the universe. In doing so, he never allows himself to be drawn in disputations which only make a man egoistic and arrogant.

47 Blessed is that servant of Rāma who is straightforward, truthful and endearing to all.

48 Blessed is that servant of Rāma who has unshakeable faith in Him, who never allows imagination to get the better of him, and who is fond of frequenting the forest for the purpose of doing silent meditation.

49 Blessed is that servant of Rāma who has made Rāma himself as his debtor on account of his devotion to

Him, and who without any selfish desire in his mind feels always thirsty for the love of Rāma.

50 Blessed is that servant of Rāma who, being full of mercy for the miserable and the needy, is always kind and helpful to them. How indeed can anger touch his mind at all ?

51 Make your life blessed by devout and daily meditation on the Name, Rāma. Then alone will you be free from all inhibitions and unconcerned with all that might befall on you.

52 Do not entertain even the slightest tinge of desire, if you wish to meditate on Rāma. For, while desire is the indication of sin, you will not be able to meet Rāma without being sinless.

53 Imagination begets imagination a thousand-fold. But this is not the way to meet Rāma. One whose mind is full of desires, and who has no love and reverence for Rāma will never be able to meet him.

54 Rāma is a wish-yielding tree or as one might say, a a wish-yielding cow, or a wish-yielding jewel. Can any thing be compared with him, or can any one be able to describe him ? For he alone is omnipotent.

55 If you are a devotee of Rāma, remember then that you are as if standing under a wish-yielding tree. If you then become sorrowful or engage yourself in disputation with God-realized souls, you shall only increase your grief.

56 Besides, your meditation will come to an end ; no longer will you feel the bliss of it. With consciousness of distinctions and disputes your mind will perforce be a store of anger, grief, and agitation. And there will be an end to your courage and resolution.

57 Your condition then will be like that of a man who possesses a wish-yielding cow but who wanders begging for butter-milk. Instead of having the knowledge of God, you will have disputations only. Alas, if in spite of having a wish-yielding jewel in hand one would beg for pieces of glass, God would certainly give them in abundance to him !

58 Perpetually wretched will be the life of him who gives himself up to the enjoyment of sensual pleasures; for his mind will be always infatuated and agitated; there will be no firm resolve; and above all, there will be in his mind no place for Rāma.

59 Remembering therefore that a fool will merely increase his sorrow, do not lead a life which is bereft of devotion and reverence for Rāma. Do not centre your desires on wealth, house and comforts only.

60 This worldly life is not only a short-lived show, but also fraught with dangers. How can one expect to be happy by eating poison? Meditate upon Rāma if you wish to find out what is really blissful.

61 Meditate upon Rāma in the early hours before sunrise. He will protect his devotees and ward off their dangers. Besides, being very powerful, bold and courageous, he is very beautiful to look at, just as dark as the cloud is.

62 Of extraordinary power is the Lord, Rāma, who holds a bow in his hand. What to speak of ordinary men before him, when even the terrible Death trembles with fear at his sight. Meditate therefore upon Rāma in the early hours before sunrise.

63 Meditate upon Rāma in the early hours before sunrise ; and leaving away jealousy and the other evil ways of life, worship him with devotion. For, he will remove the cause of your fear and make you full of joy and happiness.

64 One who has the Name of Rāma always on his tongue and has left being idle and arrogant, will for ever be free from all sorts of miseries. Necessarily, then, one must meditate on Rāma in the early hours before sunrise.

65 As the utterance of the Name Rāma is able to wash away all sins, and as it constitutes the highest merit, it will enable a man to become one with Him. Therefore, do meditate on that Name in the early hours before sunrise.

66 Has a man to spend any money, if he meditates on Rāma in the early hours before Sunrise ? He will thereby

only save himself from his great enemy in the form of this very worldly life.

67 Why should one go in for practising such penances as will torture the body, when the greatest of the calamities can be warded off by repeating the Name, Rāma? Has not the Lord Śaṅkara also resorted to meditation on that Name when he suffered from the effects of the deadly poison which he drank? Why then should not man meditate on Rāma in the early hours before sunrise?

68 There is no necessity of resorting to vows and sacrifices which involve the spending of wealth and are full of difficulties and dangers. It is enough if one meditates in the early hours before sunrise on the Name of Rāma who is all merciful for his helpless devotees.

69 Do not have any misgiving about the fact that the Name of God is the only Real thing in the world. Meditate on Rāma in the early hours before sunrise, and you will come to know the truth of this.

70 Not by actions, not by the performance of any religious duty, not by renunciation, and not by yogic practices, can God be realized. Rāmadāsa says that one who meditates on the Name, Rāma, with faith in the early hours before sunrise will alone be able to realize Him.

71 If with faith one only sings the Name and the qualities and deeds of Rāma, his mind will be free from desires and all other dualities; and he will see in the vision of Rāma his own Self who is immanent in the world.

72 Why should a devotee be afraid of what might happen to his body or befall him in his worldly life, when God can confer liberation on him. But to one who has no faith in Rāma difficulties will gather from all sides.

73 To give up meditation on God is to get oneself bewildered by the worldly anxieties. But one need not be afraid of them, if he keeps the purifying Name of Rāma fixed in his heart.

74 Hold fast the Name of the Lord of Lakṣmī. You will thereby find that He is close to you, that you have

crossed the saṁsāra by his help, and that you have gone beyond jealousy and the anxiety for earning bread.

75 Repeat always the Name of God with all reverence and without being jealous of any one. The Name is the only means of realizing God; nothing can ever be compared with it.

76 Due to misfortune one may not understand the extraordinary power of the Name, 'Rāma', which relieved even the Lord Śaṅkara of the effect of the deadly poison which he had drunk. Why should then one utter several other names?

77 Well known is the Lord Śaṅkara for having burnt Cupid, the lust incarnate, and for being the foremost among those who have got power, knowledge and the spirit of renunciation. He too along with his consort, Pārvatī, meditates on the Name of Rāma, with full faith and reverence.

78 Real rest and real bliss will be to him who has the Name of Rāma on his tongue. But doubts, weariness and grief will be in store for him who does not utter the Name.

79 No kind of desire will ever be able to afflict him who has the Name of Rāma on his tongue; courage will never forsake him. Even the strong urge of lust will be made ineffective by the devotee of God. Has not Hanumān been able to conquer the lust by being the blessed servant of Rāma?

80 Short, sweet, excellent and easy to utter is the Name, 'Rāma'. If it is meditated upon, it will root out all fear about the worldly life and bring liberation to man.

81 If you want to realize God, utter the Name of Rāma silently or at the top of your voice as you wish. But over and above this, remember the Name always whether you are taking your meals or doing any other work.

82 The divine Name has been extolled by the Vedas and by the sage Vyāsa in his Purāṇas. Therefore, one who does not meditate on Rāma has really wasted his life.

83 Proclaim the Name of Rāma with all your might and with great reverence. Do not get sick of uttering the Name; for it can be done without any cost.

84 With the loud and respectful uttering of the Name, sins will hide themselves in the caves of the distant mountains. To sing the Name of Rāma loudly had become a delightful passion with the Lord Śaṅkara.

85 It is God, who gives you food to eat. So instead of yourself being anxious about procuring food, meditate upon His Name, which can be had without any charge.

86 Make the utmost use of your body in worshipping the Personal God with great reverence and in bringing delight to the devotees of God by your humility and devotion.

87 Celebrate the Name and glory of Rāma with such great love that the consciousness that you have a body will be drowned in it. You will then be able to give up your greed and lust for wealth and women.

88 How can God be achieved by him whose desires fly with the wings of imagination, who does not know his own mind, and who talks much but does nothing?

89 Abandoning therefore the wrong path of wishful imagination which will bring in afflictions only, go by the moral path of the saints and do act as you think and speak.

90 Control your mind which has gone astray; purify your body and mind by regularly taking a bath, and by performing the twilight worship of God with devotion; have compassion for all, so that peace and tranquillity will come unto you.

91 Do not ever be angry; be not attached to anything except the company of the good and the holy; you will surely participate in the joy of liberation.

92 Be always in the company of the realized souls, so that your actions will be morally good and there will arise in you love for God. Do not speak mere hollow words unless you first act accordingly; and so converse with others without any dispute that you will arrive at truth.

93 Speak one must; but it should be to find out the truth, the spiritual Good, and to prevent the growth of scepticism by putting a stop to disputation.

94 Forgetting that God alone is the wisest of all, if a learned man becomes puffed up with pride, he would be no better than a demon.

95 To appear in different forms and as incarnations is but a sport of God. Those who do not understand His nature and realize Him are the most wretched and sinners among the creatures.

96 Even a wicked man will be changed if he remains in the company of the good. Lust is the most dangerous of all; therefore, it is very necessary to control the mind and go beyond its inclinations.

97 Meditate always upon God in solitude with the only view to realize the truth and without giving yourself in the least to idle talks and futile desires.

98 Look how the Lord Rāma had lived his life, and meditate upon Him only. He lived for the upliftment of humanity; he had nothing but truth in his mouth; and his only weapon to enforce the truth was his unerring bow.

99 Let your conduct be morally spotless; do not utter a thoughtless word, nor act in a listless manner. For, then only you will be able to give peace and consolation to those who are afflicted.

100 Even the sight of a devout saint, who has become bereft of desires and has firmly established himself in the knowledge of God, is an event of great merit. What to speak then about the touch of his grace, or of having a conversation with him ? There will not be a trace of doubt left in the mind of the seeker.

101 Know him as the king among the saints who is devoid of egoism, greed, agitation and crookedness of mind, who has no desire for God-less things, and who is always alert, tranquil, forbearing and forgiving.

102 Be in the company of the good and the holy; for thereby alone one can be able to give up the evil ways of living, and will come on the right path which will lead him to the realization of God. Before him then even the most fearful Lord of death will be powerless.

103 The whole universe is filled by the fear of death. But

the saint goes beyond fear, because he sees before him nothing but the presence of the infinite Brahman which puts an end to all fear.

104 Alas, notwithstanding what the great sages have been telling since long, man has remained as ignorant as he was. How can egoism and the consciousness of body enable him to find out his own spiritual treasure ?

105 Having once lost his spiritual treasure, he is being born again and again, and is struck with the poverty of the delusion that his real nature consists of the consciousness of the physical body alone.

106 Whereas the saint sees the whole of the space before him as filled by the presence of God, the unfortunate man sees nothing but an image of stone. How, indeed can one who has no faith acquire any merit and be able to find out his own spiritual treasure, if he has egoism only ?

107 It is on account of the three guṇas, sattva, raja and tama and of the inability to go beyond them, that man becomes miserable and unable to obtain his own spiritual treasure.

108 Rāmadāsa says that if any one wishes to realize what he really is spiritually, he must give up his egoism, and surrendering himself at the feet of the spiritual teacher serve him so assiduously that the latter might anoint his eyes with the collyrium of spiritual instruction and enable him to see the hidden treasure.

109 Ignorance prevents a man from knowing the truth; and so, being illuded he picks up a counterfeit coin and believes it to be a real one. How can illusion lead one to his spiritual Good ?

110 Be extremely humble and search out the Reality. And once you make the discovery of God, there will be an end to all illusion and ignorance.

111 Constant rumination over the objects of sense gives rise to egoism and ignorance. Meditation on the Name of God, on the other hand, makes one realize the Self and put an end to his being born again.

112 The world as perceived by the physical eyes is bound to

perish even though it might exist for thousands of years. Death puts an end to all that has come into being. The saint however discovers God and sees him always.

113 With great efforts, the saint discovers that the infinite God is one only, and that He is immovable, imperishable, unchangeable and unbreakable. How can this God, besides whom there exists nothing, be attained by one who is full of egoism ? The saint however looks at Him constantly.

114 One should search for this infinite God and become one with him by means of meditation. Though formless and indescribable by the Vedas, He alone is the support of Brahmadeva (the creator) and other beings.

115 One must make an assiduous search for the infinite God who though not capable of being seen by the physical eyes, is seen by means of the intuitive eye, and who when seen makes the devotee blind to all other worldly objects.

116 God, says Rāmadāsa, is neither yellow, nor white, nor black, nor blue; He is neither manifest nor unmanifest. But one must have faith and a will to make a thorough search to find out this God.

117 One must search and search to find out this God, and instruct his mind again and again. But all this can be accomplished by resorting to the company of the saints and by possessing a resolute mind and a loving heart.

118 With all the philosophical niceties, what is needed in the search for God is the mental insight and the practical discipline to discern the unique characteristics of God who alone is imperishable among the perishable things.

119 Neither by the knowledge of the constitution of the body, nor by that of philosophy or of music will there arise the spiritual satisfaction. It can neither be had by performance of sacrifices, nor by yogic practices, nor again by renouncing the pleasures of life. It can be had by coming in contact with the saints.

120 Just as the crescent moon of the second day of the bright half of the month, if not visible to some one, has to be pointed out to him by asking him to look in the direction of a particular branch of a tree, even so the knowledge of the five elements and other principles and of the great Vedāntic statements, such as, 'That Thou art', 'I am the Brahman,' etc. are merely an intellectual aid to the apprehension of the nature of God, who can be realized only by having a contact with a great saint.

121 If anybody says that he has known God, he must be an egoistic and inconsiderate person. Who is there who can conceive the inconceivable ? And how can egoism comprehend Him ? For, one who realizes God does not remain separate from him.

122 The more you read philosophical treatises the more will be their contradictions, and the more the confusion of your mind. This can be put an end to, if someone who has realized God will instruct you how to attain this knowledge.

123 The various sciences of the Logicians, the Mīmāṁsakas and the Vedāntins as also the Vedas, will not make you realize God. Even the great serpent, Śeṣa (on which the Lord Viṣṇu is said to lie down) had to become silent after trying hard to describe the nature of God, and to remain satisfied by merely looking at the Lord. Therefore, one should leave his egoism and remain as a silent spectator of the vision of God.

124 The egoism of man is like a fly which, if swallowed, will not let the spiritual food be digested, but will cause it to be vomited.

125 Do not have the vain desire to make people wise by disputing with them. Your egoism in doing so will make you alone miserable.

126 If the belief that the physical body is all-in-all becomes rooted in man, he is sure to forfeit the spiritual gain he could have achieved by coming in contact with the saints.

127 Know him to be a saint who always keeps his mind

filled with God, and who is never overpowered by Godless desires. How indeed can environment and belongings affect a saint, as they do the ordinary persons?

128 Meditate upon the Name of God and you will forget that you are the body and all that you egoistically think about. And as for the knowledge of the extent and the bliss of God is concerned get yourself instructed by a great saint.

129 What is real is hidden, and what is seen by the physical eye is merely the short-lived world. Howsoever you may imagine out of egoism about the Brahman which is bereft of forms and qualities, it can never be realized.

130 The original, Pure Consciousness which is one only became split as if in two forms; with reference to the sensuous objects it is known as Avidyā; while with reference to Brahman, it is known as Vidyā. But the split goes away, and the consciousness becomes one again, when man resorts to meditation.

131 If a man is thoughtful and meditative, then alone he comes to know how very stealthily the demon of egoism covers the entire field of Self-consciousness and spreads the darkness of ignorance throughout the human existence.

132 Who can ever make Him the object of his physical vision, and who can protect anything of this worldly life from that all-devouring God ? Yet, being himself the imperishable, ever-wakeful and compassionate witness of all, He takes sides with his devotees and confers on them the eternal bliss of liberation.

133 It is said that Brahmadeva as the creator of the universe writes in advance on the foreheads of all as to what is to happen in the life-time of each man. But who is He who writes on the forehead of Brahmadeva ? It is said that the Lord Śaṅkara burns this universe at the time of dissolution; but who is that God who ultimately burns this lord of destruction ?

134 It is also said that there are twelve suns, eleven Rudras and countless Indras (lords of gods). But alas, none has

found out and known the nature of the supreme God!

135 Crores and crores of gods there might be, and people might believe any one of them and worship him according as they like and as their desires are fulfilled. But alas, none is prepared to find out and realize the supreme God.

136 Alas, none utters a word regarding the Supreme God from whom have originated all these worlds. Verily, this God who remains hidden from the gaze of all can never be seen without the grace of the spiritual teacher.

137 As for the teachers, they might be lacs and crores; and the 'mantras' they impart might possess extraordinary powers to yield the desired objects. But none among these has the ability to confer the bliss of liberation.

138 Inscrutable is that saint among those who have realized the knowledge of God, who on account of his great devotion to God is neither arrogant nor attached to worldly objects. Under the garb of saintliness and devotion, he never deceives the people by practising black magic; nor is he greedy of wealth, nor is he jealous of any body.

139 One should resort only to that spiritual teacher who does as he speaks and who cherishes no Godless desire of any kind.

140 One would derive all spiritual joy from that Guru only who though learned is a devoted and realized soul, who has become free from all desires, and who is alert, forgiving, merciful and wise.

141 And then, if one makes his own search by means of meditation and by keeping himself in the company of the good and the holy, he comes to know gradually that he has become altogether a changed personality, that God who was unmanifest has manifested himself before him, and that the bliss of God-realization is beyond all description.

142 Then will he realize that the vision of Rāma which is invisible to ordinary men is not in the least different from his own Self, and that there is notrace of fear in

him. And, yet, paradoxically, the devotee should always hide himself in the vision of God.

143 If one becomes absolutely free from egoism, he will realize that Rāma is not only very close to his heart, but that there comes about an unbreakable union of his soul with God as the result of his constant meditation and of contemplation on the vision of God.

144 True it is that all things including the five elements are non-different from Self. But, in fact, they have no existence of their own in the vision of the universal Ātman. Notwithstanding therefore the various spiritual experiences and visions, one should only get himself merged in the bliss of them all, and not become proud that he has seen a particular vision.

145 The feeling that the being of oneself consists in the awareness of the physical body only should be cut into pieces by the sword of God-realization. And along with this sense of being disembodied even while one is embodied, one must ever turn his back against all God-less and immoral desires, and be merged in the bliss arising out of devout meditation.

146 One should experience that God is the creator of this world, and be liberated by the very act of visualizing Him. This will lead to the further realization that God can be seen to be bereft of any particular quality in spite of his being full of infinite qualities. Therefore the devotee too must leave attachment to all other things and be merged in the bliss of God only.

147 How can the finite individual soul be considered as the creator and the sustainer of the world ? Yet, like the Brahman, it too can go beyond the range of the four kinds of speech and become as uncontaminated as the Brahman is, if it leaves away all attachment to other things and meditates on the inconceivable Brahman alone.

148 Unless egoism and the feeling that the physical body is the core of reality are rooted out, no one can ever be able to realize the Brahman. The mind will till then be either a void or replete with ignorance.

149 Nothing can be said to have the slightest similarity with that highest Being which is inscrutable and imperishable. To realize oneself as non-different from it constitutes the best kind of contemplation on it. For, in that unique experience of bliss there is no consciousness of oneself being either non-different or identical with God.

150 The Vedas, the Purāṇas and the sciences have been unable to describe the nature of God. Even to say that He is omniscient is falsely to presuppose that the 'all' exists as different from him. And even if the object of knowledge is absent, does it mean that God ceases to be the knower ? Similarly, to say that He is visible or invisible is arbitrarily to use a human mode of predicating something about him. In fact, He is the eternal and the transcendent spectator of his own manifest or unmanifest forms.

151 All-pervading like space is that God who resides in the hearts of men. Neither does He come nor does he go out from some region to another. He is full to the brim everywhere; and there is no empty space without him.

152 Even the smallest particle is full with God. To gaze at him is to become identical with him without being aware of it.

153 If one were to contemplate upon the universal, all-pervading vision of Rāma, he would not only be free from the wrong notion that his real being is the physical body, but he would also be able to cut at the roots of the saṁsāra as a whole. And yet, his desire to look at the vision is never completely satisfied.

154 Space has enveloped the entire universe; but space too falls short in comparison with the all-pervasiveness of God. In fact, there being nothing else but God, even the attribute 'all-pervading' becomes robbed of its meaning when it is applied to God.

155 The time-old and the infinitely vast vision of God is beyond all reasoning and imagination. But what is thus unfathomable and uniquely one only, becomes easily comprehensible by the grace of the Lord himself.

156 When one sees the vision of Rāma as being present everywhere, he becomes one with him. During that supramental condition, where speech becomes dumb, even the attribute, 'omniscience' loses its meaning in the absence of any other thing except God.

157 There remains then no sense of duality and no recognition of any other being except one's own disembodied form. What a great fortune would it be if even after several births, one can meet himself and become tranquil.

158 This is all the secret knowledge which one can realize. But what is needed is the resolute will to meditate silently on the Name of God and to listen to it, as also the company of the saints.

159 Leave everything except the company of the saints. For, that alone without any other means, will put an end to all grief and bring God-realization within your reach.

160 It is the company of the saints which will destroy even the sinful effects of the erstwhile company of the unholy, put an end to the sense of duality of the aspirant, and make room for his easy and immediate liberation.

161 Rāmadāsa says that if one reads or listens attentively and with faith these two hundred verses addressed to the mind of man, he would be fit to meditate on the Name of God, and thereby would be able not only to realize God and feel disgust for all God-less things, but also acquire the power of God.

B. The Pathetic and the Confident Notes in Rāmadāsa

1 There must be a resolute will and an undaunted courage to find out God even at the sacrifice of one's own body. Then alone one can have unflinching love for God which casts aside all other objects of desire; and then alone will the formless Absolute manifest before the devotee in the form of a Personal God and protect him and assure him not to be afraid of anything.

2 Why would I have left, says Rāmadāsa, this worldly life, if I were convinced that it is not short-lived ? But I cry unto you that it is not only perishable but is also like a huge fire which will burn away completely all your inclinations and thoughts about God.

3 Like a miser then who counts and preserves his money in a secret place, meditate silently on the Name of God in a place which is secluded, if at all you wish to meet and realize Him. Let not any one know how long and where you meditate, or what your spiritual experiences would be in course of time. Even God would like to test your sincerity, love and courage in various ways. You would feel tired in doing the same meditation again and over again; doubts may enter into your mind; you may be overtaken by adversity, bereavement and disease; or false notions about holiness might make you believe that the Name is not to be uttered without a bath. But, under no circumstance, cease to meditate at the appointed hour and for the fixed period of time. The divine Name being the holiest of all, utter it at any time and in any place, whether the time is auspicious or not, or whether the place is specially made clean for the purpose of meditation or not.

4 Whether one has realized God and whether one has genuine love for Him can be judged by observing whether he likes to go again and again into seclusion for the sake of meditation or not. For, it is far more in seclusion than in the midst of a crowd that one can

enjoy the bliss of the union with God, and transcend the consciousness of body, senses, mind, intellect and egoism. Then it is that speech might become dumb, the distinction between the disciple and the Guru might vanish, and the awareness of the whole of the phenomenal world would be burnt in the flaming fire of the realization of God.

5 O Lord, you are all-powerful, an ocean of compassion and grace, and your vow is to save your helpless and miserable devotees. I am at a loss to know what I should beg of you, since I am a bundle of so many desires and doubts. Let me therefore implore you to spread the shade of your love on me and relieve me out of the fearful dangers of this worldly life, of my crookedness, desires, doubts and anxieties. Let me be devoted to you from the bottom of my heart ; let me sing your qualities and glorious Name so intensely, lovingly, always and without any egoism, that I should thereby be able not only to preserve your vision in my mind but also be able to see it exactly in the same form before my very eyes. If this is not to happen, O Rāma, then let my body fall.

6 Make haste, O Lord, make haste to meet this erring child, Rāmadāsa, of yours and save him in the flood of your grace. As days pass on, I am repenting more and more for having wasted my life without doing any devoted service to you. Alas, I concentrated all my attention and affection on my own pleasures and the pleasures of my kith and kin, and was carried away by thoughts about wealth and other temptations in life. No doubt, I came to know in course of time that people gather around some one and behave as friends only if he has got some wealth, or if they have to satisfy their own selfish ends, but that they leave him when their purpose is served. With all my knowledge, I could neither control my mind, nor keep up my resolve to serve and take shelter in you. Now, that I have been painfully convinced that all my pleasures are to end in sorrow, and that none of my relatives and friends will

be of any help to me in my hour of death, I am surrendering unto you with faith and hope that you will not desert me, but nourish me by the milk of your grace and fill my mind always with your Name, and my eyes with your beautiful vision. Kindly wash away my sins, remove the burden of the anxieties of saṁsāra from over my head, pounce like a lion upon the wolf of my desires, and make my mind fixed in being devoted to you in every way. You alone are my Master, O Rāma; treat me as your own, and give me shelter in your eternal Form.

7 How indeed can I forget, says Rāmadāsa, my spiritual teacher who made me realize the Ātmānanda and thereby feel disgusted with all other worldly objects, and who enabled me to overcome the slothfulness of my mind? It was he who instructed me in the yoga of realizing the Brahman and of being lodged there permanently. What was I except a storehouse of countless failings, egoism and ignorance? Have I ever striven for my spiritual well-being? But lo, see the greatness of my Guru. Not minding any of my shortcomings he accepted me as his own, took utmost pains to instruct me in the lore of the Brahman, and saved me by bringing me in contact with the infinite God. To repay the obligations of such a great Guru will really be impossible for me, even if I lay down my life for him. I only salute him therefore with surrender and love.

8 Time hangs heavily upon me, says Rāmadāsa, when I become separated from the saints. Of what account to me is the pleasure of living in beautiful houses, or to be endowed with other joys? Who can know the wrench of my heart, and witness the secret tears, the choked throat and the weakened limbs whenever I happen to be without the company of the saints and of Rāma? Deliberately do I try to divert my attention to other pursuits, but every hour I become more and more sorrowful and fatigued! Oh, what a great sin I must have done, in that Fate has reduced me to this helpless condition! My heart is panting to meet you, my Lord,

my mind is entangled in your noble qualities, and though my life is being exhausted day by day, you are still far away! Be gracious and meet me, and let me serve you without any break, or else, let my body fall. But be sure, I shall not worship any lesser deity, nor allow the Fate to rule over me as it likes, so long as I wait on you with intense love and longing.

9 I call myself as a servant (*dāsa*) of Rāma; but when I become aware of the world-wide difference between great saints and myself I feel that in vain have I been born. There are saints who, for the sake of realizing God, have lived in the caves of mountains and in places of pilgrimage and are doing great penance, and yet remain unknown to the world. Compared with them I feel I have done nothing, but that I have become only a burden to the earth. They are great saints indeed; for their love for God is great, and God too loves them in return. As the fruit of this mutual love, they are always in the presence of God, and they feel the direct touch of God; while I have got myself drowned in my own egoism having only verbal knowledge of God. Their power of concentrated meditation on the Name of God and of contemplation on His visions is so great that I become simply struck with wonder. Some of them have altogether given up the consideration of their bodily condition in their love for God, and so they shine with the divine lustre and possess many divine qualities; while, alas, I fly away from God with the slightest discomfort to my body! They are the incarnations of God, born, it appears, to raise high the banner of spiritual knowledge, and to establish on this earth the Kingdom of divine peace and joy; myself, on the other hand, being too selfish, have forgotten Rāma, and have become a source of affliction to myself and to others.

10 People call me as the servant of Rāma. But when I think about myself, I find that I have neither any devotion, nor any knowledge. I have neither any love for God, nor do I meditate. Instead of possessing any good quality, I become angry in no time. Yet, whenever

I prayed to Rāma, he did remove my anxiety and made me tranquil. But how long should I give him trouble and put my burden on him ? It is really impossible to repay his obligations, except by means of meditating on his Name out of gratitude.

11. Know him to be a blessed and a realized soul, says Rāmadāsa, who sees Rāma as manifested before him and who looks at him face to face. Since it is a unique character of spiritual experience that the knower, the known and the knowledge become one, Rāma will never turn his back towards his devotee if he is once seen in this manner. The devotee might look in any direction, and yet, Rāma will be seen by him face to face. He might shut his eyes, and yet all the more vividly he will see the form of Rāma. He will see Rāma simultaneously both in front of him and behind him, as well as on all sides of him as he begins to walk. He might try to forget the Name and the vision of Rāma by looking to his own person, but to his great surprise he would find that he has himself become Rāma, and yet see Rāma as before in front of him. With Rāma inside and with Rāma outside, and with his mind and eyes full of the Name and vision of Rāma respectively, he behaves as if he is mad so far as his body is concerned. There remains in him no trace of egoism or attachment for the whole of the phenomenal world including the dignity of his family.

12. And when there come about several such God-intoxicated persons, there happens to be the kingdom of Rāma on this very earth. In the absence of jealousy, anger and hatred, there would be no quarrels and fights amongst them. People would behave with each other with love and respect; there would prevail the sense of truth and justice in all. And above all, with God as the chief and central object of love, the common engagement for them all wculd be to celebrate the glory and Name of God with ever-increasing joy and love. Then the King, Rāma, will also be present amidst them in

order to shower his grace upon them, so that they should realize the Brahman.

13. Our highest ambition should be to become like Rāma, or better still, to be one with Rāma, so that we too might be able to save the people and bring them on the path of God. In order to attain this state three things are however necessary. First, we must rise spiritually higher and higher by the ladder of devotion. Constant and regular meditation on the Name of God, contemplation on the manifested forms of His vision, service of God and the saints to such an extent that they are befriended, and finally, to become one with God are the steps of this ladder. Secondly, as a result of this union with God, there should spring forth in us such a great disgust (vairāgya) for all other God-less objects that the riches and the pleasures of the whole world must be felt as insignificant as a straw. And, thirdly it must never be forgotten that notwithstanding the fact that Rāma moves round and round the devotee all the day and night and protects him and does all his work as if He is a servant of the devotee, what the devotee has to do is to behave himself as an instrument in the hands of God and in executing the plans of God.

14. With the vanishing of the whole of the perceptible world, begins the region of the spiritual experiences. Hence it is that the physical eye must make room for what is known as the spiritual or the intuitive eye which, unlike the physical eye, sees the divine lustre through every pore of the body. Naturally, by the power of the intuitive eye the physical eye also becomes capable of seeing the divine beauty. So it is that the Brahma-yogin keeps his eyes half-open and looks in the direction of the lower tip of the nose, whereby he becomes able to negate the perception of the sensible world and look at the vision of God with a steadfast gaze. The panorama of beautiful colours and other spiritual visions are seen by him; the music of the unstruck sound is heard; and in the fire of the Brahmanic knowledge is burnt the camphor of the phenomenal world.

The yogī remains rapt up in ecstasy and sings the Name of God and listens to it with one-pointed attention. This indeed is the common treasure of the great saints all over the world.

15. Beware however of the false prophets who pretend to be spiritual Gurus, but are as worthless as straw on account of their being utterly thoughtless, immoral, unjust, unspiritual, unclean, and loathsome to look at. They are like blind cattle who go astray any way they like; they are like gluttonous buffaloes, and they bark out like dogs meaningless words of philosophy and spiritual falsehoods. Their only trade is of miracle-mongering, which by itself is no test of any spiritual worth. Just see what such a Guru does.

Posing himself as an Advaitic Vedāntin, he dismisses all distinctions of good and bad, right and wrong, holy and unholy, and behaves as promiscuously as he wishes. In evidence of this, he does not hesitate to eat his own vomit, or sit and roll in places where even the excreta are thrown. He makes the cremation ground as his residence and is an expert in black magic. With his control over spirits and ghosts, he orders them to work out miracles and be useful to him in his trade of deception. He changes a clod of earth into a lump of sugar, or meat into flowers, foretells the future, makes even the animals speak, brings foliage to a withered tree, makes impotent into potent, walks over fire and over the waves of sea, eats enormously or does not eat and drink at all, becomes invisible in one place and visible in a far off place, brings the dead back to life, rides upon a tiger with the whip of a serpent in his hand, speaks out what is passing on in the minds of others, changes iron into gold, removes even incurable diseases, brings prosperity or poverty to men as he likes, and so on and so forth. But none of them ever thinks or says that God is the doer of all, or that what is of the highest value in life is the knowledge of the Ātman and Brahman. Therefore one must take utmost care to see that the Guru he wishes to resort to is one who has himself realized God and who has the capacity to make others also realize Him, though he might be indifferent to the occurrence of miracles, which he thinks, are the work of God only.

16. I shall never give up the attitude of faith and love towards Rāma even though I might be tormented by hunger and thirst and crushed down by calamities. Incapacitated may be my tongue to utter the Name of Rāma; I shall surely remember him mentally. Let death be imminent or far away, or let heavens fall on me, I shall never leave the shelter of Rāma, says Rāmadāsa.

17. It is in the company of the saints that one can give up his egoism and form the habit of meditating on the divine Name and listen to it as it is being meditated upon. I did so, says Rāmadāsa, for a very long time with faith and love; and lo, Rāma manifested before me all of a sudden. During my meditation, I had already lost the capacity of my mind to attend to other things besides the Name of Rāma. But now, when I saw the exceedingly beautiful form of Rāma face to face and on all sides of myself, when instead of myself being after him, Rāma was, so to say, after me, and when I began to visualize the same form wherever I went, I forgot to become aware of my own bodily form. In my heart and outside of me, both during day and night, at home or in the forest, in places of pilgrimage or on the top of mountains, the same resplendent vision of Rāma was my constant companion. Not only did it become impossible for me to forget meditating upon his Name and to look at his form, but I could not also recognize myself as different from him. Such being my inseparable contact (yoga) with Him, I ultimately found that there was an end to myself and to my form, and that what remained was the eternal, immortal and the disembodied Form of Rāma. All this happened in the twinkling of an eye, when Rāma showered his grace on me.

18. Leave all and find out God by coming in contact with the saints. One will then come to know how karma (Action) leads to upāsanā (devotion), and how upāsanā leads to Jñāna which means both intellectual and illuminational kinds of knowledge. At the same

time, one will come to know the limitations and the futility of karma, upāsanā and mere intellectual knowledge, if they stop short of leading men towards the illuminational knowledge of God. Leaving aside actions which are non-devotional and which therefore are totally useless in the search for God, it can be said of devotional actions, that is, of karma and upāsanā, that they constitute what is known as the 'ant's way' (Pipīlikā mārga) of reaching to God-head. Naturally, the search is bound to be slow, and the way, a long, long one. If however one is motivated only by the selfish purpose of obtaining prosperity, long life, health and other objects of desires and pleasures, neither karma nor upāsanā will lead him towards God. One may, as his fore-fathers might have done before him, wander from one place of pilgrimage to another, worship several idols of deities or copper and silver-plates with mysterious figures and letters inscribed on them, known as 'Yantras', perform innumerable sacrifices, practise many difficult yogic postures and penances, or do many an ugly and loathsome act according to the Tantra and the Śākta teachings; he can at the most gain his desired objects of the sensuous world, but will never see the face of God. In vain do the people worship the idols and images of the incarnations of God and miss the eternal, immortal God who is immanent in the universe and by whose power all the beings are protected. It is this God who ought to be directly seen by means of meditation on His Name; and then it can be said that God is realizable as immediately as the fruit on a tree by a single flight of a bird, (the Vihaṅgama Mārga). Thus it is that meditation on the Name of God becomes at once the karma and the upāsanā which culminate in the realization of God.

19. A word, when uttered, produces sound; and out of the sound comes the word. Blessed are those who go beyond the word and sound and realize the Brahman. The word makes itself and other connected words intelligible; speechlessness also would become intelligible on

account of the word being present in it ; but, what is that which exists when the word ceases to be? That is to be realized and so, it cannot be spoken. And if one tries to describe it by means of words, the description will totally fall short of Reality. True it is that the Name of God, on which one is recommended to meditate, is a symbol of God and is capable of enabling one to realize Him. But is not the existence of God prior to both the symbol and the realization of Him by one who meditates on it? The Name or the word standing as the symbol can be uttered loudly by means of the tongue, or muttered in throat, or remembered in mind, or attended to as it springs up in its subtlest form of sound from the region in the neighbourhood of the navel. It is capable of being attended to or spoken as if by what is known as the transcendent speech (parā vāṇi) rising from the navel. But, the Brahman suggested by the Name, at any of the four levels of speech, is ever transcendent of it, whether it is meditated upon or not. God is not created by the Name; He only manifests in some concrete Form, because He is pleased by the devotion of the meditator on that Name. Infinite other Names also are already there in the Brahman, but these become known only to a great and powerful realized soul, who then recommends them for being meditated upon by others. Hence it is said that speech cannot reach Him; nor can mind, nor the intellect. The imagination of the mind and the inference of the intellect are possible when there is the possibility of the existence of at least two things. But there is nothing other than God.

During the earlier stages of meditation, the devotee might be conscious of the distinction between himself as the meditator and God as meditated upon. He might also become conscious of the changing states of his mind. But as he becomes more and more assimilated with the manifested visions of God before him, his mind and intellect also become fused with God, just as camphor which is burnt becomes the fire. The devotee vanishes as a separate entity, and his Brahmanic experience alone remains. The knower and the known are merged in knowledge.

20. What a fraud that one should call himself as a follower of Jñāna-mārga (the way of knowledge) and avoid to do his duty, when he is required to do it. But if he is asked to define what he means by knowledge, he would conceal his ignorance by saying that he is only a devotee of God, and that he does not care to know what Jñāna means! Then, at the time of worshipping and praying, he would say that he is an Advaitic Vedāntin; and therefore he would say that he does not feel the necessity of praying to God, as a dualist might feel; and yet, he would be most anxious to guard his interest in his sons, daughters and other nearest relatives ! He would loudly proclaim that 'All is Brahman', and censure the good and the holy in their absence! He would teach renunciation to others, but wander from place to place in search of wealth! Alas, says Rāmadāsa, such pretenders will reap what they sow.

21. I shall not call myself a servant of Rāma, if I fail to save the fallen in the same way in which Rāma used to save them. I am not saying this out of vanity; I know full well that the saving power I possess does not belong to me, but that it has come to me on account of the grace of Rāma. In me does Rāma live ; and it is He who has ordered me to do His work of saving those who surrender unto Him. Besides, by being one with Him by my constant meditation on his Name and contemplation on his Form, I have become, says Rāmadāsa, as devoid of birth and death as Rāma is, even though I am embodied.

22. Neither do you censure and neglect the body, nor do you fondle it too much. For, it is both useful and useless. On the one hand, the consciousness that one's own body is all-in-all and the most precious thing in the world, and the consequent fattening of it, are the root-causes of egoism, vice and sin, and of the subsequent diseases, old age and miseries. On the other hand, if the body is sound, one can achieve virtue, devotion and grace of God. Then will it be possible to realize

God and enjoy the blissful condition of being immortal even while living.

23. One need not suppose that the entire phenomenal world of Māyā is dissolved back into ākāśa or the empty space, just as the waking and the dreaming conditions are being dissolved in sleep, and that there remains in both the cases nothing but a void (Śūnya) or nothingness. This is to take a partial view of the matter. For, not only there is the return of the evolutionary process of the world after its dissolution into void, and of the waking life when sleep is over, but there is also within the bosom of the void the unmanifest God or Brahman, just as within the dreamless sleep there is the unattended experience of the joy of having a sound sleep. But, if by the grace of the spiritual teacher and by the force of one's own meditation, the unmanifest God would become manifest and continue to remain face to face before the devotee in His resplendent glory, will not the devotee be able to say that what was thought of erroneously as the void, or the vacant mind, or a dreamless sleep of ignorance, has been changed into the plenitude of blissful existence or a continuous life of supra-wakeful consciousness in all the conditions of wakefulness, dream and sleep ? In the blissful presence of God, the world and the entire eight-fold Prakṛti are dissolved even while they exist; and the saint enjoys the disembodied condition even while living.

24. People go the wrong way and expect to arrive at the truth ! The remedy they use is worse than the disease; they suffer from one disease and take the medicine which is meant to cure another disease, or eat what is not to be eaten. With selfish and sinful motives they do meritorious and devotional acts and thereby become more selfish and more sinful. How can one come in the presence of the king, if he were always to mix with the ordinary people only ? Can one fill his belly by undergoing a fast ? Even so, how can one hope to realize the Brahman if he were always to engage himself in the doing of actions ? Activity which is neither

meditative nor contemplative will only bind a man and not release him.

25. Repentance for having wasted one's life without trying to realize God, or in doing useless and wicked acts, creates an initial disgust for God-less thoughts and desires, as also a devotional attitude. Along with this, if there be the company of the saints and meditation on the divine Name, there would emerge the real knowledge of God, and the devotee would become a saint. The initial Vairāgya which might occur by being repentant ought to become a way of life on account of its being rooted in the mind itself.

26 One may carry on his worldly life and be pleased with it, but one should also try to achieve his spiritual Good. If the aim of man's life is to have the pleasures of life, then let him toil and toil to have them till the end of his life, and then find that he is fatigued and frustrated. But if it is to attain the realization of God, he must surrender unto a saint and follow the path of devotion and meditation. Then will he discover that his grip on saṁsāra is being gradually loosened, that he gets complete rest, peace, contentment and joy by seeing the face of God, and that he can lead the life of actionlessness in action.

27. Preserve the Name of God in your mind, and God will protect you from all anxieties and calamities. Or else, without his grace all your efforts and hopes might end in gloom and despair. Remember always that God alone is the doer, the giver and the destroyer, and that therefore you should not feel yourself proud in his presence that you too can do or undo something by your own efforts or can achieve anything without his sanction or grace.

28. Solitude does not mean a secluded place simply. It means the non-wavering of the mind from one idea to another. The vision of the Form of God is so delicate and immaculate that it does not brook any false idea except the pure idea of the divine Name. Therefore one must make his mind steady and remember the

Name of Rāma with so great a love and intensity that the vision of Rāma will also be steady during all the time of contemplation. As the result of this, the devotee also will ever be tranquil, joyful and free from sin, egoism and the worries of the worldly life.

29. Prayer and praise do require the help of words. But how indeed can one attain to God who is beyond words and beyond the ideas created by the mind? This however ought not to be a great difficulty. For, God is both personal and impersonal (Saguṇa and Nirguṇa). Though He transcends the Name, He is also immanent in it; and the Name it is that includes in it both the praises and prayers to God. Besides, God being full of compassion and grace, he manifests himself before his devotee in a beautiful Form, on account of the devotee's constant meditation on His Name. The devotee then gets two things to attend at the same time, the Name for meditation and the Form for contemplation. And in doing this double function of the mind, he becomes so identical and mentally fixed in the contemplation of the Form, that he forgets that he is a separate entity apart from God. He becomes merged and one with God.

30. That is no real devotion which does not spring out of love and regard; and that is no real love which does not culminate in loyalty. Both love and loyalty are necessary in order to have the realization of God and the consequent liberation from the bondage of saṁsāra. But to realize God as being impersonal (nirguṇa) one must first worship the personal aspect (saguṇa) of God, by taking delight in singing the glories and qualities of God, in reading spiritual literature, and by keeping oneself in the company of the saints. God becomes then so enamoured of the devotee that He manifests before him in the form in which the devotee wishes to see him. And when the mind and the eyes of the devotee become inextricably fixed in the Form of God, he sees it everywhere, and sees it within him. In course of time, he finds that he himself has become one

with that Form. Thus it is that the devotee makes the transition from the worship of the Saguṇa to his identification with the several eternal Forms of God; and this happens because there is essentially no difference between the Name and the Form of God. In the absence of this all, to say that one has got knowledge about God is for all practical purposes not to have any knowledge about him.

31. I am not now, says Rāmadāsa, so much anxious about my worries in life as I am about how your Name, O Rāma, will continue to command my respect unless you save me first. Let me lose all, but let your Name remain ever glorified as before. I am your loyal servant; and so, even the idea that people might begin to doubt whether your Name has retained the power to save the fallen and the miserable or not, causes agony to my mind. Who will then take shelter at your feet ? Therefore, save me, your helpless servant, and be true to your promise that you are the saviour of those who love you.

32. Save me in every way, O my Lord, Rāma. Fickle-minded as I am, I cannot have any self-control; I constantly think of sensuous objects of desire. I am very slothful; I have made no use of my body in the cause of devotion; bereft is my mind of faith and love for God; I am full of egoism and anger, and I am fond of seeking faults of others; without a tinge of disgust for God-less objects, I am not tired of speaking hollow words of wisdom. Remove therefore all these faults of mine, make a radical change in my mind, and save me, O Rāma, by making me your devout and loyal servant.

33. Wonderful indeed is the vital and organic connection between God and his devotee, says Rāmadāsa. Both of them have left their native place, it appears, and have come in a foreign land; God has left his residence, the Vaikuṇṭha, and the devotee, the mortal world. As friends, therefore, now they live; and their love for each other is ever on the increase. They never live apart from each other. The devotee realizes that God

being full of compassion takes upon himself the entire burden of his devotee, and that being proud of him, He does not allow him to feel the want about anything. With his infinite hands He gives all things to his devotee, and follows him wherever he goes and says to him, 'take this; take this.' The devotee, on the other hand, is reluctant to accept anything on account of his disgust for all the objects in the world when the great God is in his presence. Thus, in a way, both of them tend to lead an ascetic life for the sake of the other,—God giving away all his possessions to his devotee, and the devotee, renouncing everything for the sake of the joy of God-realization. The devotee stores in his heart the Name and the Form of God, and God does not leave the devotee even for a moment. He protects him by keeping him in the adamantine cage of divine love and power.

34. Friendship of the ordinary people is motivated by selfish ends. It generally aims at retaining not only what one already possesses, but also at grabbing what belongs to others. But this kind of friendship does not last for a long time; for, everybody becomes sceptic about the honesty and loyalty of others. Even wicked and crafty men get themselves associated for executing a common evil plan; they eat and drink together for the purpose of gambling or stealing; but each one of them is alert to guard his own interest only. Such a friendship is suicidal in the long run. On the other hand, friendship which is guided by the sense of justice would make a clear demarcation between what belongs to oneself and what belongs to others. The profit and loss that might accrue from such an intelligently planned association or friendship is therefore shared with justice and fairness to all. Naturally, such a friendship is a source of contentment and is free from acrimony. But, there is a third kind of friendship which a large-hearted man alone can afford to form with another. It is based on the principle of generosity. The good of others even at the sacrifice of one's own interest

is the motive behind it. A saint alone is capable of having this kind of friendship which can never erode. Therefore one should strive his utmost in being befriended by the saints, so that one may be graced by them and be able to attain the realization of God.

35. That speech is known as 'Vaikharī' when the words in it are articulate, that is when they are spoken distinctly by the tongue. It is known as 'Madhyamā', when there is a sound resembling the sound of the spoken words, but without the words being articulate, just as there is the sound of the cry of a peacock. There occur however certain vibrations in the throat, as the word is being muttered there. Still more inarticulate, but remembered clearly and distinctly by the mind are the words of the speech known as 'Paśyantī'. This arises in the region of the heart, where the words are either mentally uttered or read as if they are written on the mental slate. In both the cases they are also heard by the mind occasionlly amidst the unstruck sounds. Transcending these three kinds of speech, deep in the region of the navel, springs up by way of inspiration the speech known as 'Parā' (that which transcends). Here, the mind only listens to what is silently surging up as a clear and distinct sound of word along with or without an unstruck sound of some musical instrument, or that of the roar of a lion, or of the sea, or of thunder and so on. The divine Name thus is capable of being meditated upon in four different ways, the most efficacious of which in causing the manifestation of the visions of God, is the last mentioned silent mode of listening to the Name as it springs up from within easily and unceasingly.

36. Blow silently and diligently at the spark of knowledge which the Guru has so graciously ignited in you, and make it into a huge conflagration of God-realization. Give up all idleness and meditate assiduously on the Name of God along with the in-going and out-going breaths, if you wish to bring your own experience of

God on a par with the experience of your spiritual teacher and with what you read in the scriptures. Listen to the Name of God as you utter it mentally, so that the vision of the Ātman will be clearer day by day, and the mind will be lost by being identified with it. That very moment, you will transcend the three guṇas and will become as uncontaminated as the Ātman is. And, in that supramental condition, where no other modification is possible, you will stay eternally liberated and full of bliss.

37. To attain to the experience of God as Nirguṇa, that is, as Impersonal or as bereft of any particular quality, one must have the prior experience of God as having a particular quality or form, and then of His having all of a sudden a contrary quality, or a form which is dissimilar with the first, and then again as having new or old forms and qualities as God chooses to assume. In being all and in being none, God will be realized as one who does not change with the changing forms and qualities, and as being both immanent and transcedent. In His aspect of being full of qualities and forms, He can be said to be Saguṇa; while in his aspect of not being limited by any particular quality or form, He will have to be said as Nirguṇa. Though wrathful or kind, as occasion demands, God is not limited by either of the two qualities. So, Nirguṇa does not mean that God has no quality or form, but that He is not limited by any of the innumerable qualities and forms which he possesses, and that He transcends them all. Therefore the devotee also must realize God as being Impersonal in spite of his having first realized Him as Personal.

38. To realize God as transcending the guṇas (qualities) and as uncontaminated by them, there must also be the corresponding moral effort on the part of the devotee to overcome both the guṇas of rajas and tamas by developing the sattvaguṇa in him, and then to overcome the sattvaguṇa also by the spiritual means of meditation on the divine Name and contemplation on

the divine Forms. In other words, the demoniac heritage in him should give way to the divine heritage. But in doing so, he must perforce subdue his own mental inclinations towards vice and sin by coming into contact with the saints.

39. Egoism is the worst enemy of man. Not only does it cause bickerings, quarrels and fights between man and man, but it makes him also fall away from God, even though he may be an ardent worshipper of God. It was in the process of self-assertion due to egoism that even the great five elements of ākaśa, wind, fire, water, and earth fell away from the Brahman. In the very moment they became exclusively conscious of themselves alone, they forgot that they were originally nothing but Brahman. This cleavage between God and man widened more and more at every stage when the elements from the wind to the earth forgot not only the Brahman which was the original source of all, but even the preceding element out of which it had its own being. Thus it was that wind, fire, water and earth forgot that they were before their origin ākāśa, wind, fire and water respectively. Man too in his egoism and arrogance of self-assertion, forgot all the more that he was originally nothing but Brahman; and so, he falsely identified himself with the body, the senses, the mind and the intellect. He went a step further and began to identify himself with all his belongings, relatives, social and environmental conditions and relations.

Thus, there came about the widest possible gap between God and man. Unfortunately, it was due to egoism again that every remedy he tried to shorten the gap between him and God, proved to be harmful only. His penances, philanthrophy, sacrifices, social service, moral excellence, yogic practices, intellectual attainments, and to some extent, even his devotional worship of lesser deities, became only additional sources of increasing his egoism and desires.

The only way to wipe out one's egoism completely is to resign to the will of God and to realize Him by means of meditation on his Name and contemplation on his Forms.

Thereby one would get himself merged in God and will have no consciousness of the separate existence of his own tiny individuality.

40. Sit firmly and courageously in a posture which will be found suitable and comfortable; and then withdrawing all your senses from their objects, concentrate your mind on repeating the Name of God. With your eyes open or shut as you like, fix your gaze in the direction of the tip of the nose and continue your meditation silently in your mind. In course of time, as your practice of meditation will develop you will hear various sounds, like the ringing of bells, roaring of the lion or of the sea, and so on, and see the light of the moon. Do not stop there; continue your meditation. Behold then the golden coloured, splendour of lightnings. Go on further, you will see the Sun; but it will be most difficult to look at the blazing fire. Do not lose courage; but along with enhanced force of meditation, look with fixed attention. The Sun will move aside; and you will see a number of swans, and then the moon. And when you will have a bath in the rays of the moon, your body, which was scorched by the heat of the Sun, will be immediately cool. And then you will see the Eye of your eye which will give you unlimited bliss and make you forget the consciousness of your body. The divine light will not only fill your body through and through; it will be seen as spreading outside your body and enveloping the whole space. And, as the crowning phase of this grand spiritual experience, you will see your own resplendent Form, which will put an end to all sense of duality and the fear of bodily death. O, that bliss of unison and atonement with God will be totally incommunicable to any one else. What else will you then be except that bliss ?

C. A FEW PHILOSOPHICAL ISSUES

1. *On the Personal and the Impersonal (Saguṇa and Nirguṇa) aspects of God.*

It is interesting to note how each one of the two persons who have severally experienced the Saguṇa and the Nirguṇa aspects of God extols one aspect only and belittles the other. Rāmadāsa first allows both of them to have a discussion about the two aspects, and then tells them that both of them are correct from their respective view-points, but that the experiences of both of them can be had without any contradiction, provided the beginning of the spiritual life is made with the contact of the saints. Then alone there will be the realization that what comes forth before a devotee as a particular vision of God, and as having a particular form and quality on account of his whole-hearted devotion, culminates into Absolute Reality which is eternal and which is without any form or quality, that is, as not having only one particular form and quality, but as, having infinite forms and infinite qualites. The saguṇa and the nirguṇa aspects will then no longer be talked about as being the lower and the higher aspects of Brahman, but from the view-point of a progressive devotee, as being the earlier and the later stages of one and the same process of the realization of God.

What happens generally, and therefore becomes the cause of disputation is that, on the one hand, one who is delighted at the sight of the vision of God in a particular form is content with that alone, but is reluctant to proceed further because he thinks that there may be nothing beyond that particular vision, fearing that what he has actually gained might also be lost. On the other hand, the believer in the impersonal aspect of God has either only an empty, verbal knowledge about Him, or is slow to understand how the same vision of God which he might have experienced first, presents a little while afterwards the appearance of some other form or quality. What is necessary then, according to Rāmadāsa, is that one should never leave the company of the saints, as also the devotion and service of the personal aspect of God, because it is that experience which will either change into new and ever new experiences of several other visions, or become invisible and give rise to the belief that God is formless. No one should however have the false notion that the disappearance of a particular vision (the Saguṇa aspect of God) means the destruction of it. It means only the transformation of it into the unmanifest, original, infinite source of it, namely the Brahman. In short, whether manifest or unmanifest, it is the same God or Brahman who remains the object of devotion.

In fact, to say that God is manifest or unmanifest has no meaning except from the view-point of one who is fortunate to see him. Or, we may say that God is ever manifest even if no one realizes him, just as the Sun in the sky, who can neither be said to rise nor set except from the view-point of the human beings, would remain ever shining even though the whole world be sleeping for ever. In a like manner, to say that God is saguṇa or nirguṇa is to give expression to the kind of experience which a person might have about God, and not to the real nature of God. To say that He is either this or that is to bring limitations upon his infinite powers and will, and to hide one's own ignorance about that aspect of God which, as he says, does not belong to God. As the saint says in his Dāsabodha, and as we have referred to this above, Nirguṇa means Bahuguṇa, (Bahu=many), the store-house of infinite qualities. One who has just begun to experience the grace of God would like to say that God is saguṇa, meaning thereby that God has such and such forms and qualities; while one who has come under the full blaze of the Sun of divine grace, and has, on that account, experienced not only a panorama of a few delightful visions, but also an ocean of the terrific, the majestic and the sublime visions of God, would simply be bewildered and ashamed to say that God is endowed with this or that quality or form. The moment he would begin to describe that God is so and so, he would find that He has changed into something else, and again into something else. And then the only manner which is left to him to describe the nature of God is to say about him in the famous Vedāntic negative way of description, namely, 'not this alone', 'not this alone' (*neti*, *neti*). It is this negation of qualities and forms one after another that constitutes the meaning of 'Nirguṇa'. But it ought to be clear now that Nirguṇa does not mean the cancellation of saguṇa and thereby making God a mere blank or void; it is the inclusion and the transcendence of saguṇa. Therefore, it will be proper to speak about God that He is infinite in every respect, infinite in qualities, infinite in forms, and infinite in powers, bounty and grace.

One who has not the slightest experience of God, but who supposes that what he thinks must be correct, should be left to speak as he speculates and derive an intellectual pleasure in fighting an unfruitful battle regarding whether God is saguṇa or nirguṇa. For him God is neither this nor that, though he might continue to argue that he is only this and not that.

But what is the good of merely holding dry and hollow intellectual opinions about the nature of God ? Does it bring any solace and comfort to the mind that is distressed, and to the soul that is torn by several anxieties, calamities, sorrows and miseries, due to disease, old age and death ? It is not simply the belief but the experience that God is kind and compassionate that will be of practical help to save one from the innumerable perplexities and predicaments in life. God must be first directly experienced as possessing some quality or other before he is declared as saguṇa in character. How can God who is thought of as Nirguṇa can either be wrathful or kind, and be capable of bringing destruction or protection ? Let him be transcendent or immanent,—and this also amounts to His having some quality—He cannot be moved to any action unless He is capable of possessing emotions and of giving expression to them either by being angry or compassionate.

Perhaps it might be argued that this would be merely an anthropomorphic picture of God, drawn by merely raising the human qualities to the highest degree and calling the possessor of them as God. But the charge is futile. For, it is the concrete evidence of the experience of the saints, the prophets and the saviours, especially of India, that the same Caitanya, that is, the same Conscious and Blissful Force, known as Sat-Cit-Ānanda, or the formless Absolute or Brahman who assumes various forms and qualities, and becomes effective as the creator, the protector and the destroyer of all, as and when He wills. The consciousness of man being only an infinitesimal fraction of that infinite consciousness, the view that God is anthropomorphic in character holds no water. On the contrary, man being divine in nature can recognize the divine qualities in God and be ultimately assimilated with Him, if he wishes and strives to be so, by means of devout meditation on the Name of God. And, as said above, he will first come to know a few qualities of God, and then, by his continued meditation and grace of God, come to know that God is not at all limited by them. So, he discovers ultimately that God is both saguṇa and nirguṇa, and that He can assume infinite forms and yet be formless (sākāra and nirākāra).

2. *Is Brahman immanent only, or is it transcendent also ?*

There is this controversy between those who have realized the Brahman as both transcendent and immanent and those who have realized it as immanent only. Both may be the devotees of God, both may believe that the world has been created by God and that God is immanent in all the objects. But those who say that God is immanent only call themselves as Rājayogīs or as practical Vedāntins, and so they believe that the world and its various objects and beings in which the Brahman is equally immanent are non-different from it, just as the effect is non-different from the cause. In illustration of this, they would say that the ornaments made of gold, that is, the ornaments in which gold is through and through immanent are non-different from gold. To know and enjoy any one of them is to know and enjoy gold itself. Even so, to enjoy the world is to enjoy the Brahman. Supported by this argument, the Rājayogī, in spite of his great devotion to God, will not hesitate to enjoy with ease and freedom the pleasures of life, and to engage himself in various activities, concerning the family, the society and the state, and yet remain uncontaminated by them all. Like the Brahman, he would lead the life of being immanent in all, and consider himself to be unaffected by that 'all'.

All this is a grand ideal, no doubt. And so, anyone would like to be a Rājayogī, and not a recluse or a sannyāsin who would merely look at the world as a stranger and not partake of its joys and sorrows, being perhaps afraid that he would be entangled in the snares of Māyā and be lost. Like the transcendent God, he too wishes to be transcendent and aloof from the world. He is no doubt steadfast in his devotion, but shuns to be active, and retreats to his secluded home. Brave in his love of God, he chooses to live as a coward among men. Naturally, the Rājayogī proves himself superior to him.

We need not however be hasty to come to such an easy conclusion. For in the case of the Rājayogī, and more so in the case of those who follow his counsel blindly, there is the great risk of forgetting God very soon and falling into the rut of the ignorant and the voluptuous. If one were to be always immersed in the activities and pleasures of life, and yet continue to proclaim to the world that his way of life is quite consistent with the philosophic view 'All this is Brahman', meaning thereby that 'all this is the sport (vilāsa) of Brahman', it might then be more often than not the vilāsa of himself and not of the Brahman. It will neither be the sign of boldness nor of knowledge, but the sign of obstinacy and pretence. Unless a man voluntarily and deliberately cultivates the habit of renouncing his desires and pleasures of life, and increases his devout attachment to God, unless he moves frequently away from the hubbub of the world and meditates on the Name of God in a secluded place, he will neither discover that God is ever transcendent, nor be joyfully absorbed in the unique and compelling beauty and sublimity of the various visions of God. He alone who can reap the divine harvest daily in this manner, and is, so to say, perpetually God-thirsty and God-intoxicated, is fit to declare that the whole world also is lit by the splendour of God or that God is immanent in the world. But those who say that the world is as enjoyable as God, since God is immanent in it do not necessarily give us a convincing proof that they have also the experience of enjoying God without the sensuous objects of the world. Perhaps, it is advantageous to them to speak about the immanence of God; for, under the guise of language they can enjoy the world only. The world may be enjoyed in the presence and the company of God, but to enjoy it without God is mere voluptuousness.

To speak about immanence of God is analogous to speaking about Him as being internally visible. But who knows whether what one sees in his mind is the image of his own fancy, or what one says is a fraudulent way of deceiving the credulous persons? That may be a reality or not. On the other hand, one who says that the divine vision which he sees inside is exactly the same which he sees outside with open eyes and vice versa, gives us the proof that God is just the same whether he is immanent in the body or transcends the body. To see God as immanent in oneself and immanent in all beings and objects of the outside Nature is also very essential, since it is the apprehension and consciousness of the common spiritual bond between oneself and everything else in the universe that will make him truly sympathetic and truly helpful to all those who are groaning under the burden of miseries, disease and ignorance. Unless one sees the whole world as informed by the spirit of God, one should never dream of establishing the Kingdom of God in which all are equal in freedom, joy and peace. In short, one who has got this double experience of God as being both immanent and transcendent, both internal and external, is alone justified in saying that 'All this is Brahman'.

3. *Robust Activity versus Crouching Fatalism*

In the ordinary life of the world it is but a common experience that a man who works honestly and incessantly does not meet with success, while another who is not so active but resigns himself completely to his Fate is crowned with success. We are not here much concerned with the speculative solution of this apparent incongruity, like the one given by the great German philosopher, Kant, namely, that the balance of justice will be set properly in a life beyond death. This too is a fatalistic argument and might give a temporary consolation to a disturbed mind. The moral or the spiritual consciousness will hardly be satisfied with this. And if it does, it will be a clean licence to act in any way as prudence would dictate, and to believe in God or not as will be advantageous to one. The moral life will be saved, if only one would say to himself, 'whatever may happen to me in a life beyond death, I shall behave as an honest man among the most dishonest persons, here in this world, so long as there is life in me'. The moral life is autonomous and brooks no interference from outside. Morality need not be based on the belief in a life beyond death.

But what about the spiritual life of a novice for whom mere speculation will be of no use and in whom the spiritual consciousness has not even taken root? He has necessarily to fall back upon the advice of the experts in the field. Here, however, there is no unanimity. Some would ask him to depend entirely on the grace of God, while some would tell him that there is nothing impossible for hard and sincere work. Like a shuttlecock, the novice might move from one to the other; or being impatient, he might only be bewildered and find himself where he was. What has Rāmadāsa to say in this connection? He takes us to the root of the matter. What is known as Fate or 'Prārabdha' is nothing but the result of actions done in the past lives, and is not something which is arbitrarily written by the creator as if on the forehead of a man at the time of his birth, and which must therefore inevitably happen, notwithstanding whatever the man might do to change it. This means that it is the free and voluntary human action which is the cause of what is known as Fate, and which would therefore also be the cause of overcoming or of changing that fate. Activity which is prior to the accumulated result of it known as fate, must also possess the power of undoing that fate. So, those who rely helplessly on the unseen power of Fate, saying that it is inexorable, and do not therefore stir to modify or to put a stop to it, are only giving a false excuse for their idleness and want of courage.

It is exactly these very people who would try to make a capital of their slothfulness and want of a determined will, and so would desist from the practice of meditating on the Name of God under the plea that their own efforts would do nothing to enhance their spiritual progress. They would therefore idly speak that since God's grace is competent to make them meditate and achieve the spiritual gain, they would simply depend upon and wait for the grace of God. These are the people who are worse than those who depend upon their fate for their worldly success. For, whereas the fatalists will have no complaint against the unseen power of fate, the pretenders in spiritual life would attribute their misfortunes in their worldly life and their failure in spiritual life to the absence of the grace of God, on which they falsely say they depend. No doubt, grace is the free gift of God; but why should it come to the faithless, the pretenders and the idlers ? With faith, love and sincerity, they should first put in maximum efforts to increase their moral and spiritual worth, and then expect the grace from God. They will then certainly be rewarded by God. Even then there is a duty which devolves upon them. They must be all the more devoutly faithful to God, and try their utmost to preserve that grace by meditating more and more on the divine Name and by serving Him and the saints in all possible ways. Idleness will neither deserve nor be able to preserve the grace, even if it comes chancely as a free gift in order to test the sincerity of the receiver.

4 *The reality and unreality of names and forms*

In the tenth samāsa (section) of the fourteenth Daśaka (a group of ten samāsas), Rāmadāsa gives us an interesting description of how Māyā appears to us as something which it is not, and points out in illustration of this how certain names are fondly given to persons and animals who do not possess in the least the qualities indicated by the names. A woman who is illiterate is named as Saraswati (Goddess of learning); another who is striken by poverty is named as Lakṣmī (Goddess of wealth) ; a pet dog is named as a tiger, and so on. Now, it is obvious, as students of Logic know, that proper names are non-connotative; that is they only denote a person or being, but have no connotation. Metaphysically considered, it might be said that such names are altogether unreal. They have only a nominal existence. Bubbles of coloured water are beautiful to look at, but contain no substance in them. A smoke or vapour that goes up in the air, or a cloud in the sky might take different shapes and forms, but they are all too short-lived to make us believe that they are more real than a dream or an illusory experience of a snake on the rope.

There are however other names and forms in which we are as much interested as in the names of our relatives and friends, but which carry with them more than a conventional value, and an existence which is more objective than what our subjective liking would endow upon them. For instance, a metal which is yellow, which has a specific gravity, and which stands the test of acid, is named as gold; and an ornament made of gold is named as ring, and it has got a circular form. For all practical purposes, men knowing the English language will agree in saying that the names, 'gold', 'yellow', 'ring', and 'roundness', belong to the ornament known as the ring. Here is the tacit assumption that the specified name, 'ring' and the form 'round' must be present in what is known as the golden ring. Even so, for people in general, the names and forms of the several things have got as permanent an existence as the substances to which they belong. But one who has got a scientific or a philosophic turn of mind would like to believe more in the permanent value and existence of the substance as well as in the specific qualities, than in the changing names and forms. A goldsmith, for instance, will have his eye on the metal gold, rather than on the names and forms of the various ornaments made of gold. Considered thus, one can say that names and forms may come and go, but the substance remains the same. Extending the argument, one might say that the names and forms of the phenomenal world may come and go; what lies behind the phenomena, namely, the Brahman or God is the Reality. To put it differently, whatever becomes the object of sensuous knowledge is bound to perish, while whatever is perceived non-sensuously or by the intuitive eye is real.

This last statement however is likely to create a doubt in the mind of an aspirant on the spiritual path. On the one hand, he is advised to get himself initiated by one who has realized God and obtain a Divine Name from him for meditating upon it, and to gaze with love and adoration at the forms of the visions of God; while on the other hand, as we have just seen, his attention is drawn to the philosophical opinion that the names and forms are but a passing show. Is this not like defeating the very purpose of the spiritual life? And, if it is not, we should be able to show that the names and forms in the spiritual realm are different from those in the phenomenal world, and are as abiding as the eternal Being is. Even the testimony of the great Śrī Śaṅkarācārya might appear to some as giving the lie to the view that the names and the forms of the various visions of God have got an abiding value, especially when the Ācārya says about the vision of the Viśvarūpa which Arjuna had seen according to the author of the Bhagavadgītā, that it was "Māyā—Vijṛmbhaṇam" only, meaning thereby, as these people would like to put it, the illusory show created by Māyā. And then, if the forms of the various visions are not ultimately real, the various names which are given to the Vibhūtis (manifestations) would also be equally unreal.

What we have to say in the matter is, in the first place, that Śaṅkarācārya does mean by Māyā in the context of the Viśvarūpa that it is the power of God and not the source of illusion. 'Vijṛmbhitam' would mean then simply 'extended' or projected; and the vision of the Viśvarūpa, nothing but the projections or the manifestations of God in new and newer forms, just as gold might be made into ever new ornaments. The various forms of visions therefore must be considered as real as God, just as the various ornaments made of gold are as real as gold.

To this there might come forth a counter-argument in the form that the names and forms of the phenomenal world also can be treated by parity of reasoning that they are as if the extended limbs of God, and therefore as real as God. In a way, the argument has got an element of truth in it, provided it means that an ornament is real, not because it has an independent existence of its own as distinguished and separated from gold, but because it is made of gold, and exhibits only a manner or mode of the existence of gold. It is gold which is real, and not the name and the form of the ornament which simply hang upon gold, and are only appearances. On the contrary, the names and forms of the visions of God, are neither short-lived in spite of their appearance and disappearance, nor superimposed upon God. They have got an objective, universal and necessary existence and have got the same significance to all the saints the world over, irrespective of space and time. Apart from them, none can have any idea of how God is omnipresent, immanent and transcendent at the same time, much less of His higher powers of being omniscient, ommipotent, Creator, Preserver and Destroyer of the universe. Our knowledge about God to be concrete, direct and first hand shall have to be attained first through the several visions in which God manifests on account of His grace and love for the devotees, and that these forms of manifestations are imperishable and uncontaminated can be tested by the discovery that they cannot be burnt in fire, swept away by floods of water, cut by weapons, or blown away by wind, and so on.

What we find in the phenomenal world is that names are many a time given to things corresponding to their forms, and vice versa. This is not necessary in the spiritual world. Any Name of God has the power in it to produce out of it any other divine Name as also any form of the visions of God. It has no exclusive reference to any particular divine personality or Vibhūti, as the name in the phenomenal world has to a particular thing, person, or event. Any divine Name is equally potent to manifest all the glories, all the visions and all the powers and incarnations of God, whether of the past or of the future. That Name is neither a conventional sign, nor an arbitrary symbol chosen by an ordinary man. Nor is it invented by the Spiritual Teacher. It comes to him directly by the grace of God and is transmitted by him to the disciple as a gift of God. Here one cannot say, 'what is in a name' ? For any other name chosen by the disciple but not sanctioned by spiritual teacher will not be a symbol of God. It will not sprout into any divine form which will exhibit His beauty, splendour, majesty and other excellent qualities. It will be no more than a mere, hollow skeleton, a dead word written on a parchment unable to carry the divine Form with all His power, glory and knowledge.

As the Saint Tulasīdāsa has said, and as Prof. R.D. Ranade has commented upon his view, the Name and Form, are in the Spinozistic sense the 'Attributes' (upādhis) of God meaning thereby, as we have hinted above that they are the two ways of looking at God, or rather two ways of realizing God. No doubt, we agree with Spinoza in saying that God has infinite attributes, out of which only two are capable of being comprehended by man. Name (Nāma) would stand for Spinoza's attribute of 'Thought' or 'Idea', and Form (Rūpa) for that of 'Extension' or 'Matter'. We do not however agree with him in the first place in saying that human intelligence can have any hold on them. For both of them being the gifts of God or of the spiritual teacher, go beyond the range of human intelligence, and as such have the power to open his intuitive eye, which remains closed till it is opened by the Master by means of the Name or Form of God. And further where is the necessity of these Attributes being two in number ? For any one of them is capable of producing and multiplying infinitely both the Name and Form. Generally, the disciple receives the Name from his Guru; but this need not be so. He might be able by the grace of his Guru to see the Form of God, and then as he contemplates on it, he might hear any number of divine Names. The Name imparted by the Guru is the guarantee that other Names and Forms must follow it, if the Name is meditated upon; and the Form shown by the Guru is the guarantee that other Forms and Names must follow it, if the original Form is contemplated upon regularly and with concentration, love and respect. So, in the second place, instead of saying that there are two attributes or upādhis or points of view of looking at God, we might say that there is only one point of view, namely, that which the Guru or God, makes available to us and not the point of view of any man who has not been blessed by the Guru. It is God's point of view wherefrom God will contemplate upon himself, as Aristotle holds; for man, it is only given to him to adopt that point of view, so that when the seed (whether of Name or Form) is sown in him, man will grow into God. And so, in the third place, we shall cease to talk about the Name of God as merely the Upādhi of God as if God would be some one transcending that Upādhi. For us the upādhi itself is God; and then there will be no sense from the mystical point of view in saying that God is immanent or transcendent; for these words will only help to make a cleavage between man and God. In knowing God by means of meditation on the Name and contemplation on the Form of God, man is to become God.

5. *Liberation, a process and not an event*

In Sections 25 and 51 of Dāsabodha, we have discussed the problem of Liberation and have come to know the view of Rāmadāsa that there is only one kind of liberation which is everlasting and which does not suffer from the defects of the other three kinds of it. It is known as the 'Sāyujya-mukti' which consists in the identification of the self with God, though this can be had approximately and by degrees. This obviously means that it is a process, and not an event. We shall however note here a few more points of importance in this connection.

In a passage of the Dāsabodha (1.1 : 12-15) where he describes the power of the spiritual Master, Rāmadāsa has very brilliantly shown as to how the destiny of the disciple is being gradually shaped, and how ultimately there takes place complete transmutation of his being into that of his Guru and into the being of God. A river which runs into the sea, says Rāmadāsa, loses its own name and form and becomes the sea. But before it meets the sea, it continues to be known by its own name. This means that the river partly retains its own individuality and partly loses itself in the larger individuality of the sea. The disciple, on the other hand, loses his individuality once for all; but he gains the individuality of his Master which is infinitely larger than his own and which being spiritual in nature can save the humanity in exactly the same manner in which the Master used to do. In the case of the river, it is definitely a loss; for after it has once entered into the sea, it can no longer quench the thirst of the people by its sweet water, which however it continues to do upto the point of its merging into the sea. But the disciple who attains the status of his Guru can provide spiritual water to any one who thirsts for God. In one respect, however, the disciple ought to behave like the course of the river, throughout his life. Just as the river is pouring its water into the sea every minute as it flows on, even so the disciple must every minute of his life surrender everything of what he is and has at the feet of the Lord. From moment to moment, the whole of his life must be a continuous sacrifice. Here lies the true freedom from the egoism of man's tiny individuality. Liberation does not come as an event at a particular point of time in the life of a sādhaka. It must come at every moment till his last breath. It is an infinite series, which is not capable of being cut even by death, and is composed of infinite moments every one of which is the fullest expression of freedom from bondage of any kind. And the only way to attain this living immortality of perfect liberation is ever to be in the company of God either by meditating on His Name or by contemplation on the Forms of His visions.

Another very fine illustration which Rāmadāsa cites in this connection is that of the so-called 'Pārasa' stone which is believed to change iron into gold. But, says Rāmadāsa, the Pārasa is incapable of changing iron or gold into its own nature. That is why iron may remain either as iron, or at best as gold. The disciple, on the other hand, attains to the status of the Guru without being touched by him. The Guru is Guru on account of the constant presence of God in him, and the disciple can be fortunate in having presence of the Guru and of God in him. True liberation or what is the same thing as the perfect freedom of God becomes the special privilege of the Guru, and even so, in course of time, the special privilege of the disciple, who with absolute faith in his Guru meditates on the divine Name with love and loyalty. Every single moment of his life is the confluence of himself as identified with his Guru and with the Name and the self-effulgent Form of God. The whole mission of his life consists in carrying forward the same truth and reality of the light and freedom to all those who would approach him with humility and implore him to grant it to them. Liberation cannot be the static and the exclusive property of a single man; it can be the fluid and the common property of generations after generations of men who have unflinching faith in the Guru and a will-to-do as he instructs, at all costs. Just as the light of one flame can be passed on to another wick without any loss to the flame, even so the freedom of God can pass on from person to person without any hindrance, and so, it would neither be impossible for the Guru nor for the disciple to endow the gift of liberation on any one by linking his faith to meditation on the Name of God and to contemplation on the Form of God.

INDEX